Debbie Bliss

photography by Debi Treloar

ESSENTIAL baby

over 20 hand knits to take your baby from
first days to first steps

Quadrille

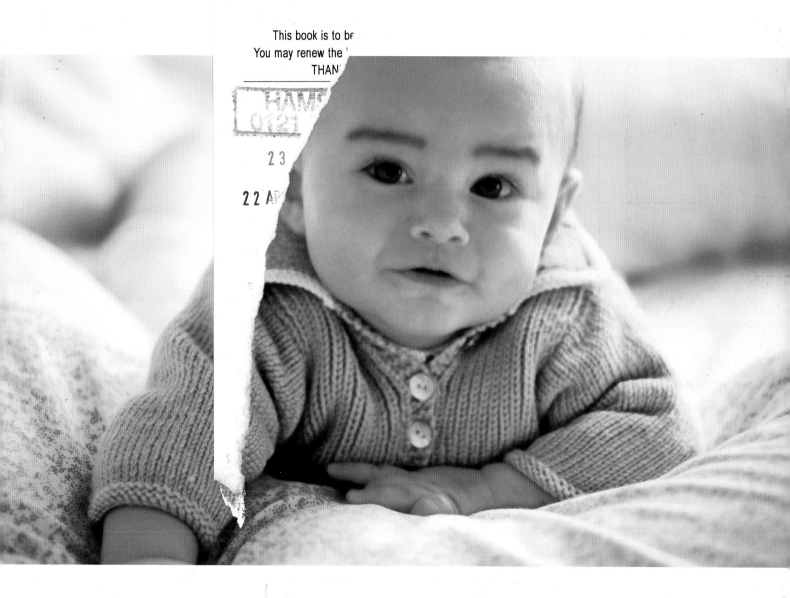

ESSENTIAL baby

This book is to be
You may renew the
THAN

HAM
0121

23

22 AP

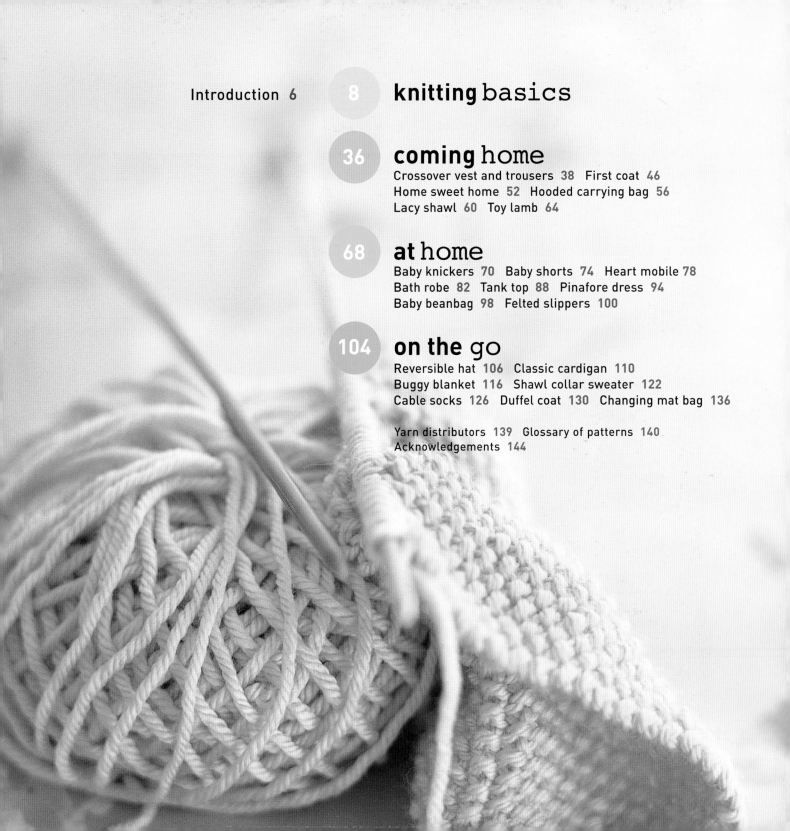

introduction

The period immediately before the arrival of a baby is a unique time for nesting, perfect for creating special hand knits to welcome a newborn infant home. With this in mind, in **Essential Baby** I have designed a capsule collection to take a baby through from his or her first few days to their first few steps.

Divided into three sections, Coming Home, At Home and On the Go, this book provides every new parent with the key knitted pieces needed for baby's first eighteen months.

Coming Home is full of baby must-haves: a snuggle-into shawl, a hooded carrying bag in a cashmere mix – gentle against a baby's delicate skin – while a simple wrapover top, trousers and matinee coat provide a contemporary feel to the classic layette. As well as everything you need to wrap up your precious little one and

keep them cosy, to welcome your baby home there are projects such as a knitted house picture and a cuddly toy lamb for baby's first room.

At Home is for downtime, with a cosy cotton bathrobe – a great wraparound for after a bath – and slip-on felted slippers. Soft vintage-style knee-length trousers and frilly romper knickers are both perfect for crawlers, while for playtime there is a squashy beanbag for baby to relax and kick back on and a heart mobile to hang over their cot.

On the Go includes outdoor basics that will keep your tot snug on trips out and about: a practical changing mat that doubles up as a carrying bag, a double-sided patchwork and striped blanket to tuck around baby in their buggy, a reversible beanie, chunky cable-knit socks and a double-breasted duffel coat.

All the yarns from my ranges have been especially chosen for comfort and practicality. There are cashmere mixes, extra-fine merino wools and classic cottons, which are all machine washable but at the same time are soft and gentle against young skin.

I have designed the projects to cover a range of knitting skills, but most are simple makes, reflecting a new life balance when nurturing may take over from knitting.

knittingbasics

types of yarns

When choosing a yarn for babies or children it is essential that you work with a fibre that is soft and gentle against a baby's skin. Babies are not able to tell you if a collar is rough against their neck or if cuffs are irritating their wrists, and as older children are often more used to the lightweight freedom of fleeces, they can be resistant to hand knits that they may consider scratchy and uncomfortable.

The yarns I have chosen for the patterns in this book are cashmere combined with merino wool (giving softness and durability), a pure cotton and an extra-fine merino. Although they create fabrics that are sumptously soft to wear, most importantly all these yarns are machine washable.

When knitting a garment, wherever possible try to buy the yarn stated in the pattern. All these designs have been created with a specific yarn in mind: the Shawl Collar Sweater is worked in a softer yarn to gently frame a baby's face, whilst the Changing Mat Bag is made in a natural cotton to give it the necessary sturdiness to maintain its shape – a floppier fibre or a synthetic yarn would create a limp fabric. From an aesthetic point of view, the clarity of a subtle stitch pattern may be lost if a garment is knitted in an inferior yarn.

However, there may be occasions when a knitter needs to substitute a yarn – if there is an allergy to wool, for example – and so the following is a guideline to making the most informed choices.

Always buy a yarn that is the same weight as that given in the pattern: replace a double knitting with a double

knitting, for example, and check that the tension of both yarns is the same.

Where you are substituting a different fibre, be aware of the design. A cable pattern knitted in cotton when worked in wool will pull in because of the greater elasticity of the yarn and so the fabric will become narrower; this will alter the proportions of the garment.

Check the metreage of the yarn. Yarns that weigh the same may have different lengths in the ball or hank, so you may need to buy more or less yarn.

Here are descriptions of my yarns and a guide to their weights and types:

Debbie Bliss alpaca silk aran:
80% alpaca, 20% silk. Approximately 65m/50g ball.
Debbie Bliss baby cashmerino:
55% merino wool, 33% microfibre, 12% cashmere. Approximately 125m/50g ball.
Debbie Bliss cashmerino aran:
55% merino wool, 33% microfibre, 12% cashmere. Approximately 90m/50g ball.
Debbie Bliss cashmerino astrakhan:
60% merino wool, 30% microfibre, 10% cashmere. Approximately 70m/50g ball.
Debbie Bliss cashmerino double knitting:
55% merino wool, 33% microfibre, 12%

cashmere. Approximately 110m/50g ball.
Debbie Bliss cotton double knitting:
100% cotton. Approximately 84m/50g ball.
Debbie Bliss rialto double knitting:
100% extrafine merino wool. Approximately 105m/50g ball.

buying yarn

The ball band on the yarn will carry all the essential information you need as to tension, needle size, weight and yardage. Importantly it will also have the dye lot. Yarns are dyed in batches or lots, which can vary considerably. As your retailer may not have the same dye lot later on, buy all your yarn for a project at the same time. If you know that sometimes you use more yarn than that quoted in the pattern, buy extra. If it is not possible to buy all the yarn you need with the same dye lot, use the different ones where it will not show as much, on a neck or border, as a change of dye lot across a main piece will most likely show.

It is also a good idea at the time of buying the yarn that you check the pattern and make sure that you already have the needles you will require. If not buy them now, as it will save a lot of frustration when you get home.

garment care

Taking care of your hand knits is important because you want them to look good for as long as possible. Correct washing is particularly important for baby garments as they need to be washed frequently.

Check the ball band on the yarn for washing instructions to see whether the yarn is hand or machine washable, and if it is the latter, at what temperature it should be washed.

Most hand knits should be dried flat on an absorbent cloth, such as a towel, to soak up any moisture. Lying them flat in this way gives you an opportunity to pat the garment back into shape if it has become pulled around in the washing machine. Even if you are in a hurry, do not be tempted to dry your knits near a direct heat source, such as a radiator.

As baby garments are small, you may prefer to hand wash them. Use a washing agent that is specifically designed for knitwear as this will be kinder to the fabric. Use warm rather than hot water and handle the garment gently without rubbing or wringing. Let the water out of the basin and then gently squeeze out the excess water. Do not lift out a water-logged knit as the weight of the water will pull it out of shape. You may need to remove more moisture by rolling in a towel. Dry flat as before.

techniques

cast on

slip-knot

Your first step when beginning to knit is to work a foundation row called a cast-on. Without this row you cannot begin to knit.

There are several methods of casting on, each can be suited to a particular purpose or is chosen because the knitter feels comfortable with that particular technique. The two examples shown here are the ones I have found to be the most popular, the thumb and the cable methods.

In order to work a cast-on edge, you must first make a slip-knot.

1 Wind the yarn around the fingers on your left hand to make a circle of yarn as shown above. With the knitting needle, pull a loop of the yarn attached to the ball through the yarn circle on your fingers.

2 Pull both ends of the yarn to tighten the slip-knot on the knitting needle. You are now ready to begin, using either of the following cast-on techniques.

cast on

thumb cast-on

1 Make a slip-knot as shown on page 15, leaving a long tail. With the slip-knot on the needle in your right hand and the yarn that comes from the ball over your index finger, wrap the tail end of the yarn over your left thumb from front to back, holding the yarn in your palm with your fingers.

2 Insert the knitting needle upwards through the yarn loop on your left thumb.

The thumb cast-on is a one needle method that produces a flexible edge, which makes it particularly useful when using non-elastic yarns such as cotton. The 'give' in it also makes it a good one to use where the edge will turn back, as on the duffel coat (see page 130).

Unlike two-needle methods you are working toward the yarn end, which means you have to predict the length you need to cast on the required amount of stitches, otherwise you may find you do not have enough yarn to complete the last few stitches and have to start all over again. If unsure, always allow for more yarn than you think you need as you can use what is left over for sewing up.

3 With the right index finger, wrap the yarn from the ball up and over the point of the knitting needle.

4 Draw the yarn through the loop on your thumb to form a new stitch on the knitting needle. Then, let the yarn loop slip off your left thumb and pull the loose end to tighten up the stitch. Repeat these steps until the required number of stitches have been cast on.

cable cast-on

1 Make a slip-knot as shown on page 15. Hold the knitting needle with the slip-knot in your left hand and insert the right-hand needle from left to right and from front to back through the slip-knot. Wrap the yarn from the ball up and over the point of the right-hand needle as shown.

2 With the right-hand needle, draw a loop through the slip-knot to make a new stitch. Do not drop the stitch from the left-hand needle, but instead slip the new stitch onto the left-hand needle as shown.

The cable cast-on method uses two needles and is particularly good for ribbed edges, as it provides a sturdy, but still elastic, edge. As you need to insert the needle between the stitches and pull the yarn through to create another stitch make sure that you do not make the new stitch too tight. The cable method is one of the most widely used cast-ons.

3 Next, insert the right-hand needle between the two stitches on the left-hand needle and wrap the yarn around the point of the right-hand needle.

4 Pull the yarn through to make a new stitch, and then place the new stitch on the left-hand needle, as before. Repeat the last two steps until the required number of stitches have been cast on.

knit

The knit and purl stitches form the basis of almost all knitted fabrics. The knit stitch is the easiest to learn and is the first stitch you will create. When worked continuously it forms a reversible fabric called garter stitch. You can recognise garter stitch by the horizontal ridges formed at the top of the knitted loops.

1 With the cast-on stitches on the needle in your left hand, insert the right-hand needle from left to right and from front to back through the first cast-on stitch.

2 Take the yarn from the ball on your index finger (the working yarn) around the point of the right-hand needle.

3 Draw the right-hand needle and yarn through the stitch, thus forming a new stitch on the right-hand needle, and at the same time slip the original stitch off the left-hand needle. Repeat these steps until all the stitches from the left-hand needle have been worked. One knit row has now been completed.

&purl

After the knit stitch you will move on to the purl stitch. If the purl stitch is worked continuously, it forms the same fabric as garter stitch. However, if purl rows and knit rows are worked alternately, they create stocking stitch, which is the most widely used knitted fabric.

1 With the yarn to the front of the work, insert the right-hand needle from the right to the left into the front of the first stitch on the left-hand needle.

2 Then take the yarn from the ball on your index finger (the working yarn) around the point of the right-hand needle.

3 Draw the right-hand needle and the yarn through the stitch, thus forming a new stitch on the right-hand needle, and at the same time slip the original stitch off the left-hand needle. Repeat these steps until all the stitches have been worked. One purl row has now been completed.

increase

increase one

1 Insert the right-hand needle into the front of the next stitch, then knit the stitch but leave it on the left-hand needle.

2 Insert the right-hand needle into the back of the same stitch and knit it. Then slip the original stitch off the needle. Now you have made an extra stitch on the right-hand needle.

make one

Increases are used to add to the width of the knitted fabric by creating more stitches. They are worked, for example, when shaping sleeves up the length of the arm or when additional stitches are needed after a ribbed welt. Some increases are invisible, while others are worked away from the edge of the work and are meant to be seen in order to give decorative detail. Most knitting patterns will tell you which type of increase to make.

1 Insert the left-hand needle from front to back under the horizontal strand between the stitch just worked on the right-hand needle and the first stitch on the left-hand needle.

2 Knit into the back of the loop to twist it, and to prevent a hole. Drop the strand from the left-hand needle. This forms a new stitch on the right-hand needle.

yarn over

yarn over between knit stitches
Bring the yarn forward between
the two needles, from the back to
the front of the work. Taking the
yarn over the right-hand needle to do
so, knit the next stitch.

yarn over between purl stitches
Bring the yarn over the right-hand
needle to the back, then between the
two needles to the front. Then purl the
next stitch.

yarn over between a purl and a knit
Take the yarn from the front over
the right-hand needle to the back. Then
knit the next stitch.

yarn over between a knit and a purl
Bring the yarn forward between the
two needles from the back to the front
of the work, and take it over the top
of the right-hand needle to the back
again and then forward between the
needles. Then purl the next stitch.

cast off

knit cast-off

1 Knit two stitches. Insert the left-hand needle into the first stitch knitted on the right-hand needle and lift this stitch over the second stitch and off the right-hand needle.

2 One stitch is now on the right-hand needle. Knit the next stitch. Repeat the first step until all the stitches have been cast off. Pull the yarn through the last stitch to fasten off.

purl cast-off

Casting off is used to finish off your knitted piece so that the stitches don't unravel. It is also used to decrease more than one stitch at a time, such as when shaping armholes, neckbands, and buttonholes. It is important that a cast-off is firm but elastic, particularly when you are casting off around a neckband, to ensure that it can be pulled easily over the head. Unless told otherwise, cast off in the pattern used in the piece.

1 Purl two stitches. Insert the left-hand needle into the back of the first stitch worked on the right-hand needle and lift this stitch over the second stitch and off the right-hand needle.

2 One stitch is now on the right-hand needle. Purl the next stitch. Repeat the first step until all the stitches have been cast off. Pull the yarn through the last stitch to fasten off.

decrease

Decreases are used to make the fabric narrower by getting rid of stitches on the needle. They are worked to make an opening for a neckline or shaping a sleeve head. As with increases they can be used to create decorative detail, often around a neck edge. Increases and decreases are used together to create lace patterns.

knit 2 together

knit 2 together ('k2tog' or 'dec one')
On a knit row, insert the right-hand needle from left to right through the next two stitches on the left-hand needle and knit them together. One stitch has been decreased.

purl 2 together

purl 2 together ('p2tog' or 'dec one')
On a purl row, insert the right-hand needle from right to left through the next two stitches on the left-hand needle. Then purl them together. One stitch has been decreased.

slip stitch over

slip 1, knit 1, pass slipped stitch over ('psso')
1 Insert the right-hand needle into the next stitch on the left-hand needle and slip it onto the right-hand needle without knitting it. Knit the next stitch. Then insert the left-hand needle into the slipped stitch as shown.

2 With the left-hand needle, lift the slipped stitch over the knitted stitch as shown and off the right-hand needle.

reading patterns

To those unfamiliar with knitting patterns they can appear to be written in a strange, alien language! However as you become used to the terminology you will see that they have a logic and consistency that you will soon become familiar with.

Do not be too concerned if you read through a pattern first and are confused by parts of it as some instructions make more sense when your stitches are on the needle and you are at that point in the piece. However, it is sometimes a good idea to check with your retailer whether your skill levels are up to a particular design as this can prevent frustration later on.

Figures for larger sizes are given in round ( ) brackets. Where only one figure appears it means that those numbers apply to all sizes. Figures in square brackets [ ] are to be worked the number of times stated after the brackets. Where 0 appears, no stitches or rows are worked for this size.

When you follow the pattern it is important that you consistently use the right stitches or rows for your size, and you don't switch inside the brackets. This can be avoided by marking off your size throughout with a highlighting pen, but photocopy the pattern first so that you don't spoil your book.

Before starting your project, check the size and the actual measurements that are quoted for that size; you may want to make a smaller or larger garment depending on the proportions of the wearer it is intended for.

The quantities of yarn quoted in the instructions are based on the yarn used by the knitter of the original garment and therefore all amounts should be considered approximate. For example, if that knitter has used almost all of the last ball it may be that another knitter with a slightly different tension has to break into another ball to complete the garment. A slight variation in tension can therefore make the difference between using fewer or more balls than that stated in the pattern.

tension

Every knitting pattern will state a tension or gauge – the number of stitches and rows to 10cm that should be obtained with the quoted yarn, needle size and stitch pattern. It is vital to check your tension before starting your project. A slight variation can alter the proportions of the finished garment and the look of the fabric. A too loose tension will produce an uneven and unstable fabric that can drop or lose its shape after washing, whilst a too tight tension can make a hard, inelastic fabric.

Making a tension square
Use the same needles, yarn and stitch pattern quoted in the tension note in the pattern. Knit a sample at least 13cm square to get the most accurate result. Smooth out the finished sample on a flat surface making sure you are not stretching it out.

To check the stitch tension, place a tape measure or ruler horizontally on the sample and mark 10cm with pins. Count the number of stitches between the pins. To check the row tension, mark 10cm with pins vertically as before and count the number of rows. If the number of stitches and rows is greater than that quoted in the pattern, your tension is tighter and you should try changing to a larger needle and trying another tension square. If there are fewer stitches and rows, your tension is looser and you should try again on a smaller needle. The stitch tension is the most important to get right as the number of stitches in a pattern are set but the length is often calculated in measurement rather than rows and you may be able to work more or fewer rows.

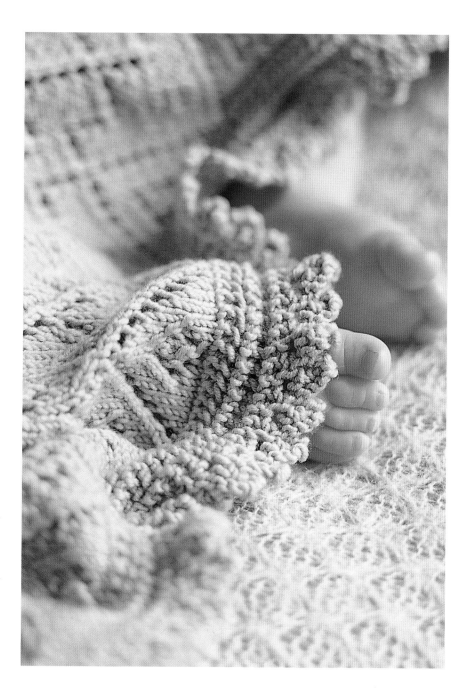

abbreviations

In a pattern book general abbreviations will usually be given at the front before the patterns begin, whilst those more specific to a particular design will be given at the start of the individual pattern. The following are the ones used throughout this book.

standard abbreviations

alt = alternate
beg = begin(ning)
cont = continue
dec = decrease (ing)
foll = following
inc = increase (ing)
k = knit
m1 = make one stitch by picking up the loop lying between the stitch just worked and the next stitch and working into the back of it
patt = pattern
p = purl
psso = pass slipped stitch over
rem = remain (ing)
rep = repeat (ing)
skpo = slip 1, knit 1, pass slipped stitch over
sl = slip
st(s) = stitch(es)
st st = stocking stitch
tbl = through back of loop
tog = together
yf = yarn forward
yon = yarn over needle
yrn = yarn round needle

cables

Cables are formed by the simple technique of crossing one set of stitches over another. Stitches are held on a cable needle (a short double-pointed needle) at the back or front of the work while the same amount of stitches is worked from the left-hand needle. Simple cables form a vertical twisted rope of stocking stitch on a background of reverse stocking stitch and tend to be worked over four or six stitches.

back cross cable

1 Slip the first three cable stitches purlwise off the left-hand needle and onto the cable needle. Leave the cable needle at the back of the work, then knit the next three stitches on the left-hand needle, keeping the yarn tight to prevent a gap from forming in the knitting.

2 Knit the three stitches directly from the cable needle, or if preferred, slip the three stitches from the cable needle back onto the left-hand needle and then knit them. This completes the cable cross.

front cross cable

1 Slip the first three cable stitches purlwise off the left-hand needle and onto the cable needle. Leave the cable needle at the front of the work, then knit the next three stitches on the left-hand needle, keeping the yarn tight to prevent a gap from forming in the knitting.

2 Knit the three stitches directly from the cable needle, or if preferred, slip the three stitches from the cable needle back onto the left-hand needle and then knit them. This completes the cable cross.

intarsia

Intarsia is used when you are working with larger areas of usually isolated colour, such as when knitting motifs. If the yarn not in use was stranded or woven behind, it could show through to the front or pull in the colour work. In intarsia you use separate strands or small balls of yarn for each colour area and then twist them together where they meet to prevent a gap forming.

vertical

rs

ws

changing colours on a vertical line
If the two colour areas are forming a vertical line, to change colours on a knit row drop the colour you were using. Pick up the new colour and wrap it around the dropped colour as shown, then continue with the new colour. Twist the yarns together on knit and purl rows in this same way at vertical-line colour changes.

right diagonal

rs

ws

changing colours on a right diagonal
If the two colour areas are forming a right diagonal line, on a knit row drop the colour you were using. Pick up the new colour and wrap it around the dropped colour as shown, then continue with the new colour. Twist the yarns together on knit rows only at right-diagonal colour changes.

left diagonal

rs

ws

changing colours on a left diagonal
If the two colour areas are forming a left diagonal line, on a purl row drop the colour you were using. Pick up the new colour and wrap it around the colour just dropped as shown, then continue with the new colour. Twist the yarns together on purl rows only at left-diagonal colour changes.

reading charts

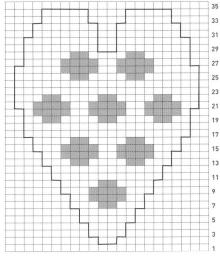

☐ A ecru   ▨ C lime

Most colour patterns are worked from a chart rather than set out in the text. Each square represents a stitch and row and the symbol or colour within it will tell you which colour to use. There will be a key listing the symbols used and the colours they represent.

Unless stated otherwise, the first row of the chart is worked from right to left and represents the first right-side row of your knitting. The second chart row represents the second and wrong-side row and is read and worked from left to right.

If the colour pattern is a repeated design, as in Fair Isle, the chart will tell you how many stitches are in each repeat. You will repeat these stitches as many times as is required. At each side of the repeat there may be edge stitches, these are only worked at the beginning and end of the rows and they indicate where you need to start and end for the piece you are knitting. Most colour patterns are worked in stocking stitch.

stranding

stranding on a knit row

1 On a right-side (knit) row, to change colours drop the colour you were using. Pick up the new colour, take it over the top of the dropped colour and start knitting with it.

2 To change back to the old colour, drop the colour you were knitting with. Pick up the old colour, take it under the dropped colour and knit to the next colour change, and so on.

stranding on a purl row

Stranding is used when colour is worked over a small amount of stitches where using two colours in a row. The colour you are not using is left hanging on the wrong side of the work and then picked up when it is needed again. This creates strands at the back of the work called floats. Care must be taken so that they are not pulled too tightly as this will pucker the fabric. By picking up the yarns over and under one another you will prevent them tangling.

1 On a wrong-side (purl) row, to change colours drop the colour you were using. Pick up the new colour, take it over the top of the dropped colour and start purling with it.

2 To change back to the old colour, drop the colour you were knitting with. Pick up the old colour, take it under the dropped colour and purl to the next colour change, and so on.

seaming

When you have completed the pieces of your knitting you reach one of the most important stages. The way you sew up or finish your project determines how good your finished garment will look. There are different types of seaming techniques but the best by far is mattress or ladder stitch, which creates an invisible seam. It can be used on stocking stitch, rib, garter and moss stitch.

The seam that I use for almost all sewing up is mattress stitch, which produces a wonderful invisible seam. It works well on any yarn, and makes a completely straight seam, as the same amount is taken up on each side – this also means that the knitted pieces should not need to be pinned together first. It is always worked on the right side of the fabric and is particularly useful for sewing up stripes and Fair Isle.

I use other types of seams less frequently, but they do have their uses. For instance, backstitch can sometimes be useful for sewing in a sleeve head, to neatly ease in the fullness. It is also good for catching in loose strands of

yarn on colourwork seams, where there can be a lot of short ends along the selvedge. Just remember when using backstitch to sew up your knitting that it is important to ensure that you work in a completely straight line.

The seam for joining two cast-off edges is handy for shoulder seams, while the seam for joining a cast-off edge with a side edge (selvedge) is usually used when sewing a sleeve onto the body on a dropped shoulder style.

It is best to leave a long tail at the casting-on stage to sew up your knitting with, so that the sewing up yarn is already secured in place. If this is not possible, when first securing the thread for the seam, you should leave a length

that can be darned in afterwards. All seams on knitting should be sewn with a large blunt-tipped yarn or tapestry needle to avoid splitting the yarn.

Before sewing up side seams, join the shoulder seams and attach the sleeves, unless they are set in sleeves. If there are any embellishments, such as applied pockets or embroidery, this is the time to put them on, when you can lay the garment out flat.

seams

mattress stitch on stocking stitch and double rib
With the right sides of the knitting facing you, insert the needle under the horizontal bar between the first stitch and next stitch. Then insert the needle under the same bar on the other piece. Continue to do this, drawing up the thread to form the seam.

mattress stitch on garter stitch
With the right sides of the knitting facing you, insert the needle through the bottom of the 'knot' on the edge and then through the top of the corresponding 'knot' on the opposite edge. Continue to do this from edge to edge, drawing up the thread to form a flat seam.

mattress stitch on moss stitch
With the right sides of the knitting facing you, insert the needle under the horizontal bar between the first and second stitches on one side and through the top of the 'knot' on the edge of the opposite side.

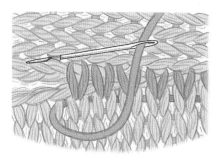

joining two cast-off edges (grafting)
1 With the cast-off edges butted together, bring the needle out in the centre of the first stitch just below the cast-off edge on one piece. Insert the needle through the centre of the first stitch on the other piece and out through the centre of the next stitch.

2 Next, insert the needle through the centre of the first stitch on the first piece again and out through the centre of the stitch next to it. Continue in this way until the seam is completed.

joining cast-off and selvedge edges
Bring the needle from back to front through the centre of the first stitch on the cast-off edge. Then insert it under one or two horizontal strands between the first and second stitches on the selvedge and back through the centre of the same cast-off stitch. Continue in this way until the seam is completed.

pickingupstitches

When you are adding a border to your garment, such as front bands or a neckband, you usually pick up stitches around the edge. A border can be sewn on afterwards but this method is far neater. If you are picking up stitches along a long edge, a front band of a jacket for example, a long circular needle can be used so that you can fit all the stitches on. The pattern will usually tell you how many stitches to pick up.

picking up stitches along a selvedge
With the right side of the knitting facing, insert the knitting needle from front to back between the first and second stitches of the first row. Wrap the yarn around the needle and pull a loop through to a form a new stitch on the needle. Continue in this way along the edge of the knitting.

picking up stitches along a neck edge
On a neck edge, work along the straight edges as for a selvedge. But along the curved edges, insert the needle through the centre of the stitch below the shaping (to avoid large gaps) and pull a loop of yarn through to form a new stitch on the needle.

Crossover vest and trousers   First coat
Home sweet home   Hooded carrying bag
Lacy shawl   Toy lamb

coming home

crossover vest

measurements

To fit ages 0–3 (3–6: 6–9: 9–12) months

finished measurements

Chest 42 (46: 50: 54)cm
Length to shoulder 26 (28: 30: 32)cm
Sleeve length 12 (13: 14: 16)cm

materials

2 (3: 3: 3) x 50g balls Debbie Bliss Baby Cashmerino in lilac (M) and a small amount in chocolate (C)
Pair each 3mm and 3$\frac{1}{4}$mm knitting needles
60cm ribbon, 7mm wide
One small button

tension

25 sts and 34 rows to 10cm square over st st using 3$\frac{1}{4}$mm needles.

abbreviations

See page 25.

back

With 3mm needles and C, cast on 65 (70: 75: 80) sts.
K 1 row.
Change to 3¼mm needles and M.
Beg with a k row, work in st st.
Work 6 (8: 10: 10) rows.
Dec row (right side) K8, skpo, k to last 10 sts, k2tog, k8.
Work 9 (9: 9: 11) rows.
Rep the last 10 (10: 10: 12) rows 3 times more and the dec row again. **55 (60: 65: 70) sts.**
Cont straight until back measures 17 (18: 20: 21)cm from cast-on edge, ending with a p row.
Shape armholes
Cast off 6 sts at beg of next 2 rows. **43 (48: 53: 58) sts.**
Cont straight until back measures 26 (28: 30: 32) cm from cast-on edge, ending with a p row.
Shape shoulders
Cast off 5 (6: 7: 8) sts at beg of next 4 rows.
Leave rem 23 (24: 25: 26) sts on a holder.

left front

With 3mm needles and C, cast on 44 (47: 50: 53) sts.
K 1 row.
Change to 3¼mm needles and M.
Beg with a k row, work in st st.
Work 6 (8: 10: 10) rows.
Dec row (right side) K8, skpo, k to end.
Work 9 (9: 9: 11) rows.
Rep the last 10 (10: 10: 12) rows 3 times more and the dec row again. **39 (42: 45: 48) sts.**
Cont straight until front measures 17 (18: 20: 21)cm from cast-on edge, ending with a p row.
Shape armhole
Cast off 6 sts at beg of next row. **33 (36: 39: 42) sts.**
Next row P to end.
Buttonhole row K to last 4 sts, yf, k2tog, k2.
Next row P to end.
Next row K to end.
Shape neck
Next row (wrong side) Cast off 5 (6: 7: 8) sts, p to end. **28 (30: 32: 34) sts.**
K 1 row.
Next row Cast off 5 sts, p to end.
K 1 row.
Next row Cast off 3 sts, p to end. **20 (22: 24: 26) sts.**
Next row K to last 2 sts, k2tog.
Cont to dec 1 st at neck edge on every foll right-side row until 10 (12: 14: 16) sts rem.
Cont straight until front measures same as Back to shoulder, ending at armhole edge.
Shape shoulder
Cast off 5 (6: 7: 8) sts at beg of next row.
Work 1 row.
Cast off rem 5 (6: 7: 8) sts.

right front

With 3mm needles and C, cast on 44 (47: 50: 53) sts.
K 1 row.
Change to 3¼mm needles and M.
Beg with a k row, work in st st.
Work 6 (8: 10: 10) rows.
Dec row (right side) K to last 10 sts, k2tog, k8.
Work 9 (9: 9: 11) rows.
Rep the last 10 (10: 10: 12) rows 3 times more and the dec row again. **39 (42: 45: 48) sts.**
Cont straight until front measures 17 (18: 20: 21)cm from cast-on edge, ending with a k row.
Shape armhole
Cast off 6 sts at beg of next row. **33 (36: 39: 42) sts.**
Work 4 rows straight.
Shape neck
Next row (right side) Cast off 5 (6: 7: 8) sts, k to end. **28 (30: 32: 34) sts.**
P 1 row.
Next row Cast off 5 sts, k to end.
P 1 row.
Next row Cast off 3 sts, k to end. **20 (22: 24: 26) sts.**
P 1 row.
Next row Skpo, k to end.
Cont to dec 1 st at neck edge on every foll right-side row until 10 (12: 14: 16) sts rem.
Cont straight until front measures same as Back to shoulder, ending at armhole edge.
Shape shoulder
Cast off 5 (6: 7: 8) sts at beg of next row.
Work 1 row.
Cast off rem 5 (6: 7: 8) sts.

sleeves

With 3mm needles and C, cast on 35 (38: 38: 41) sts.
K 1 row.
Change to 3¼mm needles and M.
Beg with a k row, work in st st and inc 1 st at each end of the 5th and every foll 6th row until there are 45 (50: 50: 55) sts.
Cont straight until sleeve measures 12 (13: 14: 16)cm from cast-on edge, ending with a p row.
Mark each end of last row with a coloured thread.
Work a further 2cm, ending with a p row.
Cast off.

button strip

With 3mm needles and M, cast on 15 (17: 19: 21) sts.
K 1 row.
Cast off.

right front edging	With right side facing, 3mm needles and C, pick up and k53 (55: 61: 63) sts evenly along right front edge. K 1 row. Cast off.
left front edging	With right side facing, 3mm needles and C, pick up and k53 (55: 61: 63) sts evenly along left front edge. K 1 row. Cast off.
neckband	Join shoulder seams. With right side facing, 3mm needles and C, pick up and k1 st across row ends of right front band, 39 (42: 43: 46) sts up right front neck, k across 23 (24: 25: 26) sts from back neck holder, pick up and k39 (42: 43: 46) sts down left front neck then pick up and k1 st across row ends of front band. **103 (110: 113: 120) sts.** K 1 row. Cast off.
to make up	Sew sleeves into armholes with row ends above markers sewn to sts cast off at underarm. Join side and sleeve seams. Cut ribbon in half and sew one piece to right front and one on left front. Sew one end of button strip to right front armhole seam 4 rows above armhole shaping then sew button to other end.

measurements

To fit ages 0–3 (3–6: 6–9: 9–12) months
finished measurements
Over nappy 41 (46: 51: 56)cm
Length 29 (33: 38: 43)cm

materials

2 (2: 2: 3) x 50g balls Debbie Bliss Baby Cashmerino in chocolate (M) and small amount in lilac (C)
Pair each 3mm and 3¼mm knitting needles
Waist length of 1.5cm wide elastic

tension

25 sts and 34 rows to 10cm square over st st using 3¼mm needles.

abbreviations

See page 25.

trousers to match

legs (make 2)

With 3mm needles and C, cast on 54 (60: 66: 72) sts.
Rib row * K1, p1; rep from * to end.
Change to M and work a further 9 rows.
Change to 3¼mm needles.
Beg with a k row, work in st st until work measures 14 (16: 17: 19)cm from cast-on edge, ending with a p row.
Shape crotch
Inc 1 st at each end of the next row and 2 (2: 3: 3) foll alt rows.
P 1 row.
Cast on 3 sts at beg of next 2 rows. **66 (72: 80: 86) sts.**
Shape for legs
Work 2 rows.
Dec 1 st at inside edge of the next row and 2 (3: 4: 5) foll alt rows. **60 (64: 70: 74) sts.**
Dec 1 st at each end of 5 (6: 7: 8) foll 6th rows. **50 (52: 56: 58) sts.**
Work 6 (6: 8: 10) rows.
Change to 3mm needles and C.
K 2 rows.
Cast off.

to make up

Join inner leg seams. Join centre front and back seam. Join elastic into a ring. Work a herringbone casing over rib at waist, enclosing elastic.

first coat

measurements

To fit ages 0–3 (3–6: 6–9: 9–12) months

finished measurements

Chest 46 (50: 55: 60)cm
Length to shoulder 28 (30: 32: 34)cm
Sleeve length 12 (13: 14: 16)cm

materials

3 (3: 4: 4) x 50g balls Debbie Bliss Baby Cashmerino in stone (M) and a small amount in ecru (C)
Pair each 3mm and 3¹/₄mm knitting needles
4 small buttons

tension

25 sts and 34 rows to 10cm square over st st and 32 sts and 34 rows to 10cm square over rib both using 3¹/₄mm needles.

abbreviations

See page 25.

back

With 3mm needles and M, cast on 75 (83: 91: 99) sts.
K 3 rows.
Change to 3¼mm needles.
Beg with a k row, work in st st until back measures 15 (16: 18: 19)cm from cast-on edge, ending with a p row.
Next row (right side) K1, * p1, k1; rep from * to end.
Next row P1, * k1, p1; rep from * to end.
Rep the last 2 rows until back measures 18 (19: 22: 23)cm from cast-on edge, ending with a wrong-side row.
Shape armholes
Cast off 8 sts at beg of next 2 rows. **59 (67: 75: 83) sts.**
Dec 1 st at each end of the next row and 3 (4: 5: 6) foll alt rows. **51 (57: 63: 69) sts.**
Cont straight until back measures 28 (30: 32: 34)cm from cast-on edge, ending with a wrong-side row.
Shape shoulders
Cast off 9 (11: 14: 16) sts at beg of next 2 rows.
Leave rem 33 (35: 35: 37) sts on a holder.

left front

With 3mm needles and M, cast on 39 (43: 47: 51) sts.
K 3 rows.
Change to 3¼mm needles.
Next row (right side) K to end.
Next row K3, p to end.
These 2 rows form the st st with garter st edging.
Cont straight until front measures 15 (16: 18: 19)cm from cast-on edge, ending with a wrong-side row.
Next row (right side) * P1, k1; rep from * to last 5 sts, p1, k4.
Next row K3, * p1, k1; rep from * to end.
Rep the last 2 rows until front measures 18 (19: 22: 23)cm from cast-on edge, ending with a wrong-side row.
Shape armhole
Cast off 9 sts at beg of next row. **30 (34: 38: 42) sts.**
Work 1 row.
Dec 1 st at beg of the next row and 3 (4: 5: 6) foll alt rows. **26 (29: 32: 35) sts.**
Work straight until front measures 24 (26: 27: 29)cm from cast-on edge, ending with a wrong-side row.
Shape neck
Next row Rib to last 10 sts, leave these sts on a holder.
Dec 1 st at neck edge on every row until 9 (11: 14: 16) sts rem.
Cont straight until front measures same as Back to shoulder, ending at armhole edge.
Shape shoulder
Cast off.
Mark positions for 4 buttons, the first on the 3rd row of rib patt and the fourth 1cm below neck shaping, with the rem 2 buttons spaced evenly between.

right front

With 3 mm needles and M, cast on 39 (43: 47: 51) sts.
K 3 rows.
Change to 3¼ mm needles.
Next row (right side) K to end.
Next row P to last 3 sts, k3.
These 2 rows form the st st with garter st edging.
Cont straight until front measures 15 (16: 18: 19)cm from cast-on edge, ending with a wrong-side row.
Next row (right side) K4, p1, * k1, p1; rep from * to end.
Next row K1, * p1, k1; rep from * to last 4 sts, p1, k3.
Buttonhole row K2, yf, k2tog, p1, rib to end.
Work rem buttonholes as set by this row to match button markers.
Rep the last 2 rows until front measures 18 (19: 22: 23)cm from cast-on edge, ending with a right-side row.

Shape armhole
Cast off 9 sts at beg of next row. **30 (34: 38: 42) sts.**
Dec 1 st at beg of the next row and 3 (4: 5: 6) foll alt rows. **26 (29: 32: 35) sts.**
Work straight until front measures 24 (26: 27: 29)cm from cast-on edge, ending with a wrong-side row.

Shape neck
Next row Rib 10 sts, leave these sts on a holder, rib to end.
Dec 1 st at neck edge on every row until 9 (11: 14: 16) sts rem.
Cont straight until front measures same as Back to shoulder, ending at armhole edge.

Shape shoulder
Cast off.

sleeves

With 3mm needles and M, cast on 40 (43: 45: 46) sts.
K 3 rows.
Change to 3¼mm needles.
Beg with a k row, work in st st and inc 1 st at each end of the 5th row and every foll 6th row until there are 50 (55: 57: 60) sts.
Cont straight until sleeve measures 12 (13: 14: 16)cm from cast-on edge, ending with a p row.
Mark each end of last row with a coloured thread.
Work a further 2cm, ending with a p row.
Shape top
Dec 1 st at each end of the next row and 3 (4: 5: 6) foll alt rows. 42 **(45: 45: 46) sts.**
Cast off.

collar

Join shoulder seams.
With right side facing, 3¼mm needles and M, slip 10 sts from right front holder onto a needle, pick up and k16 (16: 18: 18) sts up right front neck, k33 (35: 35: 37) sts from back, 16 (16: 18: 18) sts down left side of front neck, k10 sts from left front holder. 85 **(87: 91: 93) sts.**
Next row (wrong side) K1, * p1, k1; rep from * to end.
This row sets the rib.
Next 2 rows Rib to last 26 sts, turn.
Next 2 rows Rib to last 20 sts, turn.
Next 2 rows Rib to last 14 sts, turn.
Next 2 rows Rib to last 8 sts, turn.
Next row Rib to end.
Cast off 4 sts at beg of next 2 rows.
Work a further 14 (16: 16: 18) rows.
Break off yarn.
With right side facing, 3mm needles and M, pick up and k12 (14: 14: 16) sts along row ends of collar, k across sts of collar, then pick up and k12 (14: 14: 16) sts along row ends of collar.
Next row K12 (14: 14: 16), m1, k to last 12 (14: 14: 16) sts, m1, k to end.
Change to C.
Next row K to end.
Next row K12 (14: 14: 16), m1, k to last 12 (14: 14: 16) sts, m1, k to end.
Cast off.

to make up

Sew sleeves into armholes, with row ends above markers sewn to sts cast off at underarm. Join side and sleeve seams. Sew on buttons. Sew row ends of collar edging in place.

home sweet home

size
Height 30.5 cm
Width 42 cm

materials
1 x 50g ball Debbie Bliss Rialto DK each in ecru (M), duck egg blue (A), pale pink (B), grey (C) and brown (D)
Pair 4 mm knitting needles
30 x 40 cm plain birch picture frame

tension
22 sts and 30 rows to 10 cm square over st st using 4 mm needles.

abbreviations
See page 25.

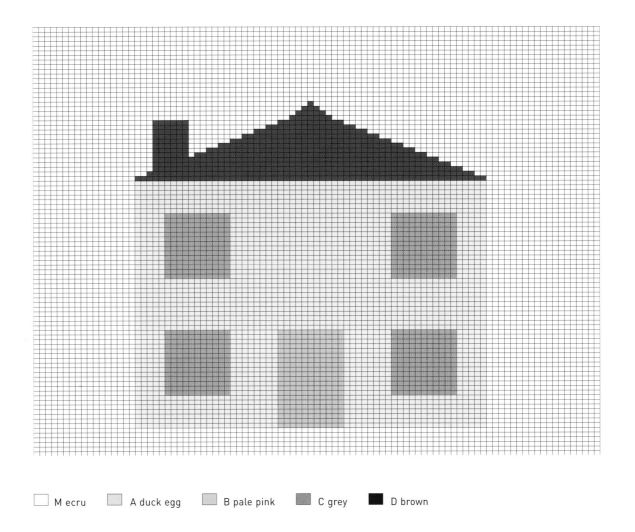

□ M ecru   ▨ A duck egg   ▨ B pale pink   ▨ C grey   ■ D brown

chart note

The chart is worked in st st. When working from the chart, k rows are read from right to left, and p rows are read from left to right. When working motif, use the Intarsia method (see pages 28–30), knitting with separate small balls of yarn for each area of colour and twisting yarns on wrong side when changing colour to avoid holes.

to make

With 4 mm needles and M, cast on 95 sts.
Beg with a k row, work in st st from chart using the Intarsia method, until all 92 rows have been worked.
Cast off.
Press according to the ball band.

to finish

Remove glass from the frame, cut a piece of card the same size as the backing board, then using double-sided tape, attach the picture to the card, insert and re-assemble frame.

measurements

To fit ages 0–3 (3–6) months
finished measurements
Length to shoulder 55 (60) cm

materials

8 (9) x 50g balls Debbie Bliss Cashmerino Aran in ecru
Pair 4$\frac{1}{2}$mm knitting needles
4$\frac{1}{2}$mm circular knitting needle
40cm zip fastener

tension

20 rows and 42 rows to 10cm square over garter st using 4$\frac{1}{2}$mm needles.

abbreviations

kfb = knit into front and back of next st.
See page 25.

hoodedcarryingbag

back, front and sleeves
(worked in one piece)

With 4$\frac{1}{2}$mm needles, cast on 54 (62) sts.
1st row Knit.
This row forms garter st and is repeated.
Cont straight until back measures 46 (48) cm from cast-on edge, ending with a wrong-side row.
Change to 4$\frac{1}{2}$mm circular needle.
Shape sleeves
Cast on 30 (36) sts at beg of next 2 rows. **114 (134) sts.**
Cont straight in garter st until back measures 55 (60) cm from cast-on edge, ending with a wrong-side row.
Place a marker at each end of last row for shoulder line.
Divide for fronts
Next row (right side) With 4$\frac{1}{2}$mm needles, k43 (53), turn and cont on these sts only for right front, leaving rem sts on the circular needle.
Shape neck
Next row (wrong side) Kfb, k to end. **44 (54) sts.**
K 1 row.
Rep the last 2 rows once more. **45 (55) sts.**
Next row Cast on 2 sts, k to end. **47 (57) sts.**
K 1 row.
Next row Cast on 3 sts, k to end. **50 (60) sts.**

K 1 row.
Rep the last 2 rows once more. **53 (63) sts.**
Next row Cast on 7 sts, k to end. **60 (70) sts.**
Mark front edge of last row with a coloured thread.
Cont straight in garter st until work measures 10 (12) cm from shoulder line marker, ending with a wrong-side row.
Shape sleeve
Next row (right side) Cast off 30 (36) sts, k to end. **30 (34) sts.**
Cont in garter st until work measures 40 cm from front edge marker, ending with a right-side row.
Next row Cast off 3 sts, slip rem 27 (31) sts onto a holder.
Return to sts on circular needle and with right side facing, slip 28 sts at centre back neck onto a holder, rejoin yarn to rem 43 (53) sts for left front, k to end.
K 1 row.
Next row (right side) Kfb, k to end. **44 (54) sts.**
K 1 row.
Rep the last 2 rows once more. **45 (55) sts.**
Next row Cast on 2 sts, k to end. **47 (57) sts.**
K 1 row.
Next row Cast on 3 sts, k to end. **50 (60) sts.**
K 1 row.
Rep the last 2 rows once more. **53 (63) sts.**
K 1 row.
Next row Cast on 4 sts, k to end. **57 (67) sts.**
Mark front edge of last row with a coloured thread.
Cont straight in garter st until work measures 10 (12) cm from shoulder line marker, ending with a right-side row.
Shape sleeve
Next row (wrong side) Cast off 30 (36) sts, k to end. **27 (31) sts.**
Cont in garter st until work measures 40 cm from front edge marker, ending with a right-side row.
Next row (wrong side) K 27 (31) sts of left front, then k across 27 (31) sts on right front holder. **54 (62) sts.**
Cont straight until front measures 55 (60) cm from shoulder line, ending with a right-side row.
Cast off.

hood

With right side facing and 4½mm needles, pick up and k22 sts up right front neck to shoulder, then work k2, [m1, k2] 13 times across 28 sts on back neck holder, then pick up and k20 sts down left front neck. **83 sts.**
Work in garter st until hood measures 20 cm from pick-up row.
Cast off.

to make up

Fold cast-off edge of hood in half and stitch to form top seam. Fold along shoulder line and stitch front to back along sleeve seams and around side and lower edges. Handstitch zip in place with left front edge sewn close to the zip teeth and right front, sewn approximately 1 cm from the edge, so forming a fly front. Catchstitch cast-off sts of lower end of fly front in place.

lacy shawl

size
94 x 110 cm, excluding edging

materials
16 x 50g balls Debbie Bliss Baby Cashmerino in pale blue
Pair 3¼ mm knitting needles
3¼ mm circular knitting needle

tension
24 sts and 40 rows to 10 cm square over centre lace patt using 3¼ mm needles.

abbreviations
sk2togpo = sl 1, k2tog, pass slipped st over.
y2rn = yarn round needle twice to make 2 sts.
See page 25.

centre square

With 3¼mm circular needle, cast on 239 sts.

1st row (right side) K2, * k1 tbl, k2, yf, skpo, k4, yf, skpo, k3, k2tog, yf, k2; rep from * to last 3 sts, k1 tbl, k2.

2nd and every foll wrong-side row P.

3rd row K2, * k1, k2tog, yf, k1 tbl, yf, skpo; rep from * to last 3 sts, k3.

5th row K1, yf, * sk2togpo, yf, k3, yf; rep from * to last 4 sts, sk2togpo, yf, k1.

7th row K2, * yf, skpo, k3, k2tog, yf, k5, yf, skpo, k4; rep from * to last 3 sts, yf, skpo, k1.

9th row K2tog, yf, * k1 tbl, yf, skpo, k3, k1 tbl, k2, yf, skpo, k1, k1 tbl, k3, k2tog, yf; rep from * to last 3 sts, k1 tbl, yf, skpo.

11th row K2, * k2, yf, skpo, k3, k2tog, yf, k1 tbl, yf, skpo, k3, k2tog, yf, k1; rep from * to last 3 sts, k3.

13th row K2, * k3, yf, skpo, k1, k2tog, yf, k3, yf, skpo, k1, k2tog, yf, k2; rep from * to last 3 sts, k3.

15th row K2, * [yf, skpo, k2] twice, yf, sk2togpo, yf, k2, k2tog, yf, k3; rep from * to last 3 sts, yf, skpo, k1.

17th row K2tog, yf, * k1 tbl, [yf, skpo, k2] twice, yf, skpo, k1, k2tog, yf, k2, k2tog, yf; rep from * to last 3 sts, k1 tbl, yf, skpo.

19th row K2, * [k2, yf, skpo] twice, k1, k1 tbl, k1, k2tog, yf, k2, k2tog, yf, k1; rep from * to last 3 sts, k3.

21st row K1, yf, * sk2togpo, yf, k5, yf, skpo, k1, k2tog, yf, k5, yf; rep from * to last 4 sts, sk2togpo, yf, k1.

23rd row K2, * yf, skpo, k6, yf, sk2togpo, yf, k7; rep from * to last 3 sts, yf, skpo, k1.

24th row As 2nd row.

These 24 rows form the centre patt and are repeated.

Cont in patt ending with the 23rd row of the 17th patt repeat (407 rows worked).

Cast off.

edging

With 3¼mm needles, cast on 10 sts.

K 1 row, then work in patt as follows:

1st row (wrong side) Sl 1, [k1, yf, k2tog] twice, k1, y2rn, k1, y2rn, k1.

2nd row [K2, p1] twice (each y2rn is treated as 2 sts, the first is worked as k1, the second as p1), k2, [yf, k2tog, k1] twice.

3rd row Sl 1, [k1, yf, k2tog] twice, k7.

4th row Cast off 4, k3, [yf, k2tog, k1] twice.

These 4 rows form the border patt and are repeated until border is long enough to fit all around the edge of the centre patt, gathering slightly at the corners, ending with a 3rd row.

Cast off.

to make up

Block centre square by placing a towel over a board and pinning knitting out to the correct dimensions. Spray lightly with water and leave to dry. Cover border in sections with a damp cloth and press lightly with a medium iron. Join ends of edging across the cast-on and cast-off edges and sew around the edge of the square.

size
Approximate height to shoulder 10cm
Approximate length from nose to tail 14cm

materials
1 x 50g ball Debbie Bliss Cashmerino Astrakhan in ecru (A)
Oddments of double knitting weight yarn in black (B)
Pair 3¾mm knitting needles
Washable toy stuffing (conforming to British Standard 5665)

tension
20 sts and 30 rows to 10cm over st st using 3¾mm needles and yarn A.

abbreviations
kfb = k into front and back of next st.
pfb = p into front and back of next st.
sk2togpo = sl 1, k2tog, pass slipped st over.
See page 25.

toy lamb

main body
(worked from tail to nose)

** With 3¾mm needles and A, cast on 2 sts.
Beg with a k row, work in st st.
Work 2 rows.
Next row Kfb, kfb. **4 sts.** **
P 1 row.
Next row (right side) Cast on 8 sts in A and 11 sts in B, k to end in correct yarns.
Next row Cast on 11 sts in B and 8 sts in A, p to end in correct yarns. **42 sts.**
Place a marker (X) on 14th st from each end of last row.
Work 4 rows in st st.
Cast off 7 sts at beg of next 2 rows. **28 sts.**
Next row Cast off 2 sts, k to last 2 sts, k2tog.
Next row Cast off 2 sts, p to last 2 rows, p2tog. **22 sts.**
Next row K2tog, k to last 2 sts, k2tog. **20 sts.**
Work 7 rows.
Cast on 3 sts in B at beg of next 2 rows and 8 sts in B at beg of foll 2 rows. **42 sts.**
Work 4 rows.
Cast off 14 sts at beg of next 2 rows. **14 sts.**
Work 2 rows.
Place a marker (Y) at each end of last row.

Shape head

Next row K4, [kfb, k1] twice, kfb, k5. **17 sts.**
Next row P5, [pfb, p1] 3 times, pfb, p5. **21 sts.**
K 1 row.
Next row P2tog, p to last 2 sts, p2tog.
Rep the last 2 rows once more. **17 sts.**
Next row K7 B, k3 A, k7 B.
Next row P8 B, p1 A, p8 B.
Work 2 rows.
Next row K2, skpo, k1, skpo, k3, k2tog, k1, k2tog, k2. **13 sts.**
P 1 row.
Next row K3, skpo, k3, k2tog, k3. **11 sts.**
P 1 row.
Next row K1, [skpo] twice, k1, [k2tog] twice, k1. **7 sts.**
Next row P1, p2tog, p1, p2tog tbl, p1. **5 sts.**
Next row K1, sk2togpo, k1. **3 sts.**
Break yarn, thread through rem sts, pull up and secure.

gusset
(worked from back to front)

With 3³/₄mm needles, cast on 11 B, 6 A, 11 B. **28 sts.**
Keeping yarns correct throughout and beg with a k, row work 4 rows in st st.
Next row Cast off 7 sts, with 1 st on needle after cast-off, k next 5 sts, k2tog, k to end.
Next row Cast off 7 sts, p to end. **13 sts.**
Next row Cast off 2 sts, k to last 2 sts, k2tog.
Next row Cast off 2 sts, p to last 2 sts, p2tog tbl. **7 sts.**
Next row K2tog, k to last 2 sts, k2tog. **5 sts.**
Work 7 rows.
Cast on 3 sts in B at beg of next 2 rows and 8 sts in B at beg of foll 2 rows. **27 sts.**
Work 4 rows.
Cast off 12 sts at beg of next 2 rows. **3 sts.**
Work 2 rows.
Next row Sk2togpo and fasten off.

ears (make 2)

With 3³/₄mm needles and B, cast on 2 sts.
K 2 rows.
Next row Kfb, k1. **3 sts.**
K 6 rows.
Cast off.

to make up

Join head from nose to markers (Y). Join back seam from tail to markers (X). Join gusset to main body with point of gusset to markers (Y), centre of cast-on edge of gusset to markers (X) and matching legs, but leave seam open between legs on one side. Stuff legs first, then head and finally body, then close seam. Sew ears in place and embroider eyes with yarn A.

Baby knickers Baby shorts Heart mobile
Bath robe Tank top Pinafore dress Baby
beanbag Felted slippers

at home

measurements

To fit ages 3–6 (6–9) months
finished measurements
Over nappy 51 (56) cm
Length 22 (24) cm

materials

2 (2) x 50g balls Debbie Bliss Baby Cashmerino in grey
Pair each $2^3/_4$mm and $3^1/_4$mm knitting needles
Waist length of 2cm wide elastic

tension

25 sts and 34 rows to 10cm square over st st using $3^1/_4$mm needles.

abbreviations

See page 25.

baby knickers

back

With $2^3/_4$mm needles, cast on 66 (76) sts.
Rib row * K1, p1; rep from * to end.
Rib a further 9 rows.
Change to $3^1/_4$mm needles.
Back shaping
Next 2 rows K to last 30 sts, turn, sl 1, p to last 30 sts, turn.
Next 2 rows Sl 1, k to last 24 sts, turn, sl 1, p to last 24 sts, turn.
Next 2 rows Sl 1, k to last 18 sts, turn, sl 1, p to last 18 sts, turn.
Next 2 rows Sl 1, k to last 12 sts, turn, sl 1, p to last 12 sts, turn.
Next 2 rows Sl 1, k to last 6 sts, turn, sl 1, p to last 6 sts, turn.
Next row Sl 1, k to end.
Inc row P3, m1, [p6, m1] 4 times, p12 (22), [m1, p6] 4 times, m1, p3. 76 (86) sts.
Beg with a k row, cont in st st.
Work 42 (52) rows.
Dec 1 st at each end of the next row and 9 (7) foll alt rows. **56 (70) sts.**
P 1 row.
Dec 1 st at each end of the next 16 (20) rows. **24 (30) sts.**
Work 20 (22) rows without shaping.
Break off yarn and leave these sts on a holder.

Side of right leg

With 3¹/₄mm needles, cast on 2 sts.

P 1 row.

Next row K1, m1, k1.

Next row P2, m1, p1.

Next row K1, m1, k to end.

Next row P to last st, m1, p1.

Rep the last 2 rows 10 (11) times. **26 (28) sts.**

Break off yarn and leave these sts on a holder.

Side of left leg

With 3¹/₄mm needles, cast on 2 sts.

P 1 row.

Next row K1, m1, k1.

Next row P1, m1, p2.

Next row K to last st, m1, k1.

Next row P1, m1, p to end.

Rep the last 2 rows 10 (11) times. **26 (28) sts.**

Next row K these 26 (28) sts, k24 (30) sts from first holder, then k 26 (28) sts from second holder. **76 (86) sts.**

Work 18 (26) rows without shaping.

Dec row [P5, p2tog] 5 times, p6 (16), [p2tog, p5] 5 times. **66 (76) sts.**

Change to 2³/₄mm needles.

Rib row * K1, p1; rep from * to end.

Rib a further 9 rows.

Cast off in rib.

leg edgings

With right side facing and 3¹/₄mm needles, pick up and k72 (78) sts evenly round leg opening.

Rib row * K1, p1; rep from * to end.

Rib 1 more row.

Change to 2³/₄mm needles.

Rib a further 3 rows.

Cast-off row Cast off 3 sts, * slip st back onto left-hand needle, cast on 2 sts, cast off 6 sts; rep from *, ending last rep cast off 3 sts.

to make up

Join side and edging seams. Join elastic into a ring. Work a herringbone casing over rib at waist, enclosing elastic.

measurements

To fit ages 3–6 (6–9) months
finished measurements
Over nappy 51 (56) cm
Length 27 (30) cm

materials

2 (3) x 50g balls Debbie Bliss Baby Cashmerino in grey
Pair each 3 mm and 3^1/$_4$ mm knitting needles
Waist length of 2 cm wide elastic

tension

25 sts and 34 rows to 10 cm square over st st using 3^1/$_4$ mm needles

abbreviations

See page 25.

baby shorts

right leg

With 3 mm needles, cast on 66 (72) sts.
Rib row * K1, p1; rep from * to end.
Work a further 9 rows in rib.
Change to 3^1/$_4$ mm needles.
Back shaping
Next 2 rows K6, turn, sl 1, p to end.
Next 2 rows K12, turn, sl 1, p to end.
Next 2 rows K18, turn, sl 1, p to end.
Next 2 rows K24, turn, sl 1, p to end.
Next 2 rows K30, turn, sl 1, p to end.
2nd size only
Next 2 rows K36, turn, sl 1, p to end.
Both sizes
Beg with a k row, cont in st st until work measures 17 (19) cm along short edge, ending with a p row.
** **Shape crotch**
Inc row (right side) K2, m1, k to last 2 sts, m1, k2.
P 1 row.
Rep the last 2 rows, 3 times more. **74 (80) sts.**
Cast on 3 sts at beg of next 2 rows. **80 (86) sts.**

Shape for legs

Work 2 rows in st st.

Dec row (right side) K2, skpo, k to last 4 sts, k2tog, k2.

Work 3 rows in st st.

Rep the last 4 rows, 4 (5) times more. **70 (74) sts.**

Leg edging

Change to 3 mm needles.

Dec row K1 (3), [k2tog, k4] 11 times, k2tog, k1 (3). **58 (62) sts.**

P 1 row.

Eyelet row (right side) K1, [yf, k2tog] to last st, k1.

Work 2 rows in st st.

Cast off.

left leg

With 3 mm needles, cast on 66 (72) sts.

Rib row * K1, p1; rep from * to end.

Work a further 9 rows in rib.

Change to 3¹/₄ mm needles.

Back shaping

Next 2 rows P6, turn, sl 1, k to end.

Next 2 rows P12, turn, sl 1, k to end.

Next 2 rows P18, turn, sl 1, k to end.

Next 2 rows P24, turn, sl 1, k to end.

Next 2 rows P30, turn, sl 1, k to end.

2nd size only

Next 2 rows P36, turn, sl 1, k to end.

Both sizes

Beg with a p row, cont in st st until work measures 17 (19) cm along short edge, ending with a p row.

Work as Right Leg from ** to end.

to make up

Join inner leg seams. Join centre front and back seam. Join elastic into a ring. Work a herringbone casing over rib at waist, enclosing elastic. Fold picot edge of legs onto wrong side and slip stitch in place.

sizes
Approximately 8 (9: 10) cm for small (medium: large) hearts

materials
Oddments of 50g balls of Debbie Bliss Cotton DK in ecru (A), duck egg blue (B), lime (C) and pale pink (D)
Pair 4mm knitting needles
120cm narrow ribbon

tension
20 sts and 28 rows to 10cm square over st st using 4mm needles.

abbreviations
kfb = knit into front and back of next st.
ssk = [slip 1 knitwise] twice, insert tip of left hand needle into fronts of slipped sts and k2tog. See page 25.

heart mobile

note
The instructions are given for the basic heart shapes and the charts are given for the designs we used for our shapes. You can draw out the shapes on graph paper and create your own designs. Carry yarns not in use across wrong side of work and weave in yarns if carried over more than 4 sts. When working large spots, twist yarns at colour change to avoid holes forming.

basic hearts
(make 2 of each size)

With 4mm needles, cast on 2 sts.
1st row P2.
2nd row (right side) Kfb, kfb. 4 sts.
3rd row P.
4th row K1, m1, k to last st, m1, k1.
Rep the last 2 rows until there are 14 (16: 18) sts, ending with a right-side row.
Work 3 rows in st st.
Next row As 4th row. **16 (18: 20) sts.**
Work 3 (5: 5) rows in st st.
Small and medium hearts only
Next row Ssk, k4 (5), k2tog, turn and cont on these 6 (7) sts only.
P 1 row.
Next row Ssk, k4 (5).
P 1 row.

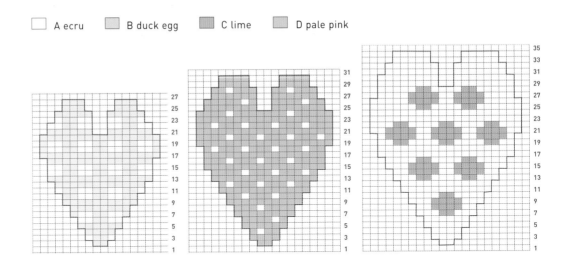

□ A ecru   ▨ B duck egg   ▨ C lime   ▨ D pale pink

Next row Ssk, k1 (2), k2tog.

P 1 row.

Cast off.

With right side facing, rejoin yarn to rem sts, ssk, k4 (5), k2tog.

P 1 row.

Next row K4 (5), k2tog.

P 1 row.

Next row Ssk, k1(2), k2tog.

P 1 row.

Cast off.

Large heart only

Next row Ssk, k to last 2 sts, k2tog. **18 sts.**

P 1 row.

Next row Ssk, k5, k2tog, turn and cont on these 7 sts only.

** Work 3 rows in st st.

Next row Ssk, k3, k2tog.

P 1 row.

Cast off. **

With right side facing, rejoin yarn to rem sts, ssk, k5, k2tog.

Work as first side from ** to **.

to make up

Join hearts together in pairs around their outer edges. Thread the ribbon through the small heart from top to bottom, leaving a loop at the top. Tie the two ends together under the heart to prevent it slipping down the ribbon. Thread the ribbon ends through the medium heart and tie at the base, then thread through the large heart and tie.

measurements
To fit ages 6 (12: 18: 24) months
finished measurements
Chest 59 (63: 67: 71) cm
Length to shoulder 42 (48: 54: 60) cm
Sleeve length (with cuff turned back) 16 (18: 21: 24) cm

materials
11 (12: 14: 15) x 50g balls Debbie Bliss Cotton DK in pink (M) and 1 x 50g ball in chocolate (C)
Pair each $3^3/4$ mm and 4 mm knitting needles
4 mm circular knitting needle

tension
20 sts and 32 rows to 10 cm square over moss st using 4 mm needles.

abbreviations
See page 25.

bath robe

back

With 4mm circular needle and M, cast on 157 (169: 185: 197) sts.

Moss st row K1, * p1, k1; rep from * to end.

This row forms the moss st and is repeated.

Work a further 31 (33: 35: 37) rows in moss st.

Dec row (right side) Moss st 42 (44: 46: 48), k3tog, moss st to last 45 (47: 49: 51), k3tog, moss st to end.

Moss st 13 rows.

Dec row (right side) Moss st 41 (43: 45: 47), p3tog, moss st to last 44 (46: 48: 50), p3tog, moss st to end.

Moss st 13 rows.

Cont in moss st, dec 4 sts as set on next row and 1 (2: 3: 4) foll 14th rows, then work the dec row once more. **137 (145: 157: 165) sts.**

Work 11 rows.

Divide for back and fronts

Next row Moss st 36 (38: 41: 43) sts and leave these sts on a holder for right front, cast off next 6 (6: 8: 8) sts, with 1 st on needle after cast-off, moss st next 52 (56: 58: 62) sts and leave these sts on a holder for back, cast off next 6 (6: 8: 8) sts, with 1 st on needle after cast-off, moss st 35 (37: 40: 42).

Working on the last set of 36 (38: 41: 43) sts for left front, work in moss st for a further 11 (12: 13: 14) cm, ending with a wrong-side row.

Shape shoulder

Cast off 16 (17: 18: 19) sts at beg of next row.

Work 1 row.

Leave rem 20 (21: 23: 24) sts on a spare needle.

Back

With wrong side facing, rejoin yarn to 53 (57: 59: 63) sts on back holder, patt to end.

Work straight until back measures same as Left Front to shoulder, ending with a wrong-side row.

Shape shoulders

Cast off 16 (17: 18: 19) sts at beg of next 2 rows.

Cast off rem 21 (23: 23: 25) sts.

Right front

With wrong side facing, rejoin yarn to 36 (38: 41: 43) sts on right front holder, patt to end.

Work straight until front measures same as Back to shoulder, ending with a right-side row.

Shape shoulder

Cast off 16 (17: 18: 19) sts at beg of next row. **20 (21: 23: 24) sts.**

Leave rem sts on a holder.

sleeves

With 4mm needles and C, cast on 29 (31: 33: 35) sts.

K 1 row.

Change to M.

Next row K1, * p1, k1; rep from * to end.

This row forms the moss st and is repeated.

Work a further 13 (13: 15: 15) rows in moss st.

Change to 3¾mm needles.

Work 14 (14: 16: 16) rows.

Change to 4mm needles.

Cont in moss st and inc 1 st at each end of 3rd (5th: 5th: 7th) row and every foll 4th row until

there are 45 (49: 55: 59) sts, taking all inc sts into moss st.
Cont straight until sleeve measures 20 (22: 26: 29) cm from cast-on edge, ending with a wrong-side row.
Mark each end of last row with a coloured thread.
Work a further 6 (6: 8: 8) rows.
Cast off.

hood

Join shoulder seams.
Using 4mm needles and M, cont as follows:
Next row (right side) Moss st 20 (21: 23: 24) sts from right front, cast on 31 (35: 35: 39) sts, moss st 20 (21: 23: 24) sts from left front. **71 (77: 81: 87) sts.**
Work 60 (62: 64: 66) rows in moss st.
Shape top
Next row Moss st 34 (37: 39: 42), work 3 tog, moss st 34 (37: 39: 42).
Next row Moss st 33 (36: 38: 41), work 3 tog, moss st 33 (36: 38: 41).
Next row Moss st 32 (35: 37: 40), work 3 tog, moss st 32 (35: 37: 40).
Next row Moss st 31 (34: 36: 39), work 3 tog, moss st 31 (34: 36: 39).
Next row Moss st 30 (33: 35: 38), work 3 tog, moss st 30 (33: 35: 38).
Next row Moss st 29 (32: 34: 37), work 3 tog, moss st 29 (32: 34: 37).
Next row Moss st 28 (31: 33: 36), work 3 tog, moss st 28 (31: 33: 36).
Next row Moss st 27 (30: 32: 35), work 3 tog, moss st 27 (30: 32: 35).
Cast off.

pockets (make 2)

With 4mm needles and M, cast on 19 (21: 21: 23) sts.
Work 24 (26: 26: 28) rows in moss st.
Change to C.
K 1 row.
Cast off in C.

tie belt

With 4mm circular needle and M, cast on 191 (201: 211: 221) sts.
Work 3 rows in moss st.
Cast off in moss st.

to make up

Join upper hood seam. Stitch cast-on edge of hood to sts cast-off at back neck. Join sleeve seams to markers, reversing seam for turn-up. Sew sleeves into armholes, with row ends above markers sewn to sts cast off at underarm. Sew on pockets.

measurements

To fit ages 0–3 (3–6: 6–9: 9–12:) months

finished measurements

Chest 45 (50: 53: 58) cm

Length to shoulder 21 (24: 26: 28) cm

materials

2 (2: 3: 3) x 50g balls Debbie Bliss Baby Cashmerino in flax

Pair each 3mm and $3^1/_4$mm knitting needles

3mm circular knitting needle

One small button

tension

25 sts and 34 rows to 10cm square over st st using $3^1/_4$mm needles.

abbreviations

See page 25.

tank top

back

With 3¼mm needles, cast on 59 (65: 68: 74) sts.
1st row (right side) K2, * p1, k2; rep from * to end.
2nd row P.
Rep the last 2 rows twice more.
Now work in patt as follows:
1st row (right side) K2 (5: 2: 5), * p1, k8; rep from * to last 6 sts, p1, k2 (5: 2: 5).
2nd row P.
These 2 rows form the patt and are repeated.
Cont in patt until back measures 11 (13: 14: 15) cm from cast-on edge, ending with a
p row.

Shape armholes
Cast off 3 (4: 4: 5) sts at beg of next 2 rows. **53 (57: 60: 64) sts.**
Dec 1 st at each end of next row and 3 (3: 4: 4) foll alt rows. **45 (49: 50: 54) sts. ****
Cont in patt until back measures 15 (17: 19: 22) cm from cast-on edge, ending with a wrong-side row.

Back neck opening
1st row (right side) Patt 22 (24: 25: 27) sts, turn and work on these sts only for first side of neck
shaping, leaving rem sts on a spare needle.
2nd row Cast on 2 sts, then work k2, p to end. **24 (26: 27: 29) sts.**
Next row Patt to last 2 sts, k2.
Next row K2, p to end.
Rep the last 2 rows until back measures 19 (22: 24: 26) cm from cast-on edge, ending with a wrong-side row.

Shape neck
Next row K15 (16: 17: 18) sts, turn, leaving rem 9 (10: 10: 11) sts on a safety pin.
Next row P1, p2tog, p to end.
Next row Patt to last 3 sts, k2tog, k1.
Rep the last 2 rows once more. **11 (12: 13: 14) sts.**
Work 3 rows in patt.
Cast off for shoulder.
With right side facing, rejoin yarn to sts on spare needle, k2, patt to end.
Next row P to last 2 sts, k2.
Next row K2, patt to end.
Rep the last 2 rows until back measures 19 (22: 24: 26) cm from cast-on edge, ending with a right-side row.

Shape neck
Next row P12 (13: 14: 15) sts, p2tog tbl, p1, turn, leaving rem 8 (9: 9: 10) sts on a safety pin.
Next row K1, skpo, patt to end.
Next row P to last 3 sts, p2tog tbl, p1.
Rep the last 2 rows once more. **11 (12: 13: 14) sts.**
Work 3 rows in patt.
Cast off for shoulder.

front

Work as given for Back to **.

Cont in patt until front measures 15 (18: 20: 22) cm from cast-on edge, ending with a wrong-side row.

Shape neck

Next row K18 (20: 20: 22) sts, turn and work on these sts only for first side of front neck, leaving rem sts on a spare needle.

Next row Cast off 2 sts, p to end.

Patt 1 row.

Rep the last 2 rows once more. **14 (16: 16: 18) sts.**

Next row P1, p2tog, p to end.

Patt 1 row.

Rep the last 2 rows 2 (3: 2: 3) times more. **11 (12: 13: 14) sts.**

Work straight until front measures same as Back to shoulder, ending with a p row.

Cast off for shoulder.

With right side facing, slip centre 9 (9: 10: 10) sts onto a holder, rejoin yarn to rem sts on spare needle, patt to end.

Next row P.

Next row Cast off 2 sts, patt to end.

Rep the last 2 rows once more. **14 (16: 16: 18) sts.**

Next row P to last 3 sts, p2tog tbl, p1.

Patt 1 row.

Rep the last 2 rows 2 (3: 2: 3) times more. **11 (12: 13: 14) sts.**

Work straight until front measures same as Back to shoulder, ending with a p row.

Cast off for shoulder.

neckband

Join shoulder seams.

With right side facing and 3 mm circular needle, slip 8 (9: 9: 10) sts from left back onto needle, pick up and k8 sts up left back neck, 21 sts down left side of front neck, k across 9 (9: 10: 10) sts from front neck holder, pick up and k21 sts up right side of front neck, 8 sts down right back neck, then work p7 (8: 8: 9), k2 from back neck holder. **84 (86: 87: 89) sts.**

1st and 3rd sizes only

1st row (wrong side) K2, p1, * k1, p2; rep from * to last 3 sts, k3.

2nd row (buttonhole row) K1, yrn, p2tog, * k2, p1; rep from * to last 3 sts, k3.

3rd row K2, p1, * k1, p2; rep from * to last 3 sts, k3.

4th row K2, [p1, k2] 4 times, p1, [k2tog, p1, k2, p1] 4 times, k2tog, p1, k0 (-: 2: -), p0 (-: 1: -), k2tog, [p1, k2, p1, k2tog] 4 times, [p1, k2] 5 times, k1.

Cast off knitwise.

2nd and 4th sizes only

1st row (wrong side) K2, p2, * k1, p2; rep from * to last 4 sts, k1, p1, k2.

2nd row (buttonhole row) K1, yf, k2tog, * p1, k2; rep from * to last 2 sts, k2.

3rd row K2, p2, *k1, p2; rep from * to last 4 sts, k1, p1, k2.

4th row K3, [p1, k2] 4 times, [k2tog, p1, k2, p1] 4 times, k2tog, p1, k- (0: -: 2), p- (0: -: 1), k2tog, [p1, k2, p1, k2tog] 4 times, [p1, k2] 5 times, k2.

Cast off knitwise.

armbands

With right side facing and 3 mm needles, pick up and k65 (71: 77: 83) sts around armhole edge.

1st row (wrong side) P5, [k1, p2] to last 6 sts, k1, p5.

2nd row K5, * p1, k2; rep from * to last 6 sts, p1, k5.

3rd row As 1st row.

1st and 3rd sizes only

4th row K5, [p1, k2tog, p1, k2] 4 (-: 5: -) times, p1, [k2tog, p1] twice, [k2, p1, k2tog, p1] 4 (-: 5: -) times, k5. **55 (-: 65: -) sts.**

2nd and 4th sizes only

4th row K5, [p1, k2, p1, k2tog] – (5: -: 6) times, p1, [k2tog, p1, k2, p1] – (5: -: 6) times, k5. **– (61: -: 71) sts.**

All sizes

Cast off knitwise.

to make up

Join side and armband seams. Sew lower end of left back button band behind right back buttonhole band. Sew on button.

pinafore dress

measurements
To fit ages 3–6 (6–9: 9–12) months
finished measurements
Chest 47 (52: 57) cm
Length to shoulder 36 (42: 48) cm

materials
3 (4: 4) x 50g balls Debbie Bliss Baby Cashmerino in grey
Pair each 3mm and 3^1/$_4$mm knitting needles
2 buttons

tension
25 sts and 40 rows to 10cm over moss st using 3^1/$_4$mm needles.

abbreviations
See page 25.

front

With 3mm needles, cast on 101 (109: 117) sts.
Beg with a k row, work in st st.
Work 2 rows.
Eyelet row K1, * yf, k2tog; rep from * to end.
Work 3 rows.
Change to 3¼mm needles.
Moss st row K1, * p1, k1; rep from * to end.
This row forms the moss st and is repeated.
Cont straight in moss st until back measures 22 (26: 30) cm from cast-on edge, ending with a wrong-side row.
Dec row (right side) K1 (2: 4), [skpo, k1, k2tog] 20 (21: 22) times, k0 (2: 3). **61 (67: 73) sts.**
Change to 3mm needles. **
K 5 rows.
Cast off 8 (9: 10) sts at beg of next 2 garter st rows. **45 (49: 53) sts.**
Change to 3¼mm needles.
Next row K3, * p1, k1; rep from * to last 4 sts, p1, k3.
This row forms the moss st with garter st borders.
Patt 1 row.
Next row K2, skpo, patt to last 4 sts, k2tog, k2.
Patt 3 rows.
Rep the last 4 rows 6 (7: 8) times more. **31 (33: 35) sts.**
Patt 1 row.
Change to 3mm needles.
K 5 rows.
Straps
Next row (right side) K6, turn.
Work on these 6 sts only for first strap until strap measures 25 (27: 29) cm.
Cast off.
With right side facing, rejoin yarn to rem sts, cast off 19 (21: 23) sts, k to end.
Work on rem 6 sts for second strap until strap measures 25 (27: 29) cm.
Cast off.

back

Work as given for Front to **.
K 3 rows.
Buttonhole row K15 (17: 19), yf, k2tog, k to last 17 (19: 21) sts, k2tog, yf, k15 (17: 19).
K 3 rows.
Cast off.

to make up

Join side seams. Fold hem to wrong side and sew in place. Sew buttons to ends of straps to fit.

size
70 x 70 cm

materials
11 x 50g balls Debbie Bliss Cotton DK in lime
Pair 4mm knitting needles
Two 73 x 73 cm pieces of cotton lining fabric
Polystyrene beads
Two 38 x 73 cm pieces of fabric for beanbag back
65 cm zip fastener

tension
20 sts and 32 rows to 10 cm square over moss st using 4 mm needles.

abbreviations
See page 25.

baby beanbag

lining bag

With right sides of lining fabric pieces together and taking 1.5cm seams, stitch around edges, leaving a 8cm gap in one side. Turn through to right side and pour in the polystyrene beads; do not over-fill – leave enough room for the beads to move around so that they will support the baby. (Use a cone of paper as a funnel when pouring in the beads and hold the open edges of the seam together when testing whether the bag is full enough.) Join the gap in the seam.

beanbag front

With 4mm needles, cast on 141 sts.
Moss st row K1, * p1, k1; rep from * to end.
This row forms moss st and is repeated.
Work in moss st until work measures 70cm from cast-on edge.
Cast off in moss st.

beanbag back

With right sides together, pin and tack the two fabric back pieces together, taking a 1.5cm seam allowance. Remove pins and stitch the seam, leaving the centre 65cm unstitched for zipper. Press seam open. Lay zipper face down onto the pressed seam and tack in place. From the right side, topstitch the zipper in place. Remove all tacking threads. Zigzag stitch around outer edge to reduce fraying of fabric.

to make up

With right sides together, lay knitted front onto fabric back and stitch around the outer edge, taking 1 moss st into the seam. Open zipper and turn beanbag through. Insert filled lining bag, close zipper.

felted slippers

size
To fit 0–3 months

materials
2 x 50g balls Debbie Bliss Alpaca Silk Aran in stone
Pair 5mm knitting needles

tension
18 sts and 34 rows to 10cm square over garter st using 5mm needles.

abbreviations
kfb = knit into front and back of next st.
See page 25.

note
The slippers will look very large and very floppy when knitted, but after washing they will shrink and the fabric will become very thick and resilient.

slipper (make 2)

With 5mm needles, cast on 24 sts.
K 1 row.
Next row Cast on 2 sts, k to end.
Rep this row once more. **28 sts.**
Next row Kfb, k to last 2 sts, kfb, k1.
K 1 row.
Rep the last 2 rows, 3 times more. **36 sts.**
Place a marker at each end of last row.
K 4 rows.

Shape instep

Next row (right side) K24, turn.
Next row K12, turn.
K 18 rows on these 12 sts only.
Break yarn.
With right side facing, rejoin yarn at base of instep and pick up and k9 sts along side edge of instep, k across 12 sts of instep, pick up and k9 sts along other side of instep, then k rem 12 sts. **54 sts.**
K 9 rows.
Break yarn.

Shape sole

Next row With right side facing, slip first 21 sts onto right-hand needle, rejoin yarn and k12, turn.
Next row K11, k2tog, turn.
Rep the last row 41 times more. **12 sts.**
Next row * K2tog; rep from * to end. **6 sts.**
Next row [K3tog] twice. **2 sts.**
Break yarn, thread through rem sts, pull up and secure, then join back seam to markers. Sew in all yarn ends.

to felt

Wash the slippers in the washing machine at 80–95°C together with something heavy – for example, an old pair of jeans or anything that will withstand a very hot wash without losing any dye. When removed from the machine, the slippers will have shrunk considerably. Pull them into shape before leaving to dry.

Reversible hat Classic cardigan Buggy blanket
Shawl collar sweater Cable socks Duffel coat
Changing mat bag

on the go

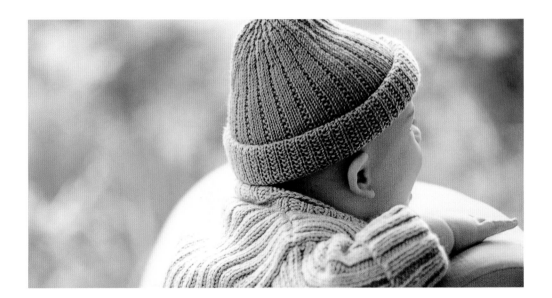

reversible hat

sizes
To fit ages 3–6 (9–12) months

materials
1 (2) x 50g balls Debbie Bliss Baby Cashmerino in each of lime (A) and grey (B)
Pair 3^1/$_4$mm knitting needles

tension
26 sts and 34 rows to 10cm square over 3 x 1 broken rib and 28 sts and 34 rows to 10cm square over 1 x 1 broken rib both using 3^1/$_4$mm needles.

abbreviations
See page 25.

inner/outer hat	With 3¼mm needles and A, cast on 98 (106) sts.

inner/outer hat

With 3¼mm needles and A, cast on 98 (106) sts.

1st row (right side) * K3, p1; rep from * to last 2 sts, k2.

2nd row Purl.

Rep these 2 rows until hat measures 14 (15) cm, ending with a p row.

1st dec row (right side) * K3, p1, k1, k2tog, p1; rep from * to last 2 sts, k2. 86 (93) sts.

Patt 3 rows as set.

2nd dec row * K1, k2tog, p1, k2, p1; rep from * to last 2 sts, k2. 74 (80) sts.

Patt 3 rows as set.

3rd dec row * K2, p1, k2tog, p1; rep from * to last 2 sts, k2. 62 (67) sts.

Patt 3 rows as set.

4th dec row * K2tog, p1, k1, p1; rep from * to last 2 sts, k2. 50 (54) sts.

P 1 row.

5th dec row K1, * k2tog, p1, k1; rep from * to last st, k1. 38 (41) sts.

P 1 row.

6th dec row * K2tog, p1; rep from * to last 2 sts, k2. 26 (28) sts.

P 1 row.

7th dec row K1, * k2tog; rep from * to last st, k1. 14 (15) sts.

P 1 row.

8th dec row K1, * k2tog; rep from * to last st, k1(0). 8 sts.

Break yarn, thread through rem sts, pull up, secure and join seam.

outer/inner hat

With 3¼mm needles and B, cast on 104 (112) sts.

1st row (right side) * K1, p1; rep from * to end.

2nd row Purl.

Rep these 2 rows until hat measures 14 (15) cm, ending with a p row.

1st dec row (right side) * [K1, p1] twice, k1, k2tog, p1; rep from * to end. 91 (98) sts.

Patt 3 rows.

2nd dec row * K1, k2tog, p1, k2, p1; rep from * to end. 78 (84) sts.

Patt 3 rows.

3rd dec row * K2, p1, k2tog, p1; rep from * to end. 65 (70) sts.

Patt 3 rows.

4th dec row * K2tog, p1, k1, p1; rep from * to end. 52 (56) sts.

P 1 row.

5th dec row * K1, k2tog, p1; rep from * to end. 39 (42) sts.

P 1 row.

6th dec row * K2tog, p1; rep from * to end. 26 (28) sts.

P 1 row.

7th dec row K1, * k2tog; rep from * to last st, k1. 14 (15) sts.

P 1 row.

8th dec row K0 (1), * k2tog; rep from * to end. 7 (8) sts.

Break yarn, thread through rem sts, pull up, secure and join seam.

to make up

Turn inner/outer hat through to the wrong side, place this inside the outer/inner hat and slip stitch the hat pieces together all around the cast-on edges. Turn up the rim.

classic cardigan

measurements

To fit ages 0–3 (3–6: 6–9: 9–12) months
finished measurements
Chest 42 (46: 50: 54) cm
Length to shoulder 20 (22: 25: 28) cm
Sleeve length 12 (14: 16: 18) cm

materials

3 (3: 3: 4) x 50g balls Debbie Bliss Baby Cashmerino in flax
Pair each 3mm and 3$^{1}/_{4}$mm knitting needles
5 small buttons

tension

25 sts and 34 rows to 10cm square over st st using 3$^{1}/_{4}$mm needles.

abbreviations

See page 25.

back

With 3mm needles, cast on 54 (58: 62: 66) sts.
1st rib row (right side) K2, * p2, k2; rep from * to end.
2nd rib row P2, * k2, p2; rep from * to end.
Rep the last 2 rows twice more, inc 1 (2: 3: 4) sts evenly across last row. **55 (60: 65: 70) sts.**
Change to 3$^{1}/_{4}$mm needles.
Beg with a k row, work in st st until back measures 10 (11: 13: 15) cm from cast-on edge, ending with a p row.
Shape underarm
Cast off 4 sts at beg of next 2 rows. **47 (52: 57: 62) sts.**
Leave these sts on a spare needle.

left front

With 3mm needles, cast on 27 (27: 31: 35) sts.
1st rib row (right side) K2, * p2, k2; rep from * to last 5 sts, p2, k3.
2nd rib row P3, * k2, p2; rep from * to end.
Rep the last 2 rows twice more, inc 1 (3: 2: 0) sts evenly across last row. **28 (30: 33: 35) sts.**
Change to 3$^{1}/_{4}$mm needles.
Beg with a k row, work in st st until front measures 10 (11: 13: 15) cm from cast-on edge, ending with a p row.
Shape underarm
Cast off 4 sts at beg of next row. **24 (26: 29: 31) sts.**
Leave these sts on a spare needle.

right front

With 3mm needles, cast on 27 (27: 31: 35) sts.
1st rib row (right side) K3, * p2, k2; rep from * to end.

2nd rib row P2, * k2, p2; rep from * to last 5 sts, k2, p3.

Rep the last 2 rows twice more, inc 1 (3: 2: 0) sts evenly across last row. **28 (30: 33: 35) sts.**

Change to 3¹/₄mm needles.

Beg with a k row, work in st st until front measures 10 (11: 13: 15) cm from cast-on edge, ending with a k row.

Shape underarm

Cast off 4 sts at beg of next row. **24 (26: 29: 31) sts.**

P 1 row,

Leave these sts on a spare needle.

sleeves

With 3mm needles, cast on 34 (38: 38: 42) sts.

1st rib row K2, * p2, k2; rep from * to end.

2nd rib row P2, * k2, p2; rep from * to end.

Rep the last 2 rows twice more, inc 3 (0: 3: 2) sts evenly across last row. **37 (38: 41: 44) sts.**

Change to 3¹/₄mm needles.

Beg with a k row, work in st st.

Work 4 rows.

Inc row K3, m1, k to last 3 sts, m1, k3.

Work 5 rows.

Rep the last 6 rows until there are 45 (50: 55: 60) sts.

Cont straight until sleeve measures 12 (14: 16: 18) cm from cast-on edge, ending with a p row.

Shape underarm

Cast off 4 sts at beg of next 2 rows. **37 (42: 47: 52) sts.**

Leave these sts on a spare needle.

yoke

With right side facing and 3¼mm needles, k across 24 (26: 29: 31) sts from right front,
37 (42: 47: 52) sts from right sleeve, 47 (52: 57: 62) sts from back, 37 (42: 47: 52) sts from left sleeve,
24 (26: 29: 31) sts from left front. **169 (188: 209: 228) sts.**

Next row (wrong side) P to end.

Next row K21 (23: 26: 28), k2tog, k2, skpo, k31 (36: 41: 46), k2tog, k2, skpo, k41 (46: 51: 56), k2tog, k2, skpo, k31 (36: 41: 46), k2tog, k2, skpo, k21 (23: 26: 28).

Work 3 rows.

Next row K20 (22: 25: 27), k2tog, k2, skpo, k29 (34: 39: 44), k2tog, k2, skpo, k39 (44: 49: 54), k2tog, k2, skpo, k29 (34: 39: 44), k2tog, k2, skpo, k20 (22: 25: 27).

Next row P to end.

Next row K19 (21: 24: 26), k2tog, k2, skpo, k27 (32: 37: 42), k2tog, k2, skpo, k37 (42: 47: 52), k2tog, k2, skpo, k27 (32: 37: 42), k2tog, k2, skpo, k19 (21: 24: 26).

Next row P to end.

Next row K18 (20: 23: 25), k2tog, k2, skpo, k25 (30: 35: 40), k2tog, k2, skpo, k35 (40: 45: 50), k2tog, k2, skpo, k25 (30: 35: 40), k2tog, k2, skpo, k18 (20: 23: 25).

Next row P to end.

Cont in this way decreasing 8 sts on every right-side row until 65 (68: 73: 76) sts rem, ending with a k row.

Next row P to end, decreasing 1 (0: 1: 0) st at centre back. **64 (68: 72: 76) sts.**

Change to 3mm needles.

1st rib row (right side) K3, * p2, k2; rep from * to last 5 sts, p2, k3.

2nd rib row P3, * k2, p2; rep from * to last 5 sts, k2, p3.

Rep the last 2 rows twice more.

Cast off in rib.

button band

With right side facing and 3mm needles, pick up and k58 (62: 70: 78) sts evenly along left front edge.

1st rib row P2, * k2, p2; rep from * to end.

2nd rib row K2, * p2, k2; rep from * to end.

Rep the last 2 rows once more and the first row again.

Cast off in rib.

buttonhole band

With right side facing and 3mm needles, pick up and k58 (62: 70: 78) sts evenly along right front edge.

1st rib row (wrong side) P2, * k2, p2; rep from * to end.

2nd rib row K2, * p2, k2; rep from * to end.

Buttonhole row (wrong side) Rib 2, [rib 2tog, yrn, rib 11 (12: 14: 16)] 4 times, k2tog, yrn, p2.

Rib 2 more rows.

Cast off in rib.

to make up

Join side and sleeve seams. Join underarm seams. Sew on buttons.

buggy blanket

size
Approximately 45 x 71 cm

materials
2 x 50g balls Debbie Bliss Cashmerino Aran each in pale blue (A) and lilac (C), and 1 x 50g ball each in mid blue (B), pale green (D) and mid green (E)
Pair 5mm knitting needles or 5mm circular knitting needle

tension
18 sts and 24 rows to 10cm over st st using 5mm needles.

abbreviations
See page 25.

note
Use the Intarsia method (see pages 28–30), knitting with separate small balls of yarn for each area of colour and twisting yarns on wrong side when changing colour to avoid holes.

front

With 5mm needles and A, cast on 83 sts.
1st row K1, * p1, k1; rep from * to end.
Rep the last row 3 times more.
1st line
Next row (right side) With A [k1, p1] twice, k15 E, k15 D, k15 C, k15 B, k15 A, with A [p1, k1] twice.
Next row With A [k1, p1] twice, p15 A, p15 B, p15 C, p15 D, p15 E, with A [p1, k1] twice.
These 2 rows set the position of the 1st line of st st squares (with 4 moss sts in A at each side) and are repeated.
Work a further 18 rows.

2nd line
Next row (right side) With A [k1, p1] twice, k15 B, k15 A, k15 E, k15 D, k15 C, with A [p1, k1] twice.
Next row With A [k1, p1] twice, p15 C, p15 D, p15 E, p15 A, p15 B, with A [p1, k1] twice.
These 2 rows set the position of the 2nd line of st st squares (with 4 moss sts in A at each side) and are repeated.
Work a further 18 rows.

3rd line
Next row (right side) With A [k1, p1] twice, k15 C, k15 D, k15 B, k15 A, k15 E, with A [p1, k1] twice.
Next row With A [k1, p1] twice, p15 E, p15 A, p15 B, p15 D, p15 C, with A [p1, k1] twice.
These 2 rows set the position of the 3rd line of st st squares (with 4 moss sts in A at each side) and are repeated.
Work a further 18 rows.

4th line
Next row (right side) With A [k1, p1] twice, k15 A, k15 E, k15 C, k15 D, k15 B, with A [p1, k1] twice.
Next row With A [k1, p1] twice, p15 B, p15 D, p15 C, p15 E, p15 A, with A [p1, k1] twice.
These 2 rows set the position of the 4th line of st st squares (with 4 moss sts in A at each side) and are repeated.
Work a further 18 rows.

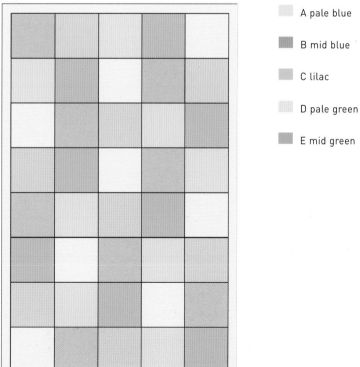

A pale blue

B mid blue

C lilac

D pale green

E mid green

5th line

Next row (right side) With A [k1, p1] twice, k15 D, k15 B, k15 A, k15 E, k15 C, with A [p1, k1] twice.
Next row With A [k1, p1] twice, p15 C, p15 E, p15 A, p15 B, p15 D, with A [p1, k1] twice.
These 2 rows set the position of the 5th line of st st squares (with 4 moss sts in A at each side) and are repeated.
Work a further 18 rows.

6th line

Next row (right side) With A [k1, p1] twice, k15 E, k15 D, k15 C, k15 B, k15 A, with A [p1, k1] twice.
Next row With A [k1, p1] twice, p15 A, p15 B, p15 C, p15 D, p15 E, with A [p1, k1] twice.
These 2 rows set the position of the 6th line of st st squares (with 4 moss sts in A at each side) and are repeated.
Work a further 18 rows.

7th line

Next row (right side) With A [k1, p1] twice, k15 C, k15 B, k15 A, k15 E, k15 D, with A [p1, k1] twice.
Next row With A [k1, p1] twice, p15 D, p15 E, p15 A, p15 B, p15 C, with A [p1, k1] twice.
These 2 rows set the position of the 7th line of st st squares (with 4 moss sts in A at each side) and are repeated.
Work a further 18 rows.

8th line

Next row (right side) With A [k1, p1] twice, k15 A, k15 E, k15 D, k15 C, k15 B, with A [p1, k1] twice.
Next row With A [k1, p1] twice, p15 A, p15 B, p15 C, p15 D, p15 E, with A [p1, k1] twice.
These 2 rows set the position of the 8th line of st st squares (with 4 moss sts in A at each side) and are repeated.
Work a further 18 rows.
Next row (right side) With A [k1, p1] twice, k75 A, with A [p1, k1] twice.
Next row With A, k1, * p1, k1; rep from * to end.
Rep the last row 3 times more.
Cast off in moss st.

back

With 5mm needles and A, cast on 83 sts.
1st row K1, * p1, k1; rep from * to end.
Rep the last row 3 times more.
Next row (right side) With A [k1, p1] twice, k75 E, with A [p1, k1] twice.
Next row With A [k1, p1] twice, p75 E, with A [p1, k1] twice.
These 2 rows form the st st with moss st edges in A and are repeated, working stripes as follows:
Keeping the moss st edges in A throughout, work a further 18 rows in E, then work in 20 row stripes of C, A, D, B, C, D, E, ending with a wrong-side row.
Next row (right side) With A [k1, p1] twice, k75 A, with A [p1, k1] twice.
Next row With A, k1, * p1, k1; rep from * to end.
Rep the last row 3 times more.
Cast off in moss st.

to make up

Join Back to Front around edges.

shawl collar sweater

measurements
To fit ages 3–6 (6–9: 9–12: 12–18: 18–24) months
finished measurements
Chest 50 (53: 60: 63: 70) cm
Length to shoulder 24 (26: 29: 32: 36) cm
Sleeve length (with cuff turned back) 14 (16: 18: 20: 22) cm

materials
3 (4: 5: 5: 6) x 50g balls Debbie Bliss Cashmerino Aran in stone
Pair each 4$\frac{1}{2}$mm and 5mm knitting needles

tension
24 sts and 24 rows to 10cm square over rib when slightly stretched using 5mm needles.

abbreviations
See page 25.

back

With 5mm needles, cast on 62 (66: 74: 78: 86) sts.
1st row (right side) K2, * p2, k2; rep from * to end.
2nd row P2, * k2, p2; rep from * to end.
These 2 rows form the rib.
Cont in rib until back measures 14 (15: 17: 18: 21) cm from cast-on edge, ending with a wrong-side row.
Shape armholes
Cast off 3 sts at beg of next 2 rows. **56 (60: 68: 72: 80) sts. ***
Cont in rib until back measures 24 (26: 29: 32: 36) cm from cast-on edge, ending with a wrong-side row.
Shape shoulders
Next row Cast off 17 (18: 21: 22: 25) sts, rib to last 17 (18: 21: 22: 25) sts and cast off these sts.
Leave rem 22 (24: 26: 28: 30) sts on a holder for collar.

front

Work as given for Back to **.
Shape neck
Next row Patt 21 (23: 27: 29: 33) sts, turn and work on these sts only for first side of neck shaping.
Work 1 row.
Dec 1 st at neck edge on next row and 3 (4: 5: 6: 7) foll 4th rows. **17 (18: 21: 22: 25) sts.**
Work straight until front measures same as Back to shoulder, ending with a wrong-side row.
Cast off.
With right side facing, rejoin yarn to rem sts, cast off 14 sts, patt to end.
Complete to match first side of neck shaping.

sleeves

With 5mm needles, cast on 42 (46: 50: 54: 58) sts.
1st row (right side) K2, * p2, k2; rep from * to end.
2nd row P2, * k2, p2; rep from * to end.
These 2 rows form the rib.

Work a further 6 rows in rib.
Change to 4¹/₂mm needles.
Work a further 8 rows in rib.
Change to 5mm needles.
Cont in rib, inc 1 st at each end of the 5th row and every foll 4th row until there are 54 (60: 66: 74: 78) sts.
Cont straight until sleeve measures 19 (21: 23: 25: 27) cm from cast-on edge, ending with a wrong-side row.
Place markers at each end of last row.
Work a further 4 rows.
Cast off.

shawl collar

With right side facing and 4¹/₂mm needles, rejoin yarn to 22 (24: 26: 28: 30) sts at back neck, cast on 4 (5: 4: 5: 4) sts, k2, p2, k0 (1: 0: 1: 0) across these sts, rib to end.
Next row (wrong side) Cast on 4 (5: 4: 5: 4) sts, p2, k2, p0 (1: 0: 1: 0) across these sts, rib to end.
Next row Cast on 4 sts, p2, k2, across these 4 sts, rib to end.
Next row Cast on 4 sts, k2, p2, across these 4 sts, rib to end.
Rep the last 2 rows 4 times more **70 (74: 74: 78: 78) sts.**
Rib a further 10 rows straight.
Change to 5mm needles.
Rib 2 rows.
Cast off loosely but evenly in rib.

to make up

Join shoulder seams. Sew sleeves into armholes with row ends above markers sewn to sts cast off at underarm. Join side and sleeve seams reversing seam for cuff. Sew cast-on edge of collar to neck edge, overlap right side of collar over left and sew row ends of collar to fronts.

cable socks

sizes
To fit ages 3–6 months

materials
1 x 50g ball Debbie Bliss Cashmerino DK in lilac
Pair 4mm knitting needles
Cable needle

tension
22 sts and 30 rows to 10cm square over st st using 4mm needles.

abbreviations
C4B = slip next 2 sts onto cable needle and hold to back of work, k2, then k2 from cable needle.
pfb = purl into front and back of next st.
See page 25.

sock (make 2)

With 4mm needles, cast on 42 sts.
1st row K2, * p1, k4, p1, k2; rep from * to end.
2nd row P2, * k1, p4, k1, p2; rep from * to end.
3rd row K2, * p1, C4B, p1, k2; rep from * to end.
4th row As 2nd row.
These 4 rows form the cable patt and are repeated once more then the first 3 rows again.
Ridge row K4, * k2tog, k6; rep from * to last 6 sts, k2tog, k4. **37 sts.**
Inc row * P2, k1, p1, pfb, p1, k1; rep from * to last 2 sts, p2. **42 sts.**
Beg with a 1st row, rep the 4 cable patt rows 4 times more, then rep the first 3 patt rows again.
1st dec row P2, * k1, p2tog, p2tog, k1, p2; rep from * to end. **32 sts.**

2nd dec row K3, * k2tog, k6; rep from * to last 5 sts, k2tog, k3. **28 sts.**

Shape heel

Next row P8, turn.

Work a further 9 rows in st st on these 8 sts only.

Dec row P2, p2tog, p1, turn.

Next row Sl 1, k3.

Dec row P3, p2tog, p1, turn.

Next row Sl 1, k4.

Dec row P4, p2tog.

Leave rem 5 sts on a holder.

With wrong side facing, slip centre 12 sts onto a holder, rejoin yarn to rem 8 sts, p to end.

Work a further 8 rows in st st on these 8 sts only.

Dec row K2, k2tog tbl, k1, turn.

Next row Sl 1, p3.

Dec row K3, k2tog tbl, k1, turn.

Next row Sl 1, p4.

Dec row K4, k2tog tbl, turn.

Next row Sl 1, p4.

Shape instep

Next row K5, pick up and k8 sts evenly along inside edge of heel, k12 sts from holder, pick up and k8 sts evenly along inside edge of heel, then k5 sts from holder. **38 sts.**

P 1 row.

Dec row K11, k2tog, k12, k2tog tbl, k11.

P 1 row.

Dec row K10, k2tog, k12, k2tog tbl, k10.

P 1 row.

Dec row K9, k2tog, k12, k2tog tbl, k9.

P 1 row.

Dec row K8, k2tog, k12, k2tog tbl, k8. **30 sts.**

Beg with a p row, work 13 rows in st st.

Shape toes

Dec row K1, [k2tog tbl, k5] 4 times, k1.

P 1 row.

Dec row K1, [k2tog tbl, k4] 4 times, k1.

P 1 row.

Dec row K1, [k2tog tbl, k3] 4 times, k1.

P 1 row.

Dec row K1, [k2tog tbl, k2] 4 times, k1. **14 sts.**

Dec row [P2tog] to end. **7 sts.**

Cast off.

to make up

Join seam across the toes, then cont to join seam along centre of sole and up the centre back, reversing seam on cuff. Turn cuff onto right side.

duffel coat

measurements

To fit ages 0–3 (3–6: 6–9: 9–12) months

finished measurements

Chest 48 (52: 57: 61) cm

Length to shoulder 21 (24: 26: 28) cm

Sleeve length (with cuff turned back) 13 (15: 17: 19) cm

materials

6 (6: 7: 8) x 50g balls Debbie Bliss Rialto DK in grey

Pair each 3¹/₄mm and 4mm knitting needles

4 buttons

tension

22 sts and 48 rows to 10 cm square over garter st using 4mm needles.

abbreviations

See page 25.

back

With 4 mm needles, cast on 53 (57: 63: 67) sts.
Work in garter st (k every row) until back measures 12 (14: 15: 16) cm from cast-on edge, ending with a wrong-side row.
Shape armholes
Cast off 4 sts at beg of next 2 rows. **45 (49: 55: 59) sts.**
Cont straight until back measures 21 (24: 26: 28) cm from cast-on edge, ending with a wrong-side row.
Shape shoulders
Cast off 11 (12: 14: 15) sts at beg of next 2 rows.
Cast off rem 23 (25: 27: 29) sts.

pocket linings
(make 2)

With 4 mm needles, cast on 12 (13: 15: 16) sts.
K 28 (30: 32: 34) rows.
Leave these sts on a holder.

left front

With 4 mm needles, cast on 38 (41: 45: 48) sts.
K 27 (29: 31: 33) rows.
Place pocket
Next row (right side) K3, cast off next 12 (13: 15: 16) sts, k to end.
Next row K23 (25: 27: 29), k across sts of first pocket lining, k3.
Cont in garter st until front measures 12 (14: 15: 16) cm from cast-on edge, ending with a wrong-side row.
Shape armhole
Cast off 4 sts at beg of next row. **34 (37: 41: 44) sts.**
Cont straight until front measures same as Back to shoulder, ending at armhole edge.
Shape shoulder
Next row Cast off 11 (12: 14: 15) sts, k to end.
K 1 row.
Leave rem 23 (25: 27: 29) sts on a spare needle.

right front

With 4 mm needles, cast on 38 (41: 45: 48) sts.
K 27 (29: 31: 33) rows.
Place pocket
Next row K23 (25: 27: 29), cast off next 12 (13: 15: 16) sts, k to end.
Next row K3, k across sts of second pocket lining, k to end.
Cont in garter st until front measures 8 (9: 9: 9) cm from cast-on edge, ending with a wrong-side row.
Buttonhole row K3, yf, k2tog, k13 (15: 17: 19), k2tog, yf, k to end.
Cont in garter st until front measures 12 (14: 15: 16) cm from cast-on edge, ending with a right-side row.

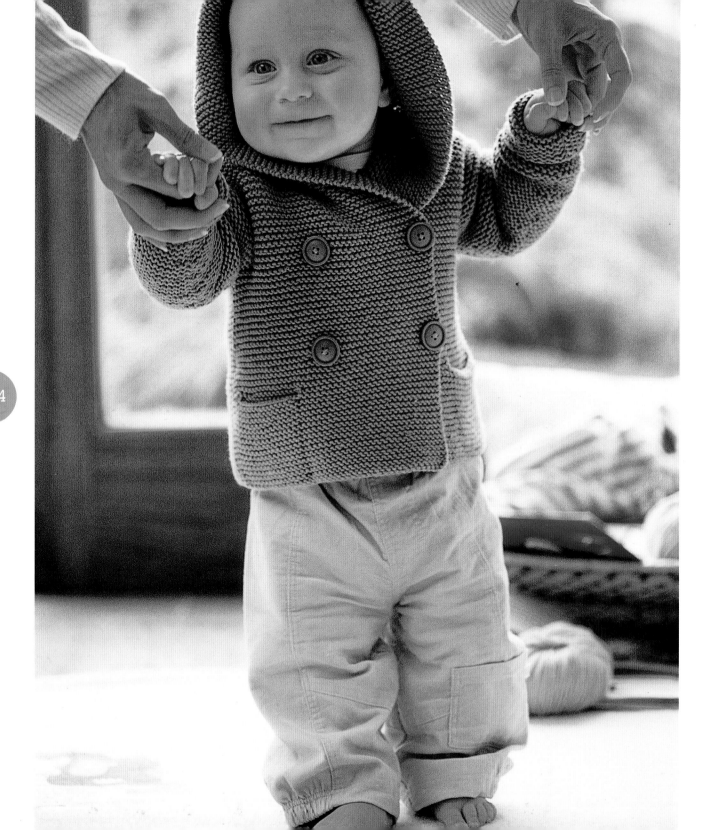

Shape armhole

Cast off 4 sts at beg of next row. **34 (37: 41: 44) sts.**

Cont straight until front measures 13 (15: 16: 17)cm from cast-on edge, ending with a wrong-side row.

Buttonhole row K3, yf, k2tog, k13 (15: 17: 19), k2tog, yf, k to end.

Cont straight until front measures same as Back to shoulder, ending at armhole edge.

Shape shoulder

Next row Cast off 11 (12: 14: 15) sts, k to end. **23 (25: 27: 29) sts.**

Do not break yarn, leave sts on the needle.

hood

Join shoulder seams.

Next row (right side) K23 (25: 27: 29) sts from right front, cast on 34 (37: 40: 44) sts, k23 (25: 27: 29) sts from left front. **80 (87: 94: 102) sts.**

Cont in garter st until hood measures 18 (20: 22: 24)cm, ending with a wrong-side row.

Cast off.

sleeves

With 4mm needles, cast on 29 (31: 33: 35) sts.

K 13 (13: 17: 17) rows.

Change to 3¼mm needles.

K 12 (12: 16: 16) rows.

Change to 4mm needles.

Inc and work into garter st 1 st at each end of the next row and every foll 8th row until there are 41 (45: 49: 53) sts.

Cont straight until sleeve measures 17 (19: 22: 24)cm from cast-on edge, ending with a wrong-side row.

Mark each edge of last row with a coloured thread.

Work a further 8 rows.

Cast off.

to make up

Fold hood in half and join top seam. Easing in fullness, join cast-on edge of hood to sts cast off at back neck. Matching centre of cast-off edge of sleeve to shoulder, sew sleeves into armholes, with row ends above markers sewn to sts cast off at underarm. Join side and sleeve seams. Sew down pocket linings. Sew on buttons.

changing mat bag

size
40 x 59 cm

materials
6 x 50g balls Debbie Bliss Cotton DK in pale blue
Pair 4mm knitting needles
43 x 62.5cm wipe-clean fabric for lining
3m tape or ribbon

tension
20 sts and 32 rows to 10cm square over patt using 4mm needles.

abbreviations
See page 25.

to make

With 4 mm needles, cast on 75 sts.
1st and 3rd rows (wrong side) Purl.
2nd row K1, * p1, k1; rep from * to end.
4th row P1, * k1, p1; rep from * to end.
These 4 rows form the patt and are repeated throughout.
Cont in patt until work measures 59 cm from cast-on edge, ending with a right-side row.
Cast off knitwise.

pocket

With 4 mm needles, cast on 13 sts for pocket bottom.
1st row (right side) K1, * p1, k1; rep from * to end.
2nd and 4th rows Purl.
3rd row P1, * k1, p1; rep from * to end.
These 4 rows form the patt and are repeated.
Work in patt for 4 cm, ending with a p row.
Shape sides
Cast on and take into patt, 9 sts at beg of next 2 rows. **31 sts.**
Cont in patt until pocket measures 15 cm from side cast-on edges, ending with a right-side row.
Cast off knitwise.

handles (make 2)

With 4 mm needles, cast on 9 sts.
Beg with a k row, work 6 rows in st st.
1st inc row K1, m1, k1, [p1, k1] 3 times, m1, k1. **11 sts.**
P 1 row.
2nd inc row K1, m1, k1, [p1, k1] 4 times, m1, k1. **13 sts.**
Place a marker at each end of last row.
1st and 3rd rows Purl.
2nd row K2, [p1, k1] 5 times, k1.
4th row K1, [p1, k1] 6 times.
Rep the last 4 rows until handle measures 25 cm from cast-on edge, ending with a 4th patt row.
P 1 row.
1st dec row K2tog tbl, p1, [k1, p1] 4 times, k2tog. **11 sts.**
P 1 row.
2nd dec row K2tog tbl, p1, [k1, p1] 3 times, k2tog. **9 sts.**
Place a marker at each end of last row.
Beg with a p row, work 6 rows in st st.
Cast off.

to make up

Join pocket side cast-on edges to row ends of pocket bottom. Position the pocket on the right side of the mat, 10 cm down from cast-off edge and 10 cm in from right-hand side edge and slip stitch in place. Fold each handle in half and join row ends to form seam between markers. Position handles onto the short ends of the mat, sewing the st st sections to the mat. Cut ribbon/tape into 8 pieces and sew to long edges of the mat, so they will tie at the sides when the mat is folded in half.
Fold 1.5 cm of lining fabric onto wrong side around all edges and place on the wrong side of the mat. Slip stitch around all edges, so hiding handle ends and raw ends of ribbon/tape.

yarn distributors

For stockists of Debbie Bliss yarns please contact:

UK & WORLDWIDE DISTRIBUTORS
Designer Yarns Ltd.
Units 8–10
Newbridge Industrial Estate
Pitt Street
Keighley
West Yorkshire BD21 4PQ
UK
t: +44 (0) 1535 664222
f: +44 (0) 1535 664333
e: david@designeryarns.uk.com
w: www.designeryarns.uk.com

USA
Knitting Fever Inc.
315 Bayview Avenue
Amityville
NY 11701
USA
t: +1 516 546 3600
f: +1 516 546 6871
e: admin@knittingfever.com
w: www.knittingfever.com

CANADA
Diamond Yarns Ltd
155 Martin Ross Avenue
Unit 3
Toronto
Ontario M3J 2L9
Canada
t: +1 416 736 6111
f: +1 416 736 6112
w. www.diamondyarn.com

BELGIUM/HOLLAND
Pavan
Meerlaanstraat 73
9860 Balegem (Oostrezele)
Belgium
t: +32 (0) 9 221 85 94
f: +32 (0) 9 221 56 62
e: pavan@pandora.be

DENMARK
Fancy Knit
Hovedvejen 71
8586 Oerum Djurs
Ramten
Denmark
t: +45 59 46 21 89
f: +45 59 46 8018
e: roenneburg@mail.dk

FINLAND
Handicraft House PRIIMA
Käsityötalo
Hämeentie 26
00530 Helsinki
Finland
t: +358 (0) 9 753 1716
f: +358 (0) 9 7318 0009
e: info@priima.net
w: www.priima.net

FRANCE
Elle Tricote
8 Rue du Coq
La Petite France
67000 Strasbourg
France
t: +33 (0) 388 230313
f: +33 (0) 8823 0169
w: www.elletricote.com

GERMANY/AUSTRIA/
SWITZERLAND
Designer Yarns
Handelsagentur Klaus Koch
Sachsstraße 30
D-50259 Pulheim-Brauweiler
Germany
t: +49 (0) 2234 205453
f: +49 (0) 2234 205456
e: kk@designeryarns.de
w: www.designeryarns.de

ICELAND
Storkurinn
Langavegi 59
101 Reykjavík
Iceland
t: +354 551 8258
f: +354 562 8252

SPAIN
Oyambre Needlework SL
Balmes, 200 At.4
08006 Barcelona
Spain
t: +34 (0)93 487 26 72
f: +34 (0)93 218 6694/368 3480
e: info@oyambreonline.com

SWEDEN
Nysta garn och textil
Luntmakargatan 50
S-113 58 Stockholm
Sweden
t: +46 (0)8 612 0330
e: info@nysta.se
w: www.nysta.se

AUSTRALIA/NEW ZEALAND
Prestige Yarns Pty Ltd.
PO Box 39
Bulli
NSW 2516
Australia
t: +61 (0) 2 4285 6669
e: info@prestigeyarns.com
w: www.prestigeyarns.com

JAPAN
Hobbyra Hobbyre
5-23-37 Higashi-Ohi
Shinagawa-ku
Tokyo 140-0011
Japan
t: +81 3 3472 1104
f: +81 3 3472 1196
w: www.hobbyra-hobbyre.com

MEXICO
Estambres Crochet SA de CV
Aaron Saenz 1891–7
Col. Santa Maria
Monterrey
N.L. 64650
Mexico
t: +52 (81) 8335 3870
e: abremer@redmundial.com.mx

For more information on my
other books and yarns, please
visit www.debbieblissonline.com

glossary of patterns

hooded carrying bag pages 56–59

baby aged (months)	0–3	3–6
back length (cm)	55	60

lacy shawl pages 60–63

length (cm)	110
width (cm)	94

toy lamb pages 64–67

height (cm)	10
length (cm)	14

baby knickers pages 70–73

baby aged (months)	3–6	6–9
over nappy (cm)	51	56
length (cm)	22	24

baby shorts pages 74–77

baby aged (months)	3–6	6–9
over nappy (cm)	51	56
length (cm)	27	30

heart mobile pages 78–81

size	small	medium	large
length (cm)	8	9	10

bath robe pages 82–87

baby aged (months)	6	12	18	24
finished chest (cm)	59	63	67	71
back length (cm)	42	48	54	60
sleeve length (cm)	16	18	21	24

tank top pages 88–93

baby aged (months)	0–3	3–6	6–9	9–12
finished chest (cm)	45	50	53	58
back length (cm)	21	24	26	28

pinafore dress pages 94–97

baby aged (months)	3–6	6–9	9–12
finished chest (cm)	47	52	57
back length (cm)	36	42	48

baby beanbag pages 98–99

length (cm)	70
width (cm)	70

felted slippers pages 100–103

baby aged (months)	0–3

reversible hat pages 106–109

baby aged (months)	3–6	9–12

classic cardigan pages 110–115

baby aged (months)	0–3	3–6	6–9	9–12
finished chest (cm)	42	46	50	54
back length (cm)	20	22	25	28
sleeve length (cm)	12	14	16	18

buggy blanket pages 116–121

length (cm)	71
width (cm)	45

shawl collar sweater pages 122–125

baby aged (months)	3–6	6–9	9–12	12–18	18–24
finished chest (cm)	50	53	60	63	70
back length (cm)	24	26	29	32	36
sleeve length (cm)	14	16	18	20	22

143

cable socks pages 126–129

baby aged (months)	3–6

duffel coat pages 130–135

baby aged (months)	0–3	3–6	6–9	9–12
finished chest (cm)	48	52	57	61
back length (cm)	21	24	26	28
sleeve length (cm)	13	15	17	19

changing mat bag pages 136–138

length (cm)	59
width (cm)	40

Dedication

to my own essential family

Editorial Director **Jane O'Shea**
Creative Director **Mary Evans**
Project Editor **Lisa Pendreigh**
Editorial Assistant **Andrew Bayliss**
Photographer **Debi Treloar**
Stylist **Julie Mansfield**
Illustrator **Kate Simunek**
Pattern Illustrator **Bridget Bodoano**
Production Director **Vincent Smith**
Production Controller **Ruth Deary**

First published in 2007 by
Quadrille Publishing Limited
Alhambra House
27–31 Charing Cross Road
London WC2H 0LS
www.quadrille.co.uk

Text and project designs © 2007 Debbie Bliss
Photography, design and layout © 2007
Quadrille Publishing Limited

British Library Cataloguing-in-Publication Data
A catalogue record for this book is available
from the British Library.

ISBN: 978 184400 501 7

Printed in Singapore

144

acknowledgements

This book would not have been possible without the contribution of the following:

Jane O'Shea, **Lisa Pendreigh** and **Mary Evans** at Quadrille Publishing who have been such
an inspirational team to work with.

Julie Mansfield, the stylist, whose input, as always, has been invaluable.

Debi Treloar, for the simply beautiful photographs, and her assistant Ciara.

Sally Kvalheim, who did such a great job baby grooming.

And, of course, the fantastic mothers and babies: **Casey** and **Evelyn**, **Charlie**, **Dylan**, **Funsho**
and **Levi**, **Grace**, **Guy**, **Hayden**, **Jake**, **Katherine**, **Kristina**, **Luca**, **Mathilda**, **Noah**, **Rachel** and
Joshua, **Rosie** and **Sydney**.

Rosy Tucker, for pattern checking and creative as well as practial support.

Penny Hill, for her essential pattern compiling and organizing the knitters.

The knitters, for the huge effort they put into creating perfectly knitted garments under
deadline pressure: **Cynthia Brent**, **Barbara Clapham**, **Pat Church**, **Pat Clack**, **Jacqui Dunt**,
Shirley Kennet, **Maisie Lawrence** and **Frances Wallace**.

My fantastic agent, **Heather Jeeves**.

The **distributors**, **agents**, **retailers** and **knitters** who support all my books and yarns, and
make all my projects possible.

the
complete
wedding
guide

A Little, Brown Book
First published in 2002 by Little, Brown and Company (UK)
New edition published in 2003

Reprinted in 2005, 2006, 2007

A CIP catalogue record for this book is available from the
British Library

ISBN 978-0-316-03034-2

Designed by Janet James
With specially commissioned photographs by Lucinda Symons

Printed and bound in Dubai

Marriage is alive and well in the 21st century – it's just a little different to the way in which couples used to celebrate their big day. Couples are much more likely to 'test the water' and live together before marriage, which has definite implications for the way in which their day is organised. One of the biggest changes is in who pays for the wedding. Until recently it was always the bride's parents who had to foot the bill. Latest readership surveys in *You & Your Wedding* have shown that the couple are now much more likely to pay for their own wedding (and so they should, as the average bride is 27 and the groom 29!). This allows them the freedom to organise the day as they want, rather than as a celebration that reflects what their parents want.

Another area which has seen big changes in recent years is wedding style. Thanks to the barrage of magazines and television programmes devoted to the subject, we are all so much more aware of lifestyle, environment and what is possible with a little creativity. All kinds of wedding suppliers tell us that couples are coming to them with files bulging with magazine tearsheets and a very firm idea of exactly how they want their wedding to look: from the design of the invitations and the colours of the flowers, to the table settings at the reception and the style of the cake. It is no longer acceptable to expect the hotel or catering company to set the style of the wedding; the bride wants the look and feel of the day to live up to all her expectations.

Weddings are increasingly likely to be celebrated with a civil rather than a religious ceremony. Church weddings are on the decrease, with more and more couples opting to wed in one of the many properties with a civil marriage licence; this in turn has led to many weddings being organised around a theme, usually to suit the style of the venue. Weddings abroad are also very popular, with European wedding venues currently rivalling sun-soaked Caribbean beaches.

In terms of what the modern couple is choosing to wear on the big day, just about anything goes! Dresses and suits are selected to complement the overall look of the wedding. Bridesmaids are getting older and are more likely to wear evening-style gowns rather than traditional bridesmaids' dresses, and if younger maids are included in the day, they are more likely to take the role of flower girl and wear something 'fairytale'.

High-profile weddings are bound to influence the modern couple's approach to their day. When so-called 'ladettes' like Zoe Ball can't wait to don a wedding dress and Madonna ties the knot in a romantic Scottish castle, it is little wonder that in our celebrity-obsessed society, others cannot wait to do the same.

Carole Hamilton, *You & Your Wedding*

Introduction

Congratulations on your engagement! You are about to begin an exciting journey that will take you towards the most memorable day of your life.

The Complete Wedding Guide is here to give you, the modern bride, a helping hand. It's packed with ideas and hints on how to make your wedding day unique, fun and inspirational.

Use the Wedding Planner to make your ideas come alive and manage your time effectively during the build up to your special day. There are heaps of tips on how to make the whole thing stress free and enjoyable – so take advantage and clear your mind.

There are tips on how to create the 'wow' factor as well as an array of products, services and ideas that you can find at your local Marks and Spencer store. For everything else there is a supplier and sources section at the back which will help with anything from wedding consultants and marquee companies to venues, cars and photographers.

Take this complete wedding guide, sit down with your partner and start to think about what would make your day special and unique. Think creatively and don't forget to include the favourite things in your lives to personalise and give the occasion your individual thumb print.

Let's get started . . .

first things first

1

The engagement
Timing is everything
How to tie the knot
The price of love
Family and friends

THE ENGAGEMENT RING IS THOUGHT TO DATE BACK TO THE ANCIENT EGYPTIANS, WHEN AN ITEM OF VALUE OR A COIN WAS GIVEN TO THE BRIDE-TO-BE BY THE MAN AS A SYMBOL OF THEIR AGREEMENT TO MARRY. OVER THE CENTURIES THIS ITEM HAS EVOLVED INTO A RING TO SYMBOLISE ETERNITY.

The engagement

Announcing the engagement

If your fiancé hasn't requested your father's permission to ask for your hand in marriage, then the bride's parents are the first people that should be told. If they live nearby, you and your fiancé could go and tell them together; if they live further afield, a telephone call will suffice. If they have not met your fiancé, arrangements should be made for a meeting as soon as possible. Then do the same for your fiancé's parents.

If either set of parents are divorced or separated you must try to ensure there is no gap between telling both parties. Either one could get very upset if they thought the ex-spouse was told first!

If either yourself or the groom have partners or children from a previous marriage, you must pluck up the courage to tell them as soon as possible. Don't let them hear it from someone else. Telling a child of their parent's forthcoming nuptials is a delicate matter. Try to involve them as much as you can in the planning and on the big day itself – it is important that they feel they are gaining a parent rather than losing one. If you are in contact with the birth father or mother, it would also be appropriate to tell them of your engagement so as to gain their acceptance and assistance in discussing issues with the children.

Newspaper announcements

It is usual for the engagement to be announced in a national or local newspaper. Placing the announcement in a national newspaper can be quite costly, but a notice in your local paper will be just as fitting and they may even include a photograph of yourself and the groom.

Contact your chosen newspaper and tell them that you want to announce your engagement. They should then talk you through the procedure and the costs involved. If you would also like your picture printed, this is the time to ask them how you go about doing it.

If the parents of the bride are divorced or separated, either one may announce the engagement, but it is usually done by whomever the bride has previously lived with. In order not to offend anyone it is sometimes easier to leave out any mention of step-parents. If either of the parents are deceased then the announcement should be made by the surviving parent with the word '(*late*)' placed after the deceased parent's name.

If the groom has been married previously, the announcement should be worded as coming from yourselves rather than your parents.

These cases aside, a typical announcement would read:

Mr and Mrs Charles Henry of Cheltenham, Gloucestershire,

announce the engagement of their daughter

Joanne Elizabeth to David Eastbury,

the son of Mr and Mrs Ian Eastbury of Sevenoaks, Kent.

Ensure that the announcement also appears in the groom's parents' local newspaper with the wording unchanged.

Engagement parties

Engagement parties are becoming increasingly popular, as they are the perfect occasion on which to announce the great news that a couple have decided to tie the knot. They are also the ideal time to introduce the two families, and to informally invite both friends and family to join in the celebrations and get to know each other early on in the planning process.

Engagement parties were traditionally hosted by the bride's parents, but nowadays there are no set rules: you and your fiancé, the groom's parents, other relatives or even close friends may want to be the hosts. If the engagement is a surprise for the guests, the bride's father or the groom traditionally makes a toast to announce the special news. The groom's father may also want to say a few words.

⟩ If formal invitations are sent they should be worded in one of the following ways:

Please join us to celebrate the engagement of . . .
Or
In honour of . . .

dos and don'ts

⟩ If the engagement announcement is to be a surprise then simply send out invitations for a party without mentioning either of the couple's names.

⟩ It is wise to invite guests to the party who will also be invited to the wedding.

⟩ Engagement gifts are generally not given and should not be expected. If guests do choose to give you a present, remember to send a thank you note!

⟩ This is your first opportunity to enjoy being in the limelight, so make the most of it!

Engagement rings

If your fiancé hasn't surprised you with a ring then it is time to go shopping!

You will wear your engagement ring for the rest of your life so it is a choice that needs to be made carefully and should not be rushed. Before you make a dash for the shops, ask your fiancé if he has a budget in mind for the ring. It is important to decide these things before you spot something you fall in love with and then find that your fiancé only wants to spend half that amount. If he is unsure how much to spend, then one month's salary is a good guide. Once a figure is agreed, stick to it.

Ask him if he has any preference for a particular style of ring or stone. Whilst it is your ring and your hand that it will be sitting on, it is important that he likes it too. Here are some pointers . . .

If you wear a lot of silver jewellery, choose either a silver, platinum or white gold ring. Platinum is the most expensive metal; silver is the least expensive. **Eighteen-carat gold** is most commonly used for engagement rings. Other carat weights to choose from include nine- and twenty-four-carat. **Whatever metal** you choose for your engagement ring, it is advisable to have the same for your wedding ring. Wearing two different metals side by side, constantly rubbing against each other, will eventually erode the metal.

Try on a variety of styles: certain shapes will suit your hand more than others. If you cannot find a style that you like then ask if you could have something made bespoke for you.

If you and your fiancé cannot afford the ring of your dreams, don't worry. Ask the jeweller for a style that could be added to later on; you could then add stones on your anniversary.

You don't have to have an engagement ring. You could have a wedding and engagement ring combined, with stones placed into the metal.

Shop around! Don't buy something from the first shop you go into. If you still love that ring after you've visited another five shops, then go back.

Ensure that you receive an insurance certificate from your jeweller when you buy the ring, and keep the receipt. Also ask the jeweller about returns, guarantees and warranties and ensure you get everything in writing.

If you are spending a great deal of money, have the ring independently examined by another qualified jeweller.

DECEMBER — turquoise
NOVEMBER — topaz
OCTOBER — opal
SEPTEMBER — sapphire
AUGUST — peridot
JULY — ruby
JUNE — pearl
MAY — emerald
APRIL — diamond
MARCH — aquamarine
FEBRUARY — amethyst
JANUARY — garnet

Stones

Diamonds are the most popular choice of stone for engagement rings. There are many shapes to choose from:

 Brilliant A round cut diamond and the most popular style

 Oval An oval diamond

 Marquise An oval diamond with a slightly pointed top and base

 Emerald A rectangular diamond

 Pear A diamond that is pointed at the top and full at the base

Try them all! They will be graded according to colour, clarity and cut, and priced accordingly. Basically, the most colourless, flawless and accurately cut diamonds are the most expensive. Ask to see different grades of stone. The human eye cannot easily distinguish one from another so you may wish to purchase a larger, lower quality stone. See if you can tell the difference!

Instead of a smaller diamond, some couples opt for a larger coloured stone, such as a sapphire, ruby, amethyst or emerald. Choosing your birth stone (see opposite) is a popular thing to do as it is said to bring luck to the person wearing it.

Achieving the perfect fit

When trying on an engagement ring or wedding band, make sure your hands are as cool as possible; this will ensure that no swelling occurs. So if you have an appointment with a jeweller, make sure you allow yourself plenty of time to get there so that you aren't hot and bothered before you start.

Your ring should slip easily over your knuckle and sit comfortably at the base of your finger. A good test is to fit a toothpick between your ring and finger to ensure there is adequate room for your finger to change in size, due to swelling for example, but also that the fit is snug enough to keep the stones of the ring facing upwards.

HAVING A CLEAR PLAN FOR YOUR WEDDING IS ESSENTIAL. IT WILL ALLEVIATE STRESS AND HELP YOU TO SET DATES WHICH ARE ACHIEVABLE WITHIN YOUR NORMAL DAILY SOCIAL AND WORK ROUTINES. IT COULD BE SAID THAT MAKING A FORMAL PLAN IS DULL AND RIGID, BUT IT DOESN'T HAVE TO BE AND IT CAN ACTUALLY HELP TO UNITE A BRIDE AND GROOM WITH FAMILY AND FRIENDS IN ALL THE ELEMENTS OF PREPARATION THAT WILL MAKE UP THE SPECIAL DAY.

Wedding Planner

We have devised three simple worksheets for you to work with. They will help you clearly define your dreams and set the ball in motion. The worksheets list topics in order of importance that you and your fiancé will need to discuss. Visualise a quiet evening in together, a nice glass of wine, a CD that you both enjoy softly playing in the background and sitting talking about your future! This should be the state of mind you both need to be in for making plans.

At the end of the third worksheet there is a list of tasks that will need to be delegated between the bride and the groom.

Let's begin....

A simple step-by-step

Sketch out your ideas on the following worksheet. This format

is normally how things flow in order of importance:

1) General outline

This worksheet gives you a chance to write down your initial thoughts and generally outline the way you see your day. Put this away and take time to absorb each other's views and come back to it when you are ready to get started on the details.

Top Tip Keep it simple and don't think too deeply about the details until you have a broad idea of what you both want.

NB: Action Points are to be used as an aid to highlight anything of importance.

Action Point

Time of year

Ceremony at home or overseas

Civil or religious ceremony

Locality of ceremony

Rough budget

(Budgets can be tough to discuss: it is hard to think romantically when you have a price tag to attach to each area – however this is just a basic sketch of what you would like and is not set in stone, so try and enjoy exploring all the elements)

Approximate number of guests

(This is the hardest thing to do – and keep to – so take your time)

Evening reception   Yes   No

Honeymoon

Cast your eye down the second worksheet a couple of days before you actually sit down to finalise your outline. Now you are ready for the next step!

2) Putting meat on the outline

Discuss ideas on what your ideal wedding would be like. Include favourite colours, films, memories and restaurants to help give depth to your thoughts

Top Tip: Try and have a similar vision

	Action Point
Choose specific dates	Confirm with family.
Locality of ceremony	Go and check availability with either religious or civil venue. If civil ceremony then provisionally book the Registrar
Rough budget	Discuss with family who's paying what (check out Price of Love chapter and don't forget to include your wedding insurance. Contact Marks and Spencer for wedding insurance 0800 316 5985)
Approximate number of guests	Give provisional numbers to families and discuss further (this will be a moving number, so don't worry!)
Locality of reception	Check out possible sites and check the availability of dates with them
Evening reception location	Check reception venue capacity
Honeymoon	If you have an ideal destination check out prices as far in advance as possible, in order to budget. (Contact Marks and Spencer for travel insurance 0800 068 3918)
Attendants	Choose your best man, bridesmaids, ushers and any other attendants

3) Getting detailed

This next worksheet will help you to become more specific with the more personal touches of the wedding.

Hopefully you will have by now a confirmed date, a ceremony venue, a reception and a budget. The foundations are firmly in place and let's get down to the nitty gritty.

Theme
Contemporary, traditional, colour-led, fantasy, seasonal. Check out the Themed weddings chapter.

Stationery
Traditional or funky? Themed? Will it include invite, order of service, menus, thankyou cards, placecards? (Marks and Spencer have a great selection of stationery for both modern and traditional brides)

Order of service
You needn't decide specifics, just roughly discuss informal or formal and some favourite hymns and readings.

Food and drink
Discuss any special preferences or wishes.

Transport
Discuss your and your guests' transportation needs and wildest dreams!

Entertainment
Outline your thoughts.

Budget
If you are paying for any proportion of the wedding then consider the financial impact (Contact Marks and Spencer for wedding insurance 0800 316 5985)

Now it's time to decide which bits you want to do together and which items you definitely need to do separately

Things to do together:

❧ Meet your ceremony officiator and discuss details
❧ Meet with your caterers and discuss food and drink
❧ Meet with reception venue and discuss all requirements
❧ Interview photographer and videographer
❧ Select wedding gifts
❧ Choose wedding rings
❧ Choose stationery
❧ Finalise guest list

Divide and conquer:

Tick off as and when you have completed the task
Put any notes in the margin
Please see the relevant chapters for the best way to approach each item

Bride:
❧ Wedding dress and accessories (Follow the chapter on dresses and the key questions you should ask and it will make things so much easier)
❧ Attendants' outfits and accessories
❧ Flowers, personal and venue
❧ Decorations for ceremony and reception
❧ Organise favours
❧ Purchase any presents for family and friends
❧ Send out invites and organise other stationery
❧ Beauty regime
❧ Order cake
❧ Change of name documentation
❧ Seating plan

Groom:
❧ Set up savings account
❧ Purchase licence and/or arrange banns
❧ Book any order of service requirements, such as choir or other musicians
❧ Organise own outfit as well as ushers and best man
❧ Arrange wedding insurance (contact Marks and Spencer 0800 316 5985)
❧ Book the photographer
❧ Book the videographer
❧ Check with ceremony venue on presence of photographer and videographer
❧ Book any entertainment
❧ Book the transport
❧ Prepare speech and confirm others
❧ Pay ceremony fees
❧ Book first night and honeymoon

Important lead times

As with many important events there are certain items that must be ordered in advance of the special day. The following information is a guide to ordering times and the scheduling of certain elements that will arise during your planning.

Wedding dress

If your wedding dress is to be designed or made, expect a minimum ordering period of twelve to fourteen weeks. This is a standard time and is not set in stone: if you do choose to have a short engagement, additional charges can sometimes be added to rush the production of a wedding dress. Be prepared to have at least two fittings. These should occur within the last four weeks leading up to your wedding day.

Attendants' outfits

Again, these will take at least twelve weeks to order. Alterations will also be required on standard sizes, even if it is simply to adjust the hem lengths.

Men's hire

Order suits at least six months ahead of the wedding date to ensure they are pre-booked for your wedding party.

Wedding rings

These can take up to four weeks to order if you are having them designed or altered.

Wedding stationery

Stationery takes up to four weeks to order and invitations should be sent out no later than six to eight weeks before the wedding; the earlier the better to enable your guests to put the date into their diaries well ahead of time.

Gift lists

If you intend to have a wedding list, be prepared to spend at least two or three days choosing the items you would like.

wedding

This is a practical calendar for you to use. Simply insert the appropriate month into the spaces. We have presumed a minimum of a five month planning period. The last month is obviously the month of your wedding!

MONTH _____

Tell friends and relatives of your plans to marry!

Choose some provisional dates!

Announce the engagement in the paper!

Arrange a meeting with your priest, rabbi or vicar and confirm date. Or book the registry office or civil ceremony venue and registrar

Set your budget!

Select your attendants

Start on your guest list

5 months to go

MONTH _____

Begin your beauty regime

Book your videographer

Book your photographer

Organise wedding insurance. Contact Marks and Spencer 0800 316 5985

Visit possible reception venues

Begin looking for attendants and your own outfits

Discuss catering and make a booking

Book your reception entertainment

4 months to go

MONTH

For a religious service, arrange the banns and discuss service

Select hymns, readings and music
Book the musicians

Book reception venue and caterers
Decide on a menu

Choose flowers and find a florist

Choose your rings

Order wedding cake

Arrange your dress fitting and plan your going away outfit

Order wedding stationery

Book your first night and honeymoon. Contact Marks and Spencer for travel insurance 0800 068 3918

Book wedding cars

2 months to go

MONTH

Organise your gift list

Check passports and arrange innoculations

Discuss hairstyles with hairdresser

Finalise order of service & print

Post invitations

Arrange favours

Buy all accessories for you and your attendants

Groom to organise his clothes

Choose presents for attendants

2 months to go

MONTH

Confirm all bookings

Send out thank yous as gifts arrive

Book hairdresser and make-up

Pay appropriate ceremony fees and purchase the certificate

Ensure everyone knows what to do!

1 month to go

MONTH

Confirm number of guests with caterer and start seating plan

Pack for honeymoon

Try on your full outfit

Confirm arrangements for honeymoon

Arrange a rehearsal

Ensure all speeches are prepared

Walk through reception arrangements

Confirm flowers, cake, cars, etc

0 months to go

IF YOU HAVEN'T THOUGHT BEYOND THE FACT THAT YOU ARE GOING TO GET MARRIED, AND ARE UNSURE OF THE WHYS AND WHEREFORES OF THE PROCESS, THIS CHAPTER WILL GUIDE YOU THROUGH THE LEGALITIES FOR A NUMBER OF THE RELIGIOUS AND CIVIL CEREMONIES THAT NOW EXIST. THIS IS THE FORMAL PART OF THE ORGANISATION PROCESS – ONCE THIS HAS BEEN DECIDED UPON THE FUN CAN BEGIN!

How to tie the knot

The Church of England

Most Church of England parishes require you to be baptised as a prerequisite to marriage.

This is under review and some churches may be lenient, so you must check prior to proceeding with the next steps listed below:

1. You will need to be over 16 years of age.
2. You and your fiancé must not be closely related.
3. You must be free and eligible to marry, if you have been married previously, you must check with your clergy as to whether they will allow you to remarry within their parish.
4. The service must take place between 8am and 6pm.
5. There must be two witnesses to the marriage.
6. The marriage must be authorised in advance in one of three ways: by banns; by Common licence; by Special licence.

Banns

This is the most common process adopted for a traditional wedding. You may choose to marry in a church that either yourself or the groom attended as a child, or at a church local to where you currently live. Whatever your thoughts you must be prepared to meet the clergy of the parish and discuss in detail why you want to marry within his parish. The vicar will want to make sure that you are not entering the sanctity of marriage lightly and that you have thought through the reasons as to why you have chosen to marry in church.

This may sound a little heavy, however the whole process of making vows of marriage within the Church is taken very seriously. The clergy is there to ensure that you understand that joining together in the eyes of the Church is an important event and needs his sanction.

The banns of marriage are read out on three consecutive Sundays within the parish of both the bride and groom prior to the wedding, as it is traditional to allow the public an opportunity to voice any concern or impediment as to why the union should not take place. If the bride and groom live in different parishes they must remain resident there during this period. In addition to this, if the couple intend to marry in a different parish they must have the banns read out at that parish as well. The clergy from the parish where the wedding will take place will require a certificate from the clergy of the other parishes to prove that the banns have been read.

If there is no objection then the marriage can be solemnized.

By Common licence

If you are in a hurry to get married and a three-week delay awaiting banns to be read does not suit you, you can opt – due to circumstances beyond your control – to request a Common licence from the clergy of the church, who can grant a licence or give details on how to go about gaining one.

There need only be one day's notice given prior to the ceremony, however the licence would need to be reapplied for if three months passes once it has been obtained and no marriage has taken place.

By Special licence

This is a licence authorised by the Archbishop of Canterbury for emergency use where a Common licence will not suffice.

TIPS

❧ If there is no obvious choice of church or chapel in which to marry, make a few informal visits to churches that have caught your eye.

❧ Approach the clergy of your chosen parish as soon as possible and look at several dates that would be good for you.

❧ Place a provisional booking with the clergy at this time. You can always change your mind, but certain dates are booked up very quickly and most parishes only hold one wedding a day.

❧ Get to know your clergy as he/she will be the one to make your vows and sermon special and personal to you both.

❧ Be prepared to answer questions about your beliefs and why you want to marry in church.

❧ Start to think about the hymns and readings you may like to have (see pages 36–40).

The Roman Catholic Church

If both bride and groom are Catholic

You will need to approach the superintendent registrar of marriages in the district in which you live to request the issue of a certificate. You will need to provide the following details: the age of yourself and the groom; residential qualifications and addresses. The marriage will be expected to take place at your local church. If bride and groom live in different districts then the superintendents within both districts will need to be approached for a certificate.

You must reside within the district in which you wish to marry for a minimum of seven days prior to the notice being given and no less than fifteen days prior to the wedding ceremony.

Although the certificate is issued by the superintendent registrar, it is the parish priest who will authorise the marriage and it is wise to talk in great detail with him as he can decline to marry you if he so wishes.

You cannot marry within the Catholic Church if you have been previously married and are now divorced.

If one partner is not Catholic

If either yourself or the groom is not Catholic and you wish to marry within the Catholic Church, you will need to give as much notice as possible to the priest so that counselling into the Catholic faith and an understanding of what is required by the Church can be given. A minimum of six months would be acceptable. Again, banns will be read out prior to the wedding to allow people the opportunity to raise objections to the union. If no objections are raised the couple are able to solemnize their vows.

TIPS

❧ The priest is an important factor in this marriage and it is wise to meet regularly so that a good rapport is established which will come across during the ceremony.

The civil ceremony

Many couples choose to marry in a civil ceremony, and since the law changed in April 1995 to allow venues to attain licences to hold marriage ceremonies, this has become an increasingly popular method as there is a great deal of flexibility regarding how and where you can marry. You may want a less formal setting for several reasons:

1. Your focus for the day is on the celebrations following the formalities.
2. Either partner may have been married previously and is now divorced.
3. It can be easier and quicker to organise.
4. You may want to personalise your wedding, organising it specifically to your requirements and taste.

Whatever your reasons, you can make your ceremony as intimate, special and as formal as you wish. The legal requirement for a civil wedding is that you attain a certificate from the superintendent registrar of the district in which you intend to marry. You must attend in person and fill in the details of name, age and residence.

TIPS

❥ Take time to find a venue or register office that feels special to you and that you know will be adaptable to your needs.

❥ Ask how long you will have for your ceremony and if there is another ceremony following yours (this usually applies to register office marriages). If you would like longer, choose the last booking of the day or a less popular day such as a Friday – your guests can make a long weekend of the celebrations!

Choosing your venue

If you want to marry in a location or place that is special to you or has a more unusual feel to it, there are now hundreds of fabulous places to choose from throughout the country, including hotels, civic buildings, stately homes, castles, museums, race courses and zoos. The only limiting factor is yourself! These venues can hold not only your ceremony but your reception as well.

The only restriction venues face when applying for a licence to marry couples is that they must not be temporary locations. So unfortunately you are unable to marry while bungee jumping, paragliding or abseiling – although if you can persuade a registrar to perform a blessing while doing any of these, there should be no stopping you! If you want to get married outside you will have to choose a conservatory, gazebo or orangery.

The Jewish ceremony

A Jewish ceremony falls within civil law as the ceremony can take place anywhere, for example in a private house, a synagogue, a hall, etc., whether it is registered for the purpose or not. Although fairly flexible, there are certain times when a Jewish ceremony would not take place:

1. Jewish Sabbath between sunset on Friday and sunset on Saturday.
2. On any festival or intermediate day of a festival.
3. On any Fast day.
4. Within the three weeks from the Fast of Tummuz to the Fast of Av.
5. During certain weeks of the Omer.

The rabbi or secretary of your synagogue will provide you with details of when it is wise to marry.

TIPS

❧ Ask your chosen venue how previous ceremonies have operated. This will give you an idea of how the layout of the venue can be best planned and suited to your needs.

❧ Check how many guests can be present at the wedding ceremony.

❧ Will the venue organise floral displays and seating plans for you?

❧ Will there be a separate room or marquee for the reception or will the room in which your ceremony takes place be turned around for the evening reception? If this is the case, make sure you are prepared to move around the venue while the changes are in progress, and inform your photographer!

❧ Meet with the registrar prior to the day to discuss readings and anything special you would like to include in the ceremony. Ask if you can write your own vows (if this appeals to you!).

Marrying abroad

Tying the knot overseas has become more popular over the past few years, offering a great alternative to marrying in the UK. The attraction of guaranteed sunshine, beautiful, unblemished beaches and fabulous luxury resorts is almost too good to miss, and many couples come to the conclusion that this would be the ideal setting in which to exchange their vows. The most popular destinations include:

St Lucia

Barbados

Florida

Mauritius

Jamaica

Antigua

Dominican
Republic

Seychelles

Maldives

Las Vegas

Cyprus

Vienna

Paris

Venice

Marriage requirements

The tour operator that organises your holiday can often also assist with the wedding arrangements and guide you easily through the legalities of each destination.

Some of the basic legal requirements for the Caribbean and the USA are as follows:

1. A minimum of 24 hours residency.
2. You will be required to produce documents such as a valid passport, and if you have been married previously you will need proof of divorce or a death certificate.
3. Return air tickets.
4. A single status affidavit.
5. If under 21 years of age you will need parental consent.
6. Most registrars/officiators will want to meet with you at least 24 hours prior to the marriage so that they can talk through their requirements and any payments. They will also run through a normal service and ensure you have a minimum of two witnesses.

Even though your wedding will be official and you will have a marriage certificate as proof, you will need to register your marriage with your local registrar on your return to the UK.

Questions for your travel agent

- What style of marriage can I have? If you're thinking of the Caribbean there should be a choice of church, beach, venue, gardens or even underwater ceremonies!

- What is included in the package that should be organised in advance: flowers; cake; photographer; transport; food; drink; registrar's/officiator's costs? Ensure you get an estimated cost of any extras that you feel will be essential while you are there. You don't want to get caught out and have to dip into your general spending money! Normally, the cost of the registrar's time and wedding certificate will be charged when you get to your destination.

- Ideally, how long should you be at your resort prior to your ceremony? You will want to spend a few days acclimatising, finding your way around, booking the flowers, cake, photographer, etc., prior to the big day. Give yourself enough time so that you aren't racing around and getting stressed.

- Are there any special deals if you take over ten friends and family away with you?

Benefits of marrying overseas

- You will have a private and very personal ceremony.

- You can invite close friends and family to share in your special day as part of a unique holiday break.

- If you have any complicated family issues it can be a good way of celebrating a marriage without the traditional constraints and without upsetting anyone.

- It can be a cheaper way of tying the knot if there are budget restrictions. On average, a marriage and two-week holiday abroad will cost between £2,000 – £4,000, depending on destination and additional extras chosen.

- It gives you a great excuse to come home and have a big party to celebrate your union!

Contact Marks and Spencer for travel insurance on 0800 068 3918 or at www.marksandspencerweddings.com

Second time around

People's perceptions of second marriages are changing fast. More couples are deciding to tie the knot for the second time, and as with first marriages the etiquette is very personal: it is completely up to yourself and your partner what you both feel comfortable doing. Go ahead and have the day that you want, and don't worry about what people may or may not think. It's a celebration of love – and that's the important thing!

The ceremony

The Catholic Church will not perform the ceremony if either bride or groom is divorced. The Church of England officially shares the same view, however the policies for marriage are always under review to keep up to date with the changing times and will be reviewed again in 2004.

If you are religious, you might consider having a civil ceremony (privately or with friends and family) so that you are married in the eyes of the law, and then have the union blessed in church. Most clergymen or -women are happy to perform a blessing and you can treat this as a proper 'wedding' (your father can walk you up the aisle, and you can request hymns and readings, etc). It can be as lavish and formal as you wish.

Otherwise, there are many beautiful venues available for civil ceremonies, and these can encompass traditions such as bridesmaids, or having your father walk you up the aisle. Alternatively, you may like your partner to meet you halfway, or have your mother escort you, or simply go it alone!

There is no need to be shy on your second or third or fourth marriage – it is a new beginning that should be celebrated. The only restrictions are with the official ceremony – then the sky's the limit!

Order of service

Your ceremony should be as personal to you as your dress. It is an opportunity to demonstrate your values and personality and you should take advantage of it. Ceremonies generally fall into one of four categories:

1. Religious: the ceremony is dictated by the beliefs of one particular religion and is performed by a priest, minister, rabbi or other ordained official.

2. Interfaith: when individuals of different faiths are married, the ceremony is performed by two representatives from each faith.

3. Civil: a judge or registrar is the officiator of the ceremony which is performed using a non-religious text.

4. Spiritual: these ceremonies place the emphasis on humanistic and spiritual beliefs rather than religious ones.

Within each category there are opportunities to make the service as individual to you as possible.

Before you start making decisions about your ceremony, talk to your official. Your choice of official is an extremely important one: be sure that you have a rapport with him or her and don't be afraid to keep looking until you have found one that you get on with. Ask them if they have a standard order of service that you can look at with your partner. Ask how long the service will last. See how flexible they are if you want to make deletions or additions. Can you write your own vows?

Now comes the fun part: choosing readings, hymns and pieces of music!

If music be the food of love . . .

Choosing the right music for your wedding day is very important as it has the power to lift the senses and set the tone for what people are about to see and experience. Firstly, choose the sort of music you would like during your service and what you would like it to be played on. Listen to different pieces of music to get some idea of what you would like and also the sounds of the various instruments. You can choose one or more of the options below, the only limiting factor being cost:

Church organ

Solo violin

Solo vocalist, accompanied or unaccompanied

String trio or quartet

Harp

Harp and flute

Church choir

Children's choir

Piano

Gospel choir

Classical guitar

Chamber music ensemble

You may have heard many beautiful pieces of music but don't have a clue who the composer is or how to find out. Listed on pages 37–39 is an array of classical music and alternative pieces that you may recognise, any of which would be the perfect accompaniment to your wedding, be it in a church, a civil venue or a register office. In addition, don't be afraid to include friends and family. Ask anyone who plays an instrument or sings well to do something for you. It saves on the cost of musicians and incorporates something personal into your day!

The bride's entrance

The music listed below is a mixture of traditional and contemporary pieces that set the tone for the service to follow.

Arrival of The Queen of Sheba *Handel*

This is a beautiful piece of music, light and delicate, and is perfect for the bride to make her entrance and walk down the aisle to. It is a fairly traditional piece and has been favoured for church weddings in the past.

Wedding March *Wagner*

Wedding March *Mendelssohn*

These are vibrant, powerful pieces of music, which can be used for both a dramatic entrance or celebratory exit and are extremely popular and the most recognised classical tunes heard at church weddings.

Spring (from Four Seasons) *Vivaldi*

This is a light and joyful piece of music that can be played at a less formal wedding for the entrance of the bride or during the signing of the register. Other great pieces of music to accompany the entrance of the bride include:

Grand March (from Aida) *Verdi*

Prince of Denmark's March *Clarke*

Alternative music

The following pieces of music are perfect for use during the signing of the register, or could be used as an alternative and less conventional accompaniment to the entrance of the bride or departure of the couple at the end of the service.

Air on the G String *Bach*
Gentle soothing tones that will complement the pause taken to sign the register. This piece of music is ideal if you have a string quartet playing at your wedding.

Ave Maria *Schubert*

This can be sung or played during the signing of the register and has a beautiful haunting quality that sounds fabulous in a church setting.

Trumpet Tune and Air *Purcell*

This is a frothy, light piece that fills in beautifully during the signing of the register or during the departure of the couple following the service. It is less conventional and would suit venue weddings and less formal occasions.

Canon in D major *Pachelbel*

This is a lovely floating melody which would be perfect for the interval offered during the signing of the register, and is a wonderful piece for string quartets. It would also suit the bride's entrance and is less traditional and uptempo.

Other great pieces of interlude music include:

O Mio Babbino Caro *Puccini*

Jesu, Joy Of Man's Desiring *Bach*

Favourite Wedding Hymns

Selecting the hymns for your wedding day can sometimes be tricky. You may have a favourite one from when you were a child or heard something that was sung at a friend, or family wedding.

If you don't recognise the title of any of the hymns below you can always buy a tape or CD with wedding compilations to help you get the right feel for your day.

Here is a helping hand to guide you through the most favoured hymns used for special occasions.

All Things Bright and Beautiful

Amazing Grace

At the Name of Jesus

Bind us Together

Colours of the Day (Light up the Fire)

Dear Lord and Father of Mankind

For the Beauty of the Earth

Give me Joy in my Heart (Sing Hosanna)

God of all Living

Guide me O Thou Great Redeemer

Immortal Invisible

I vow to Thee my Country

Jerusalem

Lead us Heavenly Father

Lord for the Years

Lord of all Hopefulness

Lord of the Dance

Lord the Light of your Love is Shining (Shine, Jesus, Shine)

Love Divine all Love Excelling

Make me a Channel of your Peace

Morning has Broken

My Song is Love Unknown

Now Thank we all our God

O Jesus I have Promised

O Lord my God (How Great thou Art)

O Perfect Love all Human Thought Transcending

O Worship the King

Praise, my Soul

Praise to the Lord, the Almighty

Tell out my Soul the Greatness of the Lord

The King of Love my Shepherd is

The Lord's my Shepherd

The departure

The departure of the couple is a celebration and the music chosen should be vibrant and powerful, creating a joyous feel to mark the end of the service.

Alla Hornpipe (from Water Music) *Handel*

A beautiful, light, happy piece of music that celebrates the union of marriage and is great for the couple to walk down the aisle to. It is very traditional and best suited to a church wedding.

Wedding March *Wagner*

Wedding March *Mendelssohn*

Again, these are very well-known pieces of music used either for the bride's entrance (see page 37) or as the couple depart from the church.

Other great pieces of music to accompany the departure of the bride and groom:

Morning (from Peer Gynt) *Grieg*

Toccata from Symphony No5 *Widor*

Music for the Royal Fireworks *Handel*

Finale from Symphony No1 *Vierne*

Readings

These can be as personal as you want them to be. There might be a particular poem, song or hymn that you empathise with, or you could choose a piece from a book of love poetry or spiritual readings. Ask a friend or relative to read it on the day, but make sure you choose someone who is confident and is able to project their voice.

Religious readings

ECCLESIASTES 3; 1–15

A passage in honour of the 'for better, for worse' part of your vows. A reminder that life has pain as well as joy.

PSALM 23

'The Lord is my shepherd'.

RUTH 1; 1–17

A passage about loyalty and love: 'Wherever you go, I will go'.

PROVERBS 31; 10–31

A passage about a 'wife of good character'.

MARK 10; 6–16

The teachings of Jesus about marriage and children.

JOHN 2; 1–11

An eyewitness account of Jesus at a wedding.

JOHN 15; 9–17

A well-known passage about the nature of true love.

1 CORINTHIANS 13; 1–13

A very popular reading at weddings that speaks of love as the greatest of all gifts.

Alternative readings

AS TRUE A HEART

Matthew Prior

LIKE A SINGING BIRD

Christina Rossetti

MARRIED LOVE

Kuan Tao-Shung

ON MARRIAGE OR LOVE

Kahil Gibran, The Prophet

TO MY DEAR AND LOVING HUSBAND

Anne Bradstreet

ESKIMO MARRIAGE SONG

Anon

THE YUEH-FU

Chinese Folk Ballad

TIPS

❧ Insist on a rehearsal prior to the big day. Go through everyone's positions and movements during the service with your official; no matter how 'spontaneous' you want your ceremony to be, you will just look foolish if you don't know what you are doing.

❧ Ask your musicians to attend the rehearsal if they possibly can. Also, find out what they are planning to wear. Church choirs often do not have the funds to stretch to uniforms so ask if they could all wear similar clothing or clothing of one colour.

❧ Ask your official if your ceremony can be videoed or photographed. Sometimes a fee will be charged for this.

❧ Don't forget to book the organ, choir and bells in advance if you wish to have them.

❧ Ask your ushers to place a few drops of an aromatherapy oil into each candle before the ceremony. As the candles burn during the ceremony, the oil will be released into the air.

❧ Never let your guests enter a space that is silent. Ask your chosen musicians to play something as the guests take their seats.

❧ Include a note in your order of service about anyone who has taken part in your ceremony, even if it is just to say that they are your brother, your best friend or your aunt! Also include something about the history of the place in which you are having your ceremony, and any other personal notes about the service, the flowers, etc. This will give the guests a nice memento of the day and something to read while they are waiting!

❧ To add a sense of drama to the occasion, count to ten before you enter once you have heard your entrance music strike up.

❧ A flower girl walking down the aisle before you scattering rose petals infused with fragrance will make a lasting memory.

❧ Ask your musicians to continue playing whilst you are having your photos taken outside the ceremony venue.

UNFORTUNATELY, LOVE COMES WITH A PRICE TAG, AND THE BUDGETING ASPECT OF ORGANISING YOUR WEDDING IS A SERIOUS MATTER TO BE TACKLED EARLY ON. BEFORE YOU CHARGE OUT AND MAKE SOME WILD DECISIONS AS TO WHAT YOU WANT TO INCLUDE ON YOUR BIG DAY, TAKE STOCK AND LIST EVERYTHING YOU COULD POSSIBLY NEED AND HOW MUCH YOU WANT TO SPEND.

The price of love

This may be a difficult task as you may not have thought about who will be paying for what at this stage. However, try and allocate an amount to each item on your list as a starting point, and if there is something that you know you really want to splash out on, this is the time to make a note of it as you may have to look at cutting back on something else.

There are a host of things that you may want to include in your budget list, covering the build-up preparations, the wedding day itself and events following the day.

Listed below are the various elements that fall into each of these categories, but there are no set rules as to what you must include. The best way to use this information is to jot down what you believe you would like to do for your wedding, then use the estimated cost guide to outline your potential spend. If the total value comes to more than you originally thought, look at redefining your priorities for the day. You can't avoid the risks from things you can't control, but you can insure against them with Marks and Spencer Wedding Insurance. Premiums from as little as £54, call 0800 316 5985 for more information.

The average costs for each section have been compiled from an independent survey held by *You & Your Wedding* magazine.

Average UK cost of a wedding in 2001

Engagement ring	£1,021
Engagement party	£429
Bride's wedding ring	£275
Groom's wedding ring	£257
Wedding dress	£941
Shoes, accessories, headdress and veil	£217
Lingerie	£97
Make-up and skincare	£87
Groom's outfit	£224
Bridesmaids' and pageboys' outfits	£367
Bride's/bridesmaids' flowers	£183
Venue flowers	£276
Wedding cars and carriages	£341
Registrar and church fees	£291
Invitations & stationery	£228
Photography	£628
Video	£452
Reception venue/marquee	£1,169
Catering	£2,248
Drinks: wine, champagne, etc.	£992
Wedding cake	£230
Going away outfit	£138
First night hotel	£193
Honeymoon	£2,566
Other expenses	£690
Total	**£14,540**

The average costs listed in the table above are based on the following criteria:
The wedding is a traditional wedding.
The groom's outfit cost includes the hire of the best man's suit.
Bridesmaids' and pageboys' outfit costs are based on an average of two attendants and one child.
The honeymoon is a longhaul overseas holiday.

If you are working to a strict budget there are several ways in which you can cut down on some of the items on the list and still achieve the effect you want. Just follow the tips and ideas throughout this book – don't panic just yet!

How to broach the topic of finances

❥ If you find it hard to contemplate the financial impact of a wedding on yourselves and your families it is best to discuss and determine the potential implications as soon as possible.

❥ It is traditional for the groom to approach his family about whether they would like to contribute to the wedding, however most parents offer their support right from the start so there shouldn't be an issue over raising the topic.

❥ The bride should also approach her family and find out their thoughts on the funding of the wedding.

Who paid for what traditionally?

Bride's family

🎗 Cost of the ceremony, including the music, flowers, registering banns and all related expenses.

🎗 The bride's wedding attire including dress, shoes and accessories.

🎗 Transportation for the bride and the bridal party.

🎗 Floral bouquets, including church, and reception decorations.

🎗 The reception costs, including the venue, food, beverages, entertainment, wedding cake, wedding favours/bonbonnière.

🎗 Photography.

🎗 Bridesmaids' attire.

Groom's family

🎗 The groom's outfit and best man and ushers' outfits.

🎗 Travel and accommodation for the groom's family.

🎗 Corsages for the parents and buttonholes for the men.

🎗 Any additional expenses they would like to contribute towards.

Bride and groom

🎗 Gifts of appreciation for the parents, the attendants and the best man.

🎗 Any expenses that exceed what was originally allocated.

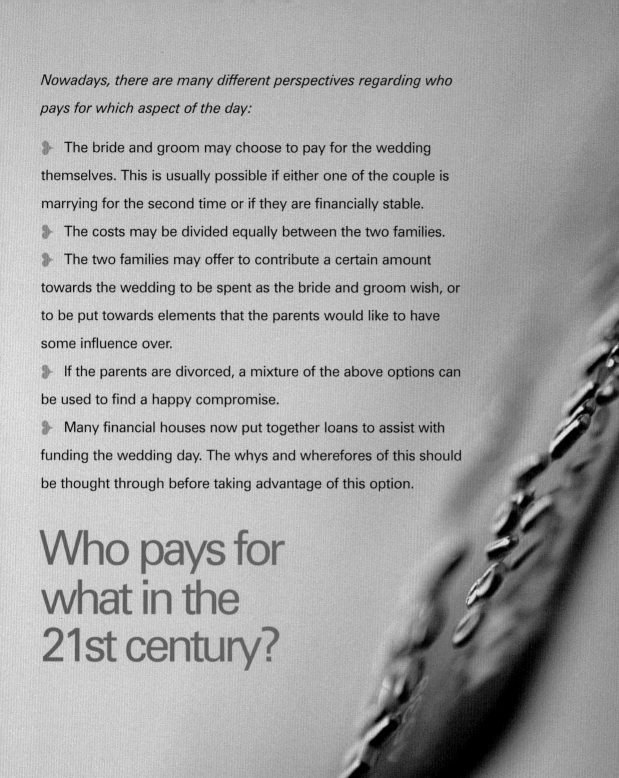

Nowadays, there are many different perspectives regarding who pays for which aspect of the day:

- The bride and groom may choose to pay for the wedding themselves. This is usually possible if either one of the couple is marrying for the second time or if they are financially stable.
- The costs may be divided equally between the two families.
- The two families may offer to contribute a certain amount towards the wedding to be spent as the bride and groom wish, or to be put towards elements that the parents would like to have some influence over.
- If the parents are divorced, a mixture of the above options can be used to find a happy compromise.
- Many financial houses now put together loans to assist with funding the wedding day. The whys and wherefores of this should be thought through before taking advantage of this option.

Who pays for what in the 21st century?

KEEPING EVERYONE HAPPY WHEN PLANNING A WEDDING IS A POTENTIAL MINEFIELD. BE ASSURED: UNLESS YOU HANDLE THE FAMILIES INVOLVED CORRECTLY, THEY COULD MAKE THE LEAD-UP TO THE WEDDING AND THE BIG DAY ITSELF A NIGHTMARE! WITH A LITTLE DIPLOMACY, HOWEVER, THIS CAN ALL BE AVOIDED . . .

Family and friends

Potential family feuds

Let's sort the family out first. Everyone's situation is unique, however the most common complaint that arises during the organisation process is the interference of 'Mothers'!

You are paying

If you are paying for the majority of the wedding, then you can pretty much do as you wish (and not invite Cousin Jane who you last set eyes on when you were ten years old!). This may not put an end to the constant stream of ideas and thoughts on how 'it should be done', however you should point out to your mother (or the groom's mother) that it is your wedding and that there are some traditions you do not wish to include. But think carefully before you actually say the words!

Be gentle, sensitive and diplomatic, as her reactions probably stem from pure emotion and nerves as the wedding gets closer. She has more than likely been dreaming of this day since you were born and sees it as an opportunity to right all the wrongs of her own big day!

Some parents feel strange about the bride and groom paying for everything, which can also prompt certain reactions or comments not normally meant or said. To make things a lot easier give Mum very specific jobs to do so she has some input and feels involved in the wedding. These jobs can include helping to send out the wedding invitations and tracking the RSVPs, ensuring the cake and the caterers arrive on time, and so on.

Parents are paying

If, as many couples still experience, your parents are paying the majority of the wedding costs, your diplomatic skills will be sorely tested. Your parents may feel that they are able to invite whoever they want to the ceremony and reception. Again, a gentle approach is required: ask if they could keep their guests to a certain number and go through the budget to help qualify what it is you are asking for and why the guest list needs to be evenly balanced between the two families and yourselves.

Meeting of minds

Try to ensure that the two families meet up before the big day. A meeting on neutral ground such as a restaurant is best. Involve the groom's mother as much as you can (or as much as she would like to be involved). It can be a very isolating experience for her otherwise. Again, ask her to do specific jobs and let her have some creative input.

Yourself and the groom should decide on the sort of wedding day that you would both like prior to sitting down with your families. Determine whether you want a civil service, a small/large reception, and so on, and then let both sets of parents know your plans right from the start. This will prevent anyone getting carried away with ideas of how it should be done. It is important that you and your fiancé present a united front. You don't want your future mother-in-law to think that you are forcing her son to do everything your way.

Friends

Another area of unease might occur between yourself and your friends, as they may feel left out. Try not to make your wedding the sole topic of conversation; their lives are continuing amidst your preparations! Ask special friends to contribute something towards the wedding day if they are not a bridesmaid or best man, perhaps a reading or the handing out of the favours at the end of the night.

The groom

You may feel that you have been left to do absolutely everything. Talk to your beloved nicely, tell him that you cannot manage everything by yourself and would really appreciate his input. Talk to him about what he may want to get involved in, such as organising the cars, alcohol, music or his outfit!

Ghastly guest lists

Guest lists can be a nightmare if they are not thought through clearly!

Before you start, estimate the number of people that you envisage coming to the church, and try to do the same for the reception. Think realistically about family, friends and work colleagues: who would you really like to be present? Then divide their names between daytime ceremony and evening reception categories. If you want them to go to both, place their names in both categories. The choice is yours.

When you start to draw up your list don't concern yourselves too much with family invitations, as this will be the basis for discussion when the families meet up. Focus on your friends (i.e. people that wouldn't be invited by either set of parents).

Try to divide the list you make into two groups: an A-list and a B-list. The A-list will consist of friends that you have known for a long time and will keep in touch with following the wedding. There will be some friends that only one of you considers should be on the A-list. At this point place them in the B-list until the numbers start to become more realistic.

Your numbers will ultimately be dictated by your budget. One thing you must not do at this stage is to change the style of your wedding to accommodate more people. For example, a stand-up finger buffet will allow for more guests than a formal sit-down meal, but to dilute your ideal wedding plans to meet guest numbers will mean that you end up pleasing no-one.

Two helpful rules to work towards are:

1. Decide on a total number of guests for the wedding, for example 100. Divide this figure by two and allocate one half to the two families, therefore asking each family to invite 25 guests, and leaving yourselves 50 guests. Always give each family a number to work towards as this will prevent you becoming embroiled in wrestling with your family's guest list as well as your own. Once this has been done they can then come back to you and say that they cannot possibly keep to the number that you suggested – so negotiate! Remember that this is your wedding.

2. If you have not spoken with some of your guests in over a year, or if you are unlikely to keep in touch with them in the future, they are probably not good enough 'friends' to stay on your A-list. Relegate them to the B-list or drop them from the guest list altogether.

Avoiding offence and saving costs

If you are trying to keep costs down but want to avoid offending people, there are a couple of things you can do.

Firstly, why not have an evening reception to which you invite everyone you want. The only additional cost is usually a buffet, with a very low charge per head. In this way the friends and family unable to make the ceremony have a chance to party and celebrate in a less formal way with you, but still feel included.

If you are working to a very tight budget then simply invite close family and friends to the ceremony and an intimate meal. Or explain to people that your budget is restricted and throw a huge party on your return from honeymoon. If you are honest and upfront about everything people are normally very understanding and supportive.

REMEMBER!

You can rely on the fact that 10 per cent of your invitations will be refused, so don't worry if you have invited 110 people to a venue that only holds 100. If you get more refusals than you are expecting (which will be the case particularly if you are getting married on one of the popular summer weekends or a bank holiday), then send more invitations out. Ensure that you do this at least one month before the wedding so people don't guess that they are last-minute additions (also, consider whether they know anyone else that would have been in the first batch of invitations and thus received theirs a month earlier, making it obvious that the later recipient is 'second choice').

Only in exceptional circumstances should you include 'and guest' on a single guest's invitation, for example if the person will know absolutely nobody else at the wedding. Remember: this is one of the most important days of your life and a very intimate occasion, not one to be shared with complete strangers.

It is a personal choice as to whether children are present on your big day. It may drastically cut down on your numbers if you do not include children. But it has to be the same rule for everyone – with no exceptions.

As you get closer to the wedding day there will be various people and/or acquaintances that will pop out of the woodwork and that you will feel obliged to invite. Remember the rules that you set yourself when you drew up the guest list and do not deviate from them. As the day approaches you will become more stressed and emotional and it is easy to make the wrong decision! If you can get away with an evening invitation and not exceed your budget then this is the best way around a tricky situation.

Choosing the best man

Selecting a friend or brother to be the best man is not easy. Not only does he have to be a fairly responsible and supportive person on the wedding day itself, but he has the task of making the groom's last days of bachelorhood as smooth and relaxed as possible!

The person chosen needs to be fairly confident and not mind stepping in and taking control of any situation thrown at him. He also needs to have the strength of character to deliver a speech to a large audience in a light-hearted and affectionate manner.

The role of best man is a special one and you need to feel that the person you choose will rise to the occasion and thrive on the privilege of being asked to play such a supportive role to the wedding party.

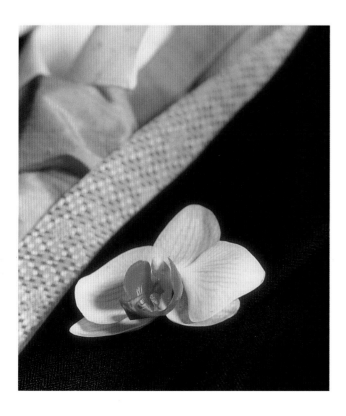

The best man's duties

The best man has a number of important duties to carry out both before and after the wedding day.

- His first and most obvious duty is to organise the stag night, so choosing someone with a modicum of responsibility is a very wise move! (See pages 116–117 for some great stag night and weekend break ideas.)
- He is responsible for acting as an intermediary between the families of the bride and groom leading up to the wedding so that everyone is kept well informed about plans and preparations.
- He will assist the groom with his responsibilities, for example sourcing the transport, photographer, and so on.
- He will accompany the groom and ushers to hire or buy their outfits and ensure that everyone is organised for the wedding day. He will call to double check that the delivery of suits (if hired) is on schedule.
- He will make sure the orders for the flowers for the bride and bridesmaids, and the buttonholes for the groom, best man and ushers, and the corsages for the mothers of the bride and groom are in hand and will be delivered on time and to the right places.
- He will organise accommodation for himself and the groom for the night before the big day.
- He is responsible for paying the church fees before the service on behalf of the groom.
- He is responsible for getting the groom to the church on time.
- He will look after the wedding rings and hand them to the groom at the right time during the service.
- He may be asked to be one of the witnesses for the signing of the marriage certificate.
- He will escort the chief bridesmaid from the church or venue and will ensure that everyone has transport on to the evening reception.
- His biggest responsibility comes at the reception, where it is traditional for the best man to initiate the toasts to the bride and groom, to make the third speech (following the groom), and to read out any telegrams and messages. If there is a toastmaster present he will liaise with him to ensure arrangements run smoothly.
- If the happy couple are departing on the day of the wedding or the following day for their honeymoon, the best man will be asked to take care of the travel documents and passports.

The best man is a key player on the wedding day. Make sure he fully understands his responsibilities and delegate those duties to him from the outset.

doing it your way

Themed weddings

Personalising your day

2

THIS CHAPTER OUTLINES SIX WEDDING THEMES THAT WILL PROVIDE INSPIRATION AND HELP YOU CREATE THE WEDDING OF YOUR DREAMS! THE SIX KEY STYLES ARE DESCRIBED IN DETAIL TO GIVE YOU A CLEAR GUIDE AS TO HOW TO SUCCESSFULLY PULL EACH ONE TOGETHER. DON'T BE AFRAID TO MIX AND MATCH SOME OF THE MORE GENERAL THEMES TO CREATE A TRULY UNIQUE WEDDING!

Themed weddings

A valentine soirée

You can lose yourself in the colours and scents of this theme, given that the rose is the symbol of love! Cherubs, hearts and linked rings are additional symbols of love and passion – emotions that can easily translate into vibrant ideas!

Time of year
14th February itself or the nearest weekend to it. Of course, you can also use the 'love' theme any time of the year if you want to!

Invitations
Traditional card invitations filled with red heart confetti that will fall out as they are opened. Or festoon your invites with hearts and cupids – true love knows no bounds!

Gown details
There are two looks that would be perfect for this theme. The first is a very simple, straight gown with embroidery detail on the bodice – imagine how dramatic vibrant red roses will look against an elegant silhouette. The second is a gown with a corseted, boned bodice and dramatic full skirt made from layers of tulle – this is wildly romantic and captures the flamboyance of love and passion.

Flowers
Red roses close-packed in a teardrop bouquet would be exquisite.

The groom
Funky and modern: a velvet three-quarter-length frock coat in a rich navy or black complemented by a satin-backed waistcoat with heart motif embroidery.

Buttonhole
A single red rose.

Attendants
Simple dresses in a colour to match your own, with posies of cream or white roses to match the dress. Add a red detail such as a wrap, red sash or Dorothy-style red shoes.

Church
Concentrate on intense displays of red roses to create an impact!

Transport
A horse-drawn carriage would add a dreamlike quality to the day.

Venue
A fairytale castle would provide a magnificent backdrop.

Reception drinks
Pink champagne served in flute glasses with a strawberry at the bottom.

Table decoration
Scatter silver dragees and tiny heart-shaped confetti over the table, and have a vase of red roses as a centrepiece. Lay a single red rose across the place setting of each lady. Alternatively, bedeck the tables with rose petals and weave ribbon down the centre.

Chair back

Use ribbon to tie a heart-shaped container filled with chocolate dragees to the back of the chair for your guests to enjoy!

Place settings

Bake heart-shaped biscuits and ice the guests' initials on top. Why not attach the heart-shaped pastry cutter used as an extra treat! Another alternative is to cut a piece of card into the shape of a cupid and write the guests' names in gold pen. Tape them onto florists wire and spiral the wire into a spring so that they stand up.

Favours

Chocolate hearts, lollipops or biscuits – even scented candles or massage oil! 'Loveheart' sweets for the children.

Food

Think pink! Smoked salmon to start, followed by chicken in a red peppercorn sauce, and fresh blackberries, red berries and strawberries covered in lashings of cream to finish.

Cake

One hundred little fairy cakes, iced and decorated with a single fondant heart.

Entertainment

A harpist for the church and drinks, followed by a Harry Connick Jnr-esque crooner to while away the wee small hours!

Buffet

A mixture of red, yellow and orange peppers stuffed with cous-cous: delicious for vegetarians and carnivores alike!

Easter celebration

This theme is inspired by new beginnings. Springtime is fresh and full of new life – think of the light colours, such as fresh lemons, whites and soft greens, captured in spring flowers. It's time for Easter bonnets, eggs and bunnies!

Time of year
Easter weekend would be ideal, or even the weekend before.

Invitations
Ask a chocolate company to enclose your invite in a small chocolate egg, then instruct the recipient to open and consume immediately! Request that women come in their best Easter bonnet!

Gown details
A gown of light fabric such as floating chiffon or feather-light organza would be beautiful. Accessories could include a chiffon stole, a wrist-length veil with small pearl detail to frame the face, and a delicate tiara or individual fresh flowers on wires dotted through the hair. Use either pure white or pale pastels coupled with a matching wrap.

Flowers
Spring flowers: soft antique white lily-of-the-valley or pastel sweet peas with their delicate scents. Alternatively, daffodils or crocuses can add a flash of colour to the soft surroundings!

The groom
Go for a traditional morning suit, top hat and tails, with a striking waistcoat in either the ivory or pastel shades of the flowers and attendants' outfits. Lilac looks great, especially when teamed with a silver cravat – but try to avoid pink!

Buttonhole
A single gardenia: simple yet stylish.

Attendants
Dresses in beautiful pastel shades. Each bridesmaid could wear a different colour: pale pink, blue and lilac, with bouquets to match (each carrying a different colour to that of their dress).

Church
Have at least two large floral displays of your chosen spring flowers; the scent will carry and fill the air. Why not have a string quartet play 'Spring' from Vivaldi's 'Four Seasons' while you walk down the aisle.

Transport
An open-top Rolls-Royce.

Venue
With spring in mind, try to find somewhere with a garden.

Reception drinks
A fruity punch or a Pimms with all the trimmings would go down well as a refreshing start to the afternoon reception.

Table decoration

Scatter the table with light, white feathers and small eggs – use a gingham tablecloth for a real spring feel. Alternatively, paint terracotta pots in your chosen colours and plant some bulbs (daffodils, crocuses, tulips and snowdrops) that will flower in time for your wedding day – you can create a striking mass of colour with just a little forward planning! If you are using a marquee, decorate the poles with cascading ribbons to resemble Maypoles – guests may even be tempted to perform the real thing!

Chair back

Tie a small posy of spring flowers to the back of the chair for a fragrant treat!

Place settings

Ask a calligrapher or friend with good handwriting to write your guests' names on eggs and lay them on a nest of ribbon and feathers. Alternatively, ice the first name of each of your guests on to small plaques of chocolate. This gives them something to nibble on halfway through the speeches!

Favours

Easter biscuits wrapped in see-through cellophane and tied with beautiful ribbon.

Food

A light buffet or sit-down meal would be appropriate. A fresh salad with edible flowers and an unusual dressing – something tangy or fruity – would be lovely, followed by tender roast lamb with a caper sauce and a baked Easter cheesecake.

Cake

Treat your guests to a traditional Easter cake – Simnel cake is a delicious fruit and saffron cake decorated with marzipan. Fresh flowers and a few miniature bunnies could be added as additional decoration.

Entertainment

A great line dance will get all your guests on their feet and in the party spirit. It's a fun way to learn new steps and adds a new element to the entertainment!

Buffet

Savoury pastries and hot cross buns.

Under the sea

This is a great theme as it conjures up a number of different elements: a warm sea of turquoise, azure and aquamarine shades; white sandy beaches and masses of shells; sea horses, starfish and fishing boats; warm sunshine and lazy days; shipwrecks and tropical island hideaways – there's so much to choose from!

Time of year
Ideal for a summer wedding.

Invitations
Try a 'message in a bottle' theme. Handwrite your invites on textured paper then roll them carefully into a scroll and place into the neck of a (clean!) plain glass bottle. Place some small shells and sand in the bottom of the bottle first.

Gown details
There are two gorgeous looks that would suit this theme well. The first is a gown made from floating ivory chiffon teamed with a soft pale blue chiffon stole – very elegant and whimsical. Alternatively, if you have a great figure, make the most of it with a bias-cut sheath dress and a magnificent godet train! This look is not only sexy, striking and elegant, but gives a slight 'mermaid' feel to the proceedings!

Flowers
A tight posy of white or sand-coloured flowers interspersed with wired shells. Use fragrant flowers with scents that will linger in the air – jasmine, orange blossom or gardenia.

The groom
If your groom is tanned or can wear soft colours well then an informal linen suit, perhaps in cream, with a pale blue waistcoat would look superb! Alternatively, go for a stylish navy suit with an ivory waistcoat and a navy or turquoise taffeta cravat.

Buttonhole
One single white flower to mimic the bride's bouquet.

Attendants
White or pale blue dresses in chiffon to match the bride. For children, use layered white net-skirted dresses with a pale blue sash.

Church
Use huge arrangements of white flowers. Also, place large shells and smooth stones all the way up the sides of the aisle and loop net along the pews.

Transport
An old-fashioned Morris Minor!

Venue
Anywhere by the sea! Cornwall is extremely picturesque. If the seaside is not an option, why not try the London Aquarium or a venue with a swimming pool in the gardens.

Reception drinks
Bloody Marys in large glasses complete with a stick of celery to stir them with.

Table decoration
Cover the table with swathes of blue fabric and scatter it with silver-wrapped chocolate fishes. Candles placed around the table will recreate the ambience of a warm sunset, and for your centrepiece place a candle inside a goldfish bowl to continue the 'fishy' theme.

Chair back
Hang a 'treasure bag' from the back of each chair, filled with silver-covered chocolate coins or treasures of your choice!

Place settings
Fishing lines dangling from the tallest glass: tie some nylon thread around a smooth pebble, then cut out fish shapes from pale grey or blue card and write the guests' names on them. Attach the fish to the thread and drop the pebble into the glass so that the fish is hanging from the thread. Tie the napkins into knots or tie a piece of thin rope around them.

Favours
Chocolate fish or ceramic mermaids.

Food
Coquille-St-Jacques, served in the original scallop shells, followed by sublime lobster ravioli with basil sauce, then baked chocolate mousse with Cornish clotted cream.

Cake
A plain white fondant Victoria sponge cake in three tiers and covered with starfish.

Entertainment
An old-fashioned piano during the drinks, followed by some riotous dancing!

Buffet
Cornish pasties.

Autumnal flair

This is a great time of year, with a choice of rich hues of orange, red and aubergine. Berries, willow and satsumas spring to mind, and of course the seasonal Halloween and Bonfire Night celebrations can provide a dramatic background for a wedding celebration!

Time of year
31st October, 5th November, or any time in the autumn.

Invitations
Handwrite your invites as though they were old luggage labels, punch holes in the end and use old garden twine to tie them to sparklers.

Gown details
An A-line or princess-line skirt would be ideal for this theme as it is a soft look that flows beautifully away from the body. Many designers use rich shades of silk, and a champagne gold or rich ivory colour would capture the feel of the time of year perfectly. There are also some very pretty embroidery details that can be added: ask for a deep red highlighted with tiny pearls for a striking finish.

Flowers
A hand-tied bouquet of a mass of orange and red flowers, with willow and berries for a little drama. The bouquet should lay along the side of your arm – as if you were holding a baby!

The groom
A smart black frock coat would fit beautifully with this autumnal theme. Complete the look with a waistcoat in a rich red design or fabric and add a champagne gold cravat or tie.

Buttonhole
Berries and leaves.

Attendants
Pick out different hues from your theme to create a dramatic effect: for example, two shades of burnt orange and two shades of burnt red with matching bouquets. Colour co-ordinate the ushers with waistcoats to match each bridesmaid.

Church
Autumn is a season of scents, all of which evoke memories. Try sprinkling the aisle with fresh herbs: as they are trampled underfoot they will release beautiful scents. Tie bunches of dried herbs to the ends of each pew using rustic materials such as brown twine.

Transport
A classic old Daimler.

Venue
Somewhere historic – an old manor house or monastery, or how about the London Dungeon for some real drama!

Reception drinks

Try buttered rum, a rich, hot drink that will take the chill out of the bones on a damp day.

Table decoration

Gather together fallen leaves and place them between two sheets of newspaper, then put something heavy on top. Place the pressed leaves on the tables and then lay net, organza or muslin over the top of them. Place pomanders (oranges spiked with cloves and dried herbs) tied with a beautiful ribbon on the tables to create a beautiful scent. Ask your florist to create centre-pieces from willow, seasonal berries, oranges and flowers. Create huge carved pumpkins and place them around the reception.

Chair back

Attach a cellophane bag of gold-covered chocolate hearts to the back of each chair.

Place settings

Dry baby oak leaves and stick them on to plain white place cards. Write the guests' names in gold pen underneath.

Favours

Toffee apples – or if it is Halloween, why not alternate a trick or treat for each guest. The trick can be fun children's toys like bald wigs, cut off fingers, Dracula teeth, or glasses

with eyes on springs! The treats can be mini sweets. Wrap them up and place them at each setting – the guests will love them!

Food

A bonfire night buffet! Pile baked potatoes wrapped in foil into a huge pyramid. Next to them have a range of delicious fillings for guests to help themselves to. Serve hot dogs and burgers with a difference: how about apple and pork sausages with a range of yummy relishes, or Stilton and beef burgers in unusual buns, such as caraway seed. To finish, use the wedding cake tartlets (see below) or something light and fruity for contrast.

Cake

Try baby fruit tartlets as an alternative! Cape gooseberries are delicious set into an elderflower jelly. Arrange the tartlets in tiers.

Entertainment

Fireworks and an exuberant barn dance will warm the guests up and dance off the rich food!

Buffet

A Welsh favourite is a gorgeous Cawl soup made of pieces of lamb, leeks, potatoes, carrots and swede, which has to be eaten with crusty white bread and lumps of cheese – it's delicious!

autumnal

Christmas cheer

A wedding with this theme should conjure up the magical feel that Christmas inspires. Picture the wonderful rich colours associated with this time of year – warm golds, luscious reds and deep greens. Think of softly lit candles and roaring log fires, the aromatic smell of mulled wine or brandy to warm you on a cold winter's night, and don't forget the infectious laughter and fabulous goodwill that Christmas brings!

This should get your senses working towards thinking about the elements you would like to include in this style of wedding. Remember to ask your venue what decorations will be in place before you book your reception so that you can link in with any themes already in place.

Time of year
Any time in December, pre-Christmas.

Invitations
Choose a traditional thick white card and have your invitations gold embossed. It will set the tone of the wedding day.

Gown details
Think opulence! A gown of duchess satin or velvet encrusted with small crystal and pearl details to complement the icy weather. Accessories could include a velvet cloak edged with fake fur, a fur muff, long satin gloves, and a crystal tiara on a band of gold.

Flowers
There are two possibilities. Go for a bouquet of pure white or ivory roses with holly, wrapped in ivy. Or for a more dramatic look try a hand-tied bouquet with deep gold roses, red holly berries and gold-sprayed willow with eucalyptus.

The groom
A black velvet frock coat with a heavily brocaded waistcoat in a deep gold, accessorised with a deep green or red taffeta cravat.

Buttonhole
One single rosebud with holly berries and ivy to match the wedding bouquet.

Attendants
Dresses in deep greens and reds, with elegant stoles or capes to match. Each should carry the opposite colour bouquet to that of their dress.

Church
Candle-lit and bedecked with a splendid Christmas tree, amaryllis flowers and deep holly and ivy floral displays. Twinkling candles should be the only form of lighting – it will look magical.

Transport
A large white 1920s Rolls-Royce with white ribbon, holly and ivy secured to the front. This will allow plenty of room for a full dress!

Christmas

Venue
A Gothic castle or stately home with marvellous fireplaces and high vaulted ceilings. Complete this effect with a Scottish piper to pipe you down the aisle and later into the main reception. The reception room should have at least one large, spectacular Christmas tree.

Reception drinks
To keep guests warm and in party mood why not offer mulled wine or egg nog! Offer the children warm blackcurrant – they will think they have been treated to the real thing!

Table decoration
The centrepieces should continue the candle-lit theme, with large bowls of deep green foliage and red roses, amaryllis or early hyacinths. Alternatively, collect pine cones in different sizes, spray them silver and gold, and place them in a bowl with holly and berries for a contrast of colour. Use long stem candles in tall candleholders to throw a soft light over them, creating a glorious festive centrepiece. As a finishing touch, scatter the table with gold dragees and foil-covered chocolate hearts.

Chair back
Tie Christmas baubles to the back of the chair with festive ribbon.

Place settings
Why not write your guests' names in gold pen on large holly or ivy leaves. If these seem too small, try a rubber plant leaf – as long as it's a deep green, what does it matter! Attach the leaves to a piece of gilded fresh fruit – a pear is ideal. Or take individual pine cones and add a name tag written in either silver or gold ink. The napkins can be tied with wired ivy, or gold or red organza ribbon.

Favours
Mini-Christmas stockings or homemade crackers.

Food
Start with a rich soup such as Stilton and celery, followed by roast goose with all the trimmings, then a light Christmassy dessert such as Christmas pudding ice cream. Think traditional – with a twist!

Cake
A traditional Christmas cake laced with plenty of brandy! It can be decorated with red holly berries and individual gold candles which can be lit during the cutting ceremony.

Entertainment
For the welcome drinks why not have an angelic choir singing carols to set the scene, whilst for the evening entertainment, start the festive proceedings with some riotous Scottish dancing followed by a disco to end the celebrations.

Buffet
Cheese and port, followed by wedding cake.

Contemporary

If you are a couple that really moves with the times, then you will be looking to create a minimalist 21st-century wedding! Think cool shades of white, cream and green. There should be little fuss and definitely no frills or fancy accessories – everything must be minimal and chic. This can be a very classy look, but make sure you don't overdo it; cool and classy can turn into lifeless and sterile if you're not careful – so try some of the following tips!

Time of year
Any time!

Invitations
Black print on plain white card. Alternatively, get a graphic designer to create your very own computer invitation and e-mail it to everyone!

Gown details
A sassy trouser suit or a contemporary little dress that suits your looks and personality to a T. For a more formal look, go for a gown with a sleek silhouette – the contemporary feel should be encompassed in the quality of the fabric and the cut of the dress.

Flowers
Three arum lilies.

The groom
A smart designer suit from Armani, Paul Smith or Ozwald Boateng. They all use wonderful fabrics and the cut of their suits is perfect for this style of wedding.

Buttonhole
Small calla lily or huge orange gerbera!

Attendants
Give each one a swatch of material in a striking colour (purple, orange, etc.) and tell them they can wear anything they like so long as it is exactly that colour!

Church
A register office in the city – Chelsea would be ideal!

Transport
A TVR, Porsche Boxter or helicopter!

Venue
The trendiest restaurant in town; ask to hire a private room.

Reception drinks
Manhattans or dry martinis garnished with a stuffed olive.

Table decoration
Go for an oriental theme, with simple white flowers, white candles and chopsticks instead of cutlery. Request candlelight or soft ambient lighting.

...D WISH WILL COME TRUE

Chair back

Not necessary – minimalism is the order of the day.

Place settings

Take a selection of smooth stones and ask a calligrapher to write guests' first names on them in permanent ink.

Favours

Fortune cookies in individual boxes.

Food

Oyster shooters accompanied by frozen vodka, followed by wild mushroom tart with asparagus, and passion fruit crème brûlée.

Cake

Tall and plain. The three layers should each be filled with a different liqueur centre, and miniature lilies scattered on each layer.

Entertainment

A funky live band or state-of-the-art disco.

Buffet

Gravadlax on rye bread served with shots of aquavit.

contemporary

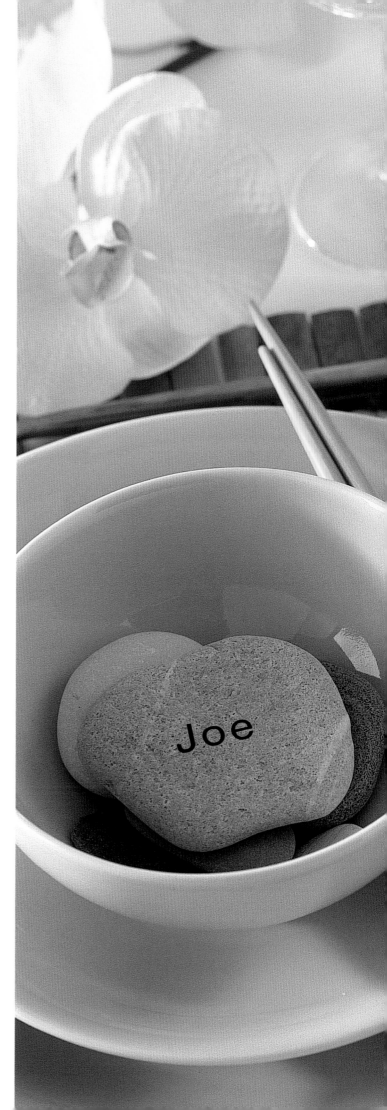

Medieval

Go for a dramatic, full, corseted gown, an old castle setting, invites that resemble old manuscripts – even dress the children up as court jesters! Serve ale and mead in silver tankards, feed your guests on whole suckling pig, and be entertained by wandering musicians. Decorate the reception venue with rich colours and fabrics, and why not host a jousting competition!

Other great themes

Caribbean

Think blue skies and palm trees! Serve Caribbean punch laced with rum, Creole cuisine and gumbo to the sound of a timpani band. Conjure up a carnival atmosphere full of vibrance and fun.

New Year's Eve

If you really want your wedding to go with a 'bang!', you can't choose a better date than New Year's Eve! Think glitz and glamour – use silver as your colour theme, with silver stars, glitter, crystals and disco balls. Count down to midnight and release hundreds of balloons from the ceiling, then see your guests off with bags of cream cheese-filled bagels and a copy of *The Times* dated 1st January.

Hollywood glamour

Think of your favourite film star: Marilyn Monroe, Elvis, Audrey Hepburn, Grace Kelly, James Bond – the list is endless! Think white tuxedos, vodka martinis (shaken not stirred), limousines and huge marquees. Flamboyance and the 'wow!' factor will give a true LA feel. Ask your guests to follow a black and white colour code on the day.

Historical fantasy

Conjure up the era of your choice. Think beautiful Greek goddesses, Grecian urns, bunches of luscious grapes, Roman pillars, cherubs in flight, togas, etc. There is a wealth of inspiration for this theme!

Flower power

Choose your favourite flower – daisies are a popular choice – and link key elements into it: bridesmaids in lemon, a wedding gown with tiny daisy details on the skirt, and so on.

Unique

IT'S THE LITTLE DETAILS THAT
PEOPLE REMEMBER. THE DRESS,
THE CAKE OR THE FLOWERS
MAY ALL BE ORIGINAL,
BUT EVERY WEDDING THAT
YOUR GUESTS GO TO WILL
INCORPORATE THESE
ELEMENTS. SO DO SOMETHING
ORIGINAL, DO SOMETHING
THAT WILL NOT BE SEEN AT ANY
OTHER WEDDING, AND YOUR
DAY WILL BE REMEMBERED BY
ALL WHO WITNESS IT.

Personalising your day

It is always the thoughtful, personal details
that are appreciated and enjoyed the most!
To follow are some ideas that could be
incorporated into your day to make it as unique
as possible.

Send out distinctive invitations. Why not attach them to mini-bottles of champagne or balloons! Dare to be different, and create the sort of excitement that you want your guests to feel on the day.

Instead of having a traditional wedding gift list, put a small note into each invite asking guests to give you: 'Something to read, something to drink, something to eat, something to look at', etc.

Create a welcome basket for each of your guests and have them waiting in their hotel rooms on their arrival. Include a scented candle or bubble bath, fruit and cookies or chocolates, or even a lottery ticket, along with a note thanking them for coming. Alternatively, arrange for the baskets to be put into the hotel rooms while the guests are at the wedding. They will arrive back from the reception to find them.

Present the female guests with small nosegays (two or three flowers) as they enter the church. This is especially effective with sweet-smelling flowers such as sweet peas. At the reception venue someone can either collect them and put them into water, to be claimed at the end of the day, or a large shallow vase can be placed at the entrance (with a notice saying 'Please claim at the end of the day') and the guests can place them there themselves.

Place two special flowers in your bouquet: on your way up the aisle present one to your mother, and on your way back down present one to your new mother-in-law.

If you have a lot of female friends and would like to include them in the wedding but do not wish to choose between them for bridesmaids, then as you reach the top of the aisle at the beginning of the wedding service, each friend could come up to you in turn and present you with a flower (for best

effect use flowers that together make a beautiful posy, such as lilies, gerberas or roses). The last friend, or perhaps your mother, can simply tie them with a ribbon to become your bouquet.

Ask both parents to give you away. You may feel that the ancient tradition of a daughter being a property that the father 'gives' to the groom is somewhat outdated, or you may simply want your mother to play a part.

While the service is taking place, ask the ushers to slip out and decorate the guests' cars with ribbons on the aerials and doors.

Have cones of dried rose petals ready after the ceremony for people to throw. Children could be given bubble blowers so that they can also join in!

Place a polaroid camera and guest book on a table at the reception (somewhere along the receiving line would be ideal). Ask guests to take a picture of themselves, stick it into the book and then write a message to the bride and groom underneath.

Ask the videographer to film each guest giving you a piece of advice for your life together.

Place disposable cameras around the reception venue, with tags saying: 'Snap me, Flash me, Point me, but please, please don't take me'.

Ask your male guests to move around two places between each course.

Instead of tossing your bouquet, ask all the wives of married couples to come onto the dance floor. Ask those who have been married less than five years to leave, then less than eight, twelve, and so on, until you are left with the longest married wife. Present the bouquet to her and ask her to lead everyone in a dance.

Choose an unusual form of wedding transport and orchestrate a dramatic exit as the guests' last memory of you both on your wedding day!

Touches of inspiration for your table

Use silver Christmas baubles (the ones that look like disco balls), add a tag with the guest's name written in silver ink and they provide the perfect sparkling place setting. **Scatter silver sparkle** confetti on the table. There are lots of designs and styles, including hearts, bells, dots, stars, top hats and doves. Mix them up and have fun sparkling, while at the same time giving a soft ambience to the table!

Feathers have become very fashionable and make fabulous additions to table settings, as well as to a bride's outfit. Ask a florist to add a selection of beautiful feathers to your centrepieces. Or why not take a coloured feather, tie a ribbon around the end with a tag attached, and get a calligrapher to write your guests' names on the tags as place settings. The feathers can be in neutral soft whites and ivories for an elegant, soft look, or in bright, vibrant colours for a strongly coloured themed setting.

Bubble blowers in the shape of cakes, doves, champagne bottles, or plain and simple bottles that you can surround in tulle, are great little table decorations.

Place a big bowl of chocolate dragees in the centre of the table. These can come in edible silver, gold or sugar-finished and can be nibbled by guests throughout the function.

Lay a miniature rose on each napkin, tie with ribbon and place it in the centre of the plate. Add an etched piece of paper with a few special words from the bride and groom and add the guest's name. This is an ideal keepsake.

Order some miniature bottles of spirit with your names and wedding date on them. You can add a wired card to the top of each bottle and display guests' names in this way! Make sure the children get the 'virgin' versions!

For a unique centrepiece, spray paint a whole range of stones, both large and small, and place them on a plate. Glue them together in a pyramid and insert some bright flowers such as gerberas or roses, or simply cascade ivy or foliage from the top.

Tie a name tag around the stalk or pin a tag to the top of pieces of fruit, such as pears, oranges or apples, and place on the side plate as a place setting. This looks great as part of a fresh spring or summer theme, where the colours are whites, ivories and greens.

The accompanying centrepiece can be a glorious fruit bowl of wild and exotic fruits that not only look fabulous but smell and taste divine!

If friends or family are good in the garden, a novel idea is to ask them to grow some seasonal flowers that will be perfect for your wedding date. These can be planted into brightly painted pots with ribbon tied around them. For colour and vibrance, choose geraniums or fuchsias; for crisp, clean simplicity go for foliage such as ivy and hebes; for soft ivories and golds why not look at lilies and hollyhocks.

It is really quite cheap to put together fun packs for the children that will be invited to the day. You should provide treats for all your guests, especially children, who can add such fun and excitement to the occasion. To keep this excitement focused it is good to supply alternative distractions, such as bags containing a Kinder Surprise, a puzzle book, washable crayons, balloons, party poppers, streamers, lollipops, and so on. Some caterers will work with crèche facilities which offer face painters and magicians.

Fill miniature terracotta pots or zinc buckets with an assortment of sweets, such as Smarties, Dolly Mixtures and Jelly Beans, and add a name tag – this is a really colourful way to display place settings for your young guests and something they can nibble at or take home with them.

behind
the scenes

The bride

The groom

The guests

Heaven scent

You've been framed

The reception

Last-minute checklist

FOR ANY BRIDE, SELECTING
THEIR DRESS IS PROBABLY THE
MOST EXCITING ASPECT OF
PLANNING THE WEDDING.
WHETHER YOU ARE NERVOUS,
UNSURE, WORRIED ABOUT
YOUR FIGURE OR JUST PLAIN
EXCITED, THIS SHOULD
BE A FUN EXPERIENCE AND
ONE YOU MUST THOROUGHLY
INDULGE IN AND ENJOY.

The bride

Finding the wedding dress is fairly high up on the planning agenda. Once the engagement ring has been selected and you have a basic idea of where you want to marry, the next step for any bride will be 'What shall I wear?'. It's important that before you set out to buy your dress, you prepare yourself for what is in store for you. The purchase of your wedding dress is like no other experience, and there are some good tips to follow to make you feel confident and in control, and to help you to build a picture of what you will be wearing on the day.

Buy a few wedding magazines (if you haven't already done so!) to get a general idea of the styles of gowns and accessories around.

Most major designers and stores advertise towards the front of magazines, however there will be a host of specialist stores and shops that may be closer to your hometown towards the rear.

Cut out anything that catches your eye. It doesn't matter if it's only the look, the colour, the model or the accessories – keep anything that makes you think 'I really like that!'.

Put together a scrapbook of all your cuttings and list under each one what it is you like about the picture. At this early stage you may not have thought about a theme, a colour or a style for your big day, so you can be as creative as you want.

Try and decide on the style of gown you like. The silhouette is important, however you will only know what looks good on your figure when you start trying dresses on.

Call the stores in advance of your day out to see if you need to make an appointment. Most stores like to offer a personal service and have a consultant to take you through the range of dresses on offer. Do not be intimidated if you do need to make an appointment: they are designed to give you guidance on a purchase that is very special.

Wear your best underwear on the day you go to try on dresses. If you wear a bra that fits well and underwear that is of neutral or white colouring you will be happier with the end results.

Only take one or two people with you when you go shopping: your mother, best friend or sister – someone who will give you an honest opinion and has your best interests at heart.

Take your scrapbook of cuttings with you when you go for your appointment. This will help the assistant to direct you to what you have in mind.

Be prepared to try on a number of different styles of dress that you wouldn't normally have chosen. Most gowns do not have hanger appeal and need to be seen on the body to appreciate the full beauty of the cut and styling.

Do not expect to find a dress on the first day. Look at it as a process of elimination. Each time you try something on, look at the dress and decide why you don't like it: is it the neckline, the fullness of skirt, the fabric? This will help you to make your final decision.

Straight or sheath

Bias-cut

Full

Two-piece straight

A-line

Princess

You will come across various dress silhouettes during your search. The following is a guide as to which suit particular body shapes.

Straight or sheath
This suits a range of figure shapes. It accentuates a tall figure by elongating the line of the body, and flatters a fairly straight, rectangular figure with small bust and hips.

Bias-cut
This is great for petite frames and for slim torsos with shapely hips. The fish-tail effect at the bottom sweeps out beautifully into a very graceful train.

A-line
This gown has an empire-style bodice which cuts under the bust. This can be extremely flattering for those brides with small or large busts. Smaller busted women should go for a scoop neckline and a small amount of accenting around the bodice, such as embroidery or beading. Larger busted women should go for a square or cowl neckline which accentuates the curve but hides a little cleavage to create a sensual effect.

Full
This glamorous style is designed for large cathedral-style events, and makes the bride look extra special and elegant. It isn't very often that you can wear such a gown, but with the fabulous corsetry and soft floating skirts it can make any figure look like it has a tiny, nipped in waist.

Two-piece straight
Two-piece dresses are great for figures that are not necessarily in proportion. If you have a size 12 torso and a size 14 hip, but still want to accentuate your great figure, a corseted bodice with separate skirt may be just what you are looking for.

Princess
This gown looks great on all shapes and sizes. It flows from bodice to skirt without defining lines, apart from darts and accents that will bring out the best in your figure and the gown itself.

silhouettes

Sizes

You will find that wedding dress stores have a selection of what are called 'sample gowns'. These are usually in standard sizes – 10, 12 and 14 are the most common – however there are also a number of fabulous designs that now come in standard sizes 16 – 30. When you book your appointment, ask what size their samples go up to. If you have a larger figure, be proud; mention it and make sure that the store can accommodate your needs. It is the shop's problem if they are unable to help, not yours.

Fabrics

The gown that you try on in the store is not necessarily the only version of that style. Ask your consultant to discuss fabrics with you and show you swatches of all possible choices. You may come across one or more of the following fabrics during your search.

Duchess satin

One of the heaviest, most beautiful natural fabrics. Although it has a fabulous rich finish, it may be slightly too heavy for a hot summer day in mid-June or July.

Dupion and Thai silks

This silk has a natural slub in the fabric; this means that you will see a texture to the thread. Dupion has a heavier texture than Thai, but both are beautiful, light fabrics perfect for a summer wedding.

Silk georgette

A light, floaty fabric that is slightly transparent in nature. It is usually added as a top layer, to drape and glide over the body of the gown. It is extremely sensual to the touch and adds a softer line to the silhouette of the gown.

Chiffon

This is a lighter fabric than the georgette. It has a translucent appearance and designers use it to softly craft or accent sleeves or drapes that elegantly cover arms or necklines.

Italian satin

Certain fabrics are termed Italian satin or defined as a mixed silk/satin blend. This is when the fabric is not completely natural and has been developed to give a different texture or quality that natural fabrics are unable to harness. There are some beautiful satins available that are more resilient to creasing and can be more adaptable to certain designs. These can often be a less costly alternative to the more expensive natural silks on the market.

The practicalities

❧ Your wedding dress will be ordered for you from the sample that you try on in the store. Remember that most designers request a 12–14-week lead time on making your wedding gown.

❧ Some wedding dresses can be made faster but there is often a rush charge placed on these as production is altered to accommodate your dress. The lead time is reduced to 6–10 weeks and the added cost is around 10 per cent of the cost of the gown.

❧ Most stores will require a minimum 50 per cent deposit when placing an order.

❧ Unless you are having a designer make the gown as a made-to-measure piece, you will be measured to the nearest size on the designer's size chart. For example, an average size 12, 14, 16, etc.

❧ Ask the consultants at the store if any alterations will be needed once the gown has been delivered. Most stores charge additional alteration fees for minor adjustments.

❧ You will usually be asked to sign a disclaimer form. Read this carefully as it gives all the details that the consultant has recorded. *The information should include:*

the style of the gown chosen

the measurements taken and the nearest size to be ordered with your agreement

any changes that you have requested. For example, extra fabric, different colour fabric from the sample tried, and so on

the total cost of the gown, the deposit paid and the outstanding balance

the date of your wedding and the order duration

All these details should be discussed prior to paying your deposit and you should request a copy of the form for your records.

Choosing a dress
dos . . .

✔ make sure you visit as many stores as you can so that you can make an informed decision

✔ visit stores during the week; it is easier to get an appointment and you will have more time with a consultant than during a busy weekend

✔ call to make appointments to help schedule your day

✔ ask as many questions as you can while you have a consultant with you

✔ make a note of any questions you want answered prior to the meeting; with all the nerves and excitement it is easy to forget key points.

and don'ts

✗ go on any crash diets! If you are planning to lose weight, make sure you inform your consultant. They may decide to measure you closer to the wedding date, otherwise you may have to pay to alter the gown

✗ go to the gym and work out before the wedding. Again, this will alter your body measurements and could cause problems with the fit of your gown

✗ let yourself be bullied into anything you don't want.

Accessorising the bride

Although important, the wedding dress is only one part of the whole ensemble. The wrong shoes or veil can detract from your outfit, so think about how you can maximise the beauty of your gown with complementary accessories. Imagine trying to complete a portrait of yourself from head to toe: think about what to wear in your hair, what to wear at your neck and ears, what to wear under your gown, what to wear on your feet and what to hold in your hands. To start with, you must decide whether you are going for a traditional look or whether you want to add an element of fun or drama to your styling. The gown will be a big factor in this decision, and your consultant can help you to understand what will flatter and look best with your chosen dress.

TRADITIONALLY, THE BRIDE WORE A VEIL AS A FORM OF MODESTY. IT COVERED HER FACE AS SHE WALKED DOWN THE AISLE AND KEPT HER HIDDEN FROM THE GROOM UNTIL THE LAST MOMENT. THE IDEA WAS TO PULL BACK THE VEIL AT THE BEGINNING OF THE WEDDING CEREMONY SO THAT THE GROOM COULD SEE HIS FUTURE WIFE'S FACE, SOMETIMES FOR THE FIRST TIME: AN UNVEILING OF HIS PRIZE.

The veil

Today there are some great looks that are both contemporary and chic, depending on your preference and surroundings. Most brides still choose to wear a veil, but it is used in a more creative way, to flatter and accent some of the details of the gown as opposed to being worn to cover up. The veil helps to frame the face, soften the complexion, and draw your eye towards the gown in a flattering, flowing line. Some brides like to have a veil with more than one tier so that they have the choice of pulling a tier forward over their face as they walk down the aisle, but in the main the different tiers and lengths discussed on page 97 are aimed at maximising the full effect of the gown and figure of the bride.

54-inch veil

This veil reaches to the shoulders and gives a fresh, punchy effect that is superb for a contemporary style. It can come in a number of tiers, from one to four, that are usually around the same length. Obviously, the more tulle or silk tiers you have the more volume and drama you create.

This is a great length for brides with a long sheath silhouette gown, or for brides with short hair who want to create some height and impact. This is also the veil to choose if you want to give an element of tradition to a less formal outfit.

72-inch veil

This is a popular length as it ends at the waist. Again, it can come in one to four tiers, and these cascade down the back to fingertip length giving volume and movement to the style. Whether you go for a simple ribbon-edged veil or a scatter pearl and crystal veil, you can accentuate your look with this very elegant accessory.

This length of veil looks great with princess-line or empire gowns. It also flatters full gowns and creates a very pretty softening effect which helps to highlight the beauty of the dress.

108-inch veil

This veil reaches to the floor and creates a little puddle train effect. It is a beautiful length and has a more traditional feel as it highlights the soft lines of most gowns. Most preferred styles at this length have three tiers, which cascade to just below the shoulder, to the waist, and the last cascade being to the floor.

This is the perfect design for straight gowns as it gives a little volume towards the hemline that is sometimes appropriate for the formality of the event. It is also fabulous with full gowns in a church or chapel setting as it adds softness to the lines of the skirt.

126- and 144-inch veils

These are known as cathedral-length veils and look spectacular at church and cathedral weddings as the tulle or silk flows out behind the bride giving the gown a glamorous and highly romantic finish. This style traditionally accompanies full and princess-line dresses, however they also suit a minimal, straight dress and look exquisite flowing behind a bias-cut gown with a godet train.

Have fun and experiment to see what suits you and your dress!

Headdresses

There are some really exciting accessories that you can add to your hair to complete your perfect look. Go for flowers, tiaras or individual diamanté clips – the choice is yours! Make sure you try on several different styles of accessory. Try using the same process that helped you to decide on your gown.

Consider the following questions:

What features of your gown do you love the most? Are there any special details such as embroidery, crystal or pearls that will help direct the choice of accessory?

Do you have long or short hair? If you have long hair, will you be wearing it up or down?

Will you be wearing a veil?

Tiara

This is the most popular hair accessory and there are hundreds of fabulous styles to choose from. Tiaras come in soft hues of colour and in various shades of gold or silver. These can often complement the theme of your wedding or capture the warmth of your gown. For example, silver goes well with white or antique white gowns and maximises the sparkle of crystals as the silver reflects the light. Champagne gold tiaras give warmth and vibrance to pearls and crystals and provide a stunning complement to champagne and ivory gowns. Tiara designs can be contemporary, such as daisies on prongs, stars on malleable stays, or clean lines and abstract clusters of pearls and crystals. They can also be more traditional, with peaks of pearls and stones that sit high in the centre of the design at the front of the head. Classic shapes and contours can be used to make a tiara elegant and timeless.

A tiara is ideal if:

❧ you are planning to wear a veil. A tiara can sit beautifully in front of the comb to disguise where the veil is attached

❧ you would like to add height to your look and elongate your frame

❧ you are after a special touch of sparkle!

Lingerie

The lingerie you wear is critical to the overall fit of the gown and is also a very personal statement by the bride. It is possible that the lingerie you would most like to wear is not suitable to be worn beneath your wedding dress – but who's to say that you can't change into something more comfortable later!

Garter

The garter was originally used to hold up hosiery. The modern-day tradition of wearing a garter on the wedding day is so that the groom can remove it at the end of the day and fling it out into the crowd of male guests – whoever catches it will be the next to marry. Keep the tradition going and see who the lucky chap will be!

Shoes

The priority is comfort! Remember that you will be on your feet all day, so don't go for anything too high or too pointed. There is a huge array of styles available – try them all, perhaps picking out a small detail to complement your dress.

TIPS

❧ If you have a gown with a corseted bodice you will not need lingerie with additional boning. In fact, boned bodices are so well constructed these days that no bra is necessary. However, most brides want to wear something – especially if they have a larger bust. So the best thing is to go for something that will fit well, give comfortable support and is not too lacy.

❧ Some straight gowns in crêpe or slipper satin can hug the figure, so lingerie sometimes shows through. Do not go for white or ivory lingerie; go for a bra and thong in a nude colour, with no visible seams. This will keep the lines of the gown smooth.

❧ Strapless dresses or dresses with shoe strap bodices need to be worn with a supportive strapless bra or basque. Basques are good as they give added support and stay up a little better. However, there are some extremely good products on the market that can lift and support even without straps.

❧ If you need to fill out your bust line slightly, a good tip is to try what are known as 'chicken fillets'. These are synthetic gels that can be placed inside dresses or lingerie to give added fullness to a bust line or to even a bust line out. Many models use them to give shape to their bodies and they are extremely good.

❧ The best tip is to choose lingerie that is as comfortable as possible. Ask your consultant for advice when trying on your dress so that when you go for your first fitting you are prepared and have the right lingerie to hand.

Essential hair and beauty tips

There are many women's magazines on the market that offer a wide range of advice on hair, skin and make-up and advertise a diverse range of products that you may have seen and want to try. However, on the lead-up to your wedding day there are some additional points to bear in mind to ensure that you look your best on the day itself!

Start thinking about your hair and make-up as soon as possible. Preparation is a must and if you have a few months lead time to your wedding day you can use it effectively, not only to take care of the quality and texture of your hair and the clarity of your complexion, but also to pamper and revitalise yourself after all your planning.

Hair flair!

Many brides have an idea of what they want to look like on their big day long before they receive a proposal of marriage! This image will obviously change slightly during the process of buying your gown and accessories, but it rarely alters dramatically.

You know what makes you look good and feel beautiful and comfortable, so don't deviate from this too much – remember, your fiancé is marrying you for the way you look now, not for some imaginary person you create for one day!

You and your hairdresser

Make sure you have a good hairdresser who knows and understands you well. You want to feel confident that he/she can create a look that you will be thrilled with and that will accentuate your features and complement your gown and accessories perfectly.

If you don't have a regular hairdresser that you feel confident with, try to find someone as far in advance of your wedding as possible. Ask friends and family for recommendations or go to a reputable company that may have a hairdresser dedicated to styling for special occasions.

Once you have found a hairdresser/stylist, go to this person as soon as you can to establish a rapport and a feeling of confidence about their ability. If you are not happy, don't be afraid to say so; you can always go elsewhere.

If you have short hair and want to wear it in a longer style for the wedding, discuss with your hairdresser the reality of growing it. Sometimes it is not always a good idea to change your hair dramatically, unless you have a long time to plan ahead. You may want to think about creating volume and length by using hairpieces, styling lotions or extensions instead of worrying about whether your hair will grow in time. Hairpieces and extensions are extremely well made these days and can look very realistic if used properly. Don't be afraid to experiment!

When you have chosen your gown, take a photograph of it to your hairdresser and discuss with him/her the best look and hair accessories for you. It may be that you have a full gown and need a more dramatic headpiece to create volume on the crown of your head; or you may have gone for a slender gown that can be complemented by a sassy hairstyle with minimal accessories.

Make regular visits to your hairdresser before your wedding to keep your hair in tip-top condition.

Make sure you have a practice run to create your chosen hairstyle at least two weeks before the wedding day. This will give you an idea of how long your hair will take to style on the morning of the wedding and will give you a chance to see how comfortable it is and to make any small changes necessary to get your look just right.

Think!
healthy eating

- Your hair will shine if you are eating a healthy diet. Do not go on crash diets before your wedding and starve yourself as this can affect both your complexion and your hair.
- Eat plenty of fruit and vegetables and a good source of protein such as red meat and fish; you could even start taking vitamin supplements to promote healthy growth. All this will ensure you have glossy hair that is full of body and easy to style.
- If you have six months before your wedding, this is the perfect time to start a healthy eating regime – not only will you look great but it will give you energy that you never knew you had!

Skin care

❧ To apply make-up successfully you need a healthy, glowing complexion as a canvas. If you don't have a daily skin routine, now is the time to start! The experts all state that if you cleanse, tone and moisturise on a daily basis, your skin will be at its best and all the dirt and grime that life in general tends to throw at it will be removed.

❧ Choose products that you feel comfortable using. If you have sensitive skin, look for products with hypoallergenic ingredients, as you don't want to start a new beauty routine by breaking out in a rash!

❧ Don't forget that healthy eating and exercise help to make you look and feel great.

❧ Cleanse your system by drinking lots of water. This will help to flush away toxins and make your eyes and skin sparkle.

❧ Treat yourself to a few early nights and dedicated relaxation sessions which take you away from the stresses of planning the wedding. This will help reduce any dark circles that may be lurking around the eyes.

❧ Why not treat yourself to a facial sauna or deep cleansing treatment with a trained beautician and acquire some more good tips on how to maintain a glowing complexion.

❧ Don't forget your eyebrows! Plucking and shaping can have an amazing effect, especially if you go to an expert to have it done. Make sure you do this a few days before the wedding – you don't want any redness around the eyes on your special day!

Make-up

❧ The essential thing to remember when trying out different styles of make-up is that you want to look as natural as possible on the day. Most women are not used to wearing ivory or white and so tend to use far deeper colours than are necessary.

❧ Your make-up needs to last all day and it also needs to photograph well. Treat yourself to a make-up session with a trained beautician; they will give you tips on how to recreate the look for the big day!

❧ Make sure you buy a good base foundation that gives your skin a matt finish and complements your skin tone. This might be the most expensive product you buy, but when you see the photographs you will definitely consider it money well spent. Choose shades of eyeshadow that you are used to wearing, and practise different styles of application to ensure you can get the results you want.

❧ Waterproof mascara is a good idea – you never know when you may be overcome by emotion on the day! Finally, choose a shade of lipstick that is flattering to your skin tone. For longer lasting lipstick, apply a lip liner followed by a layer of pressed powder to set it. Apply your first layer of lipstick, then blot your lips on tissue paper before applying another layer of pressed powder which helps to seal the colour before applying your second coat. A coat of gloss on the bottom lip can add a sensual, luscious finish to your lips that will make them look fabulous and very kissable!

❧ For a completely stress-free time, why not hire a make-up artist who will come to your house on the morning of your wedding and do your make-up for you.

The following tips on applying your make-up and remedying potential disasters have been supplied courtesy of Molton Brown:

■ If eyebrows are sparse in spots, fill in using eyeshadow with a brow brush and brush with eye groomer in an upward motion.

■ If eyelashes are sparse, dot darker, smoky kohl liner lightly along the lash line.

■ If foundation looks too pale when applied, a yellow shade of powder will correct imbalance.

■ If foundation looks too artificial or uneven, apply a little moisturiser onto the palms of your hands and press them gently onto the face. This will dilute the foundation. As a last resort, smooth the face with a sponge or brush.

■ If concealer looks cakey, smooth it over with damp fingers.

■ If eyeshadow or blusher looks too intense, dilute by applying some face powder onto a brush and then over the face.

■ To soften harsh eyebrow colour, dilute by applying some face powder onto a brush and onto the brow area to tone it down.

■ If blusher looks too bright, layer a neutral colour on top.

■ If lip colour is too thick or heavy looking, lighten by blotting with a tissue.

■ If lip colour is too matt, apply lip balm and/or lip gloss to create a shinier look.

■ If lip colour is too dark, bring it down in intensity by applying a beige or pale pink on top.

■ To reduce shine on the face, use a matt moisturiser before foundation is applied.

■ To tone down redness in the face, use a yellow tinted powder.

Molton Brown

The bride's attendants

Most brides have at least one attendant on their wedding day, whose responsibility it is to make the bride feel special and take care of her on the day itself. It is rare for a bride to choose just little ones as attendants without an adult accompanying them, however there are no rules and you can have as many attendants as you feel will suit your day.

Choosing your attendants

❧ Make sure you choose friends or family that you know you will always be in touch with and get on well with. In years to come you don't want to look back at your photographs and struggle to remember the names of your attendants!

❧ If you are going to have children as attendants, it's wise to talk through with the mothers exactly what you are hoping to achieve and allow them to keep the children informed. Children will react and cope better with all the excitement and build-up to the wedding if they know what is going on.

❧ If you are planning to have more than one attendant it is a good idea to get them all together prior to the big day, if they don't already know each other. It is also a good idea to tell them what you are looking for in terms of outfits and accessories, and what their responsibilities will be on the day so that there are no misunderstandings.

❧ Try not to be coerced into having an attendant simply because they have never been one before or because it is important to your mother or mother-in-law! You may start to begrudge them being involved if they do not show the interest and excitement that you would like, and this will only upset you as the wedding gets closer.

THE PRESENCE OF ATTENDANTS ORIGINATES FROM THE ROMAN LAW THAT DEMANDED TEN WITNESSES BE PRESENT AT A WEDDING IN ORDER TO DUPE EVIL SPIRITS WHO WERE BELIEVED TO ATTEND MARRIAGES. THE ATTENDANTS ALL DRESSED IN IDENTICAL CLOTHING TO THE BRIDE AND GROOM SO THAT THE EVIL SPIRITS WOULDN'T KNOW WHO WAS GETTING MARRIED.

Selecting the attendants' outfits

This can be a daunting task as you may have a range of ages, sizes and personalities to accommodate. You should by now have chosen your own outfit or have a good idea of what style you are going for. This will help to focus your ideas as to what you want the bridesmaids to wear. It will also help if you have decided on a colour or theme for the day as this will make it easier to choose appropriate colours and styles. Remember, your attendants are there to complement you.

Look at bridesmaid and pageboy outfits on your own or with your mother or partner before you take any of the attendants on a shopping trip. This will give you an idea of what you want and you will not be sidetracked by the personal preferences of each attendant.

If you like a certain fabric, colour or style, ask the store if they have a picture or a swatch of fabric that you can take away to show your attendants and compare to your other colour schemes. Don't look to match your colours identically with your chosen theme. Different fabrics absorb colours in different ways. As long as colours complement and don't clash you will have a lovely end result.

There is no rule that says each bridesmaid must wear the same outfit, but it helps if the dresses complement each other in colour and style.

Be open minded when shopping around; what you originally like may not look great on the chosen attendants. Don't become disheartened if you don't find what you are looking for instantly.

Order all your attendants' dresses at the same time. The dresses will be produced from the same roll of fabric, however if one is ordered later it may be cut from a different bolt of fabric and there may be a slight variation in colour.

If you are planning to make the dresses yourself, have a look in bridal magazines and choose designs that you like. You can then go to a dressmaker or store and ask for a similar pattern.

The choice of dresses and outfits available for bridesmaids is extremely large. The traditional frilly, full, three-quarter-length dress is now a thing of the past. Modern dresses are designed along the lines of eveningwear and can often be worn for other functions.

Don't forget about the accessories. These should also complement your outfit and most bridal stores now offer to dye shoes to match gowns – make sure you have a piece of fabric available as a guide for the dyeing process.

The hen party!

It's your last night of freedom – so be original and enjoy it!

Whether you call it a hen party or a bridal shower, the concept is the same: to gather a group of close friends and family of the future bride together and take her out for a great time on one of her last nights as a single woman. The celebration is usually organised by the chief bridesmaid or matron of honour, often the bride's closest friend or a family member. They are responsible for arranging an event that will suit the bride down to the ground and allow her to indulge in a night or weekend of fun – which she will deserve after all the preparations for her special day!

Take your pick from the following suggestions of how to celebrate…

Weekend adventures

Most hen parties are planned over a long weekend, so there is the chance to enjoy partying mayhem, long leisurely chats and late morning awakenings.

UK

Why not try out some classic English fun! A fabulous company that offers a huge repertoire of activities to suit a range of tastes and pockets is Red Letter Days:

 Have 'A Day at the Races'. There are many race courses to choose from and the day can include enclosure tickets, racecard, a glass of champagne on arrival, a three-course meal and the opportunity to back a winner!

 Or you might prefer 'In the Circus'. If you've ever dreamed about running away with the circus, now is the time to learn some tricks and have a go at acrobatics, juggling and the flying trapeze. If all this seems a little too tame, why not try the alternatives – knife throwing, whip cracking and lassoing!

 A group 'Make Over' may be just what the doctor ordered! Why not experience a full makeover session, where your hair, make-up and clothes are selected for you and you have a fabulous picture taken as a keepsake of your fun day.

For a laid back, fun weekend trip why not try one of the popular English resorts, such as Butlins or Pontins. There are a host of them dotted around the seaside resorts of the UK. They have some excellent facilities on site and can offer a wide choice of organised entertainment within a stone's throw of where you are staying. Get your chief bridesmaid to do some research and see how these resorts have been updated to meet 21st-century living!

Camping weekends can also be great fun as they are relaxed and bring back memories of childhood holidays. They can offer anything from bingo, amusement arcades, fun fairs and cabaret evenings, to nightclubs and organised entertainers. Every day you can be adventurous and do something completely different without having to travel any great distance.

Sophisticated alternative

If all that partying is a little too hectic for you and you want a calmer, more relaxing weekend break, why not really pamper yourselves and visit a health farm or beauty parlour. This is a very popular alternative to the clubbing/partying scene and can be a wonderful way to seal close friendships and take time out to indulge in a range of treatments that will relax, pamper and beautify everyone involved.

There are a huge variety of health spas to choose from. Why not try one of the following:

The Sanctuary Spa, Covent Garden, London
Champneys, Tring and Piccadilly, London
Hoar Cross Hall, Yoxall, Staffordshire
Nirvana Spa, Wokingham, Berkshire

Europe

For the travel minded, why not look to Amsterdam or Paris for a weekend of fun and adventure. There are many cheap and cheerful weekend break options available – try lastminute.com for some late special offers on excursions and flights. Or for more personal assistance, Thomas Cook at Virgin Bride specialise in wedding-related travels, be it for the bride and groom or for the stags and hens – they can get you to wherever you want to go, so make a list of preferred activities and places of interest and let the experts take the strain.

Jet set

If you fancy going further afield, why not jet off to New York for a great getaway trip of sightseeing, shopping, eating and partying. The Big Apple has so much to offer and you'll need at least three days to capture the buzz! Virgin offers some great deals on flights, or why not use a company like Funway Holidays to organise a flight and hotel package.

A classy night out

Celebrate with your closest friends and family in a restaurant or special venue that either holds memories of brilliant past gatherings, or is somewhere you have all wanted to go but have never had the opportunity! Pre-book the food and drink to make the evening easy, and add some special surprises to the event...

A fun accessory!

A great idea for spicing up a hen night is a 'Marriage Survival Kit' – a bag full of goodies for the bride to open before the festivities begin! A Marriage Survival Kit is essential for all brides, and the chief bridesmaid or best friend should take responsibility for putting it together. It can contain wild and wonderful toys, photos, games or clothing to tease and have fun with!

If this seems a little daunting, a company called Party Gifts Limited offers an array of gift packs dedicated to this theme. Leave it to them to find some unique and fun presents whilst you take on the responsibility of finishing off the gifts with a few personal touches!

Here are some suggestions to start you on your merry way . . .

Chocolate willy or other obscene confectionery!

Lingerie that the bride must wear over her clothes throughout the evening.

Play dice that dictate what you must do during the evening.

Miniature bottles of bubbly or the bride's favourite alcohol.

Veil with L plate.

T-shirt emblazoned with a statement such as 'I'm single tonight – come and kiss me!' or a picture of the bride during her adolescence.

Garter.

Feather boa – preferably bright pink or crazy coloured.

Bubbles to blow.

A rattle/shaker/anything noisy to draw attention to the bride.

Some nice bits and pieces for pampering at a later date: bubble bath, body lotion, bottle of bubbly, beauty treatment voucher.

Wrap each of the pressies in bright wrapping paper and place them into a large box or gift bag. Why not add confetti or rice to the packages and tell the bride to shake out each present so that she is covered in confetti by the end.

Kiss me!

es to blow!

The choice of what to do for a hen party must reflect the bride's personality. Make sure whoever is organising the event keeps the bride in mind and plans the night or weekend in the knowledge that it will be something that she will really love.

survival kit

THE GROOM IS THE MOST
IMPORTANT MAN AT THE
WEDDING, BUT IS OFTEN THE
LAST TO BE CONSIDERED
WHEN IT COMES TO
CHOOSING WHAT TO WEAR.
IT IS THE GROOM'S ROLE TO
COMPLEMENT THE STYLE OF THE
BRIDE AND HER ATTENDANTS,
SO THERE IS A CONTINUITY
TO THE COLOUR SCHEME AND
THEME OF THE WEDDING.

The groom

This doesn't mean that he has to blend into the background – far from it! Nowadays, the groom, the best man and the ushers can also be vibrant and spectacular! The 21st-century groom is blessed with a selection of retailers to focus on his every need, as there is now a broad range of suits and accessories available that can be either hired or purchased. The groom can therefore choose something fashionable to suit his personality and the needs and character of the wedding. He should not only feel comfortable, but look stylish, handsome and ooze confidence on his special day.

There are few occasions on which men can dress up to the nines, and it can be a daunting task for them to be suddenly faced with choosing a formal dress suit. Luckily, there are some gorgeous suits available and some great new looks that are totally up-to-date.

For hire...

The most common route for the groom and his ushers to take is to go to a local men's hire shop. There are a number of good retailers that offer a broad range of styles, but the traditional frock coat and morning suit are still the most popular for the groom's party. The assistants will be able to style your man from top to toe.

It's the finishing touches that count, and the diverse range of accessories that are on offer, from waistcoats, cravats, shirts in a range of colours and collar styles, to cufflinks, handkerchiefs and buttonholes will help create the image you desire.

The high street

High street stores offer a broad range of suiting for those strong-minded, fashion-conscious men who would like to stamp their own style on their wedding day and buy an outfit that they can keep forever! They also offer a great selection of garments for those wanting to marry in sunnier climes or in a less formal style. Soft hues of colour, such as a dove grey wool suit, or a navy suit with a stylish pinstripe, or even a muted camel shade, would be perfect for a modern summer wedding which has a less formal theme. The cut of the suit is important, and to keep a modern edge to the look he should go for a single-breasted style. Make sure he tries on several makes as they each place a different emphasis on the length of the suit jacket and on different details inlaid onto breast panels and trousers.

TIPS

❧ Be gentle with your partner as he may feel very self-conscious on his first outing to try on suits. Remember how nervous and excited you felt when trying on wedding dresses for the first time, and empathise with him.

❧ Unless you are extremely lucky, most men dislike being dragged from one shop to another! So to make your life a lot simpler, do some investigation into what you would like him to wear and then you can direct him to fewer places to try on outfits. He'll be thrilled!

❧ What size suit does your partner wear? If you don't know, the first thing you should do is ask an assistant to take his measurements.

❧ Make sure your fiancé tries on at least three different styles of formal suit to ensure you find a look that he feels comfortable in. A good tip is to watch how he stands in the suit. If he stands tall and proud without his hands fiddling with his cuffs or his suit jacket, and he has a beaming smile on his face, you have found a winner!

❧ The groom must stand out on the big day, so his accessories are particularly important. He should choose a distinctive cravat, waistcoat or buttonhole that will define his position to the rest of the guests. Why not find a special item that you like and give it to him as a wedding gift for him to treasure!

The designer option

If there was ever a time to splash out on a designer outfit, this is the moment!
When you enter a designer store the service you receive should reflect the money
that you will be spending. A consultant should meet you and go through exactly
what you are trying to achieve for your special day and lead you to the best
starting point to get there. Ask lots of questions and give as much information to
the assistant as possible. This will not only help to find the right suit but will also
reduce the number of suits that will need to be tried on and the length of time
spent shopping.

Remind your man that this whole shopping experience is meant to be fun and
will produce an outfit that will make him look and feel fantastic. Try and enjoy the
time spent pulling together outfits; your time is precious and you don't want to
spend it feeling stressed and unhappy.

The stag night!

Stag nights or bachelor parties are always the biggest dread for any bride. Horror stories about raunchy nights out or being stripped and left to get home alone spring to mind when the words are even mentioned! The best thing for the bride is to know that the best man is responsible and will take care of her fiancé; although a fun-filled night will be planned for the groom, you can be reassured that you'll be able to recognise him on his return.

Be adventurous!

As with hen parties, the desire to party over a weekend is very popular. Again, Red Letter Days offers a wide variety of great activities that will suit the groom and his mates down to the ground. Why not try one of the following:

'The Ferrari Experience' – choose from an array of sports cars such as Lotus, Porsche or an E-type! Book the groom in for a test drive and experience the buzz of Silverstone.

Or why not try 'Hot Air Ballooning' – 15-man baskets are available so book far enough in advance and the sky's the limit!

'White Water Rafting' is a huge adrenaline buzz and can keep the chaps in shape and out of harm's way!

If your man believes he's James Bond then why not entice the stag party to try out the 'James Bond Experience' – learn how to abseil, or try unarmed combat, hostage rescue and expert gun play! They promise to leave the guys shaken but not stirred!

Adventure weekends can also be arranged, and can include go-karting, motor racing, paint balling, quad biking and other outward bound activities. Any of these activities would suit a competitive group of guys wanting to prove themselves!

City nights

Why not try a professionally organised club or bar crawl – all you have to do is jump on and off a bus! This is a safer option than leaving things to chance and will ensure the groom has a great evening.

Many major stag night organisers can design an evening out in the city of your choice – London, Manchester, Birmingham, Leeds, Glasgow, and so on – including accommodation for the evening; this might prove a nice, stress-free option for the best man to follow!

Overseas!

Amsterdam is a popular destination for obvious reasons. lastminute.com can organise a special group trip for you, designed around specific requirements. So make a list and get cracking!

Bands of gold

It is the groom's job to take care of the wedding rings. The wedding band is a true sign of the love and commitment that a couple feel for each other, and the gesture of exchanging rings during the wedding ceremony cements the relationship in a very visible way. Whilst most women like to wear their wedding and engagement rings all the time, it is good to see that over 70 per cent of men now wear wedding rings, compared to very few in the past.

21st-century styles

Traditionally, wedding jewellery is mainly gold, with several colours and carats available – yellow gold, rose gold and white gold being the most prominent. 18-carat gold is a harder wearing gold than the 9-carat or 24-carat gold on the market and complements most engagement rings, which are usually set on an 18-carat band.

❧ There are so many designs of wedding band to choose from that it is well worth hunting around to find what you like and to see how the various styles match up with your engagement ring.

❧ Unusual bands include the Russian wedding ring, which combines a mixture of two or three of the coloured golds to give a beautiful effect and can sit well with an engagement ring or on its own.

❧ Platinum is the most expensive band as it is a rare metal and is very hard wearing. It is also very fashionable and is the ideal base metal against which to set diamonds.

❧ Whatever your preference, your wedding rings will form a lasting symbol of love and can even be engraved on the inside with initials or words of your choice for a unique and personal touch that will make them even more special.

Maintenance

It's good to be aware of how best to care for your rings, for safety reasons as well as to keep them in tip top sparkling condition!

When you take your rings off, place them into their original jewellery box for safe keeping.

Clean your rings regularly with a jewellery cleaner; use a toothbrush on any hard-to-remove dirt.

If you wear your rings constantly, try to remove them when working with strong cleaning fluids or when you are doing rough, heavy work with your hands. This will prevent any injury to your fingers, and save the rings from getting bashed around too much.

Take photographs of your rings and store them in a safe place for insurance purposes. Make sure you take out insurance on them as sometimes household policies do not cover individual high value items.

ANNOUNCING YOUR

FORTHCOMING WEDDING TO

YOUR FRIENDS AND FAMILY

IS EXTREMELY EXCITING.

THE FIRST TIME MOST GUESTS

WILL HEAR OF THE EVENT

IS VIA YOUR WRITTEN WORD –

THE WEDDING INVITATION!

SO USE THIS OPPORTUNITY

TO SET THE THEME AND

TONE OF THE WEDDING.

The guests

Most people think wedding stationery is one of the last things they need to take care of. You should, however, order your wedding stationery at least three to four months prior to your wedding date as it can take up to four weeks to get it just right, and the invitations should be sent out at least six weeks before the wedding date.

Wedding stationery can include the following:

◆ wedding invitations

◆ evening invitations

◆ order of service sheets

◆ menus

◆ thank you cards

◆ place cards

◆ reception albums

◆ napkin rings

◆ cake boxes

Stylish announcements!

There are many sources of interesting and unique styles of wedding stationery. Marks and Spencer have an array of modern and classic designs so why not start here – or you may know a printer who can do exactly what you are looking for.

The wedding stationery should complement the style you have chosen for your wedding. If there is a silver theme, include an element of silver in the invitation; this could be just the type rather than a particular design. The invitations can be jazzy and upbeat or traditional and classic. Whatever style you choose will symbolise the start of a wonderful union and will be appreciated by all who are invited to join in the celebrations.

The wording

These days there are so many different options for the wording of the invitations that it can be quite a worry to make sure you follow the right style. Here are a few examples that should cover most situations…

Mr and Mrs John Hardy
Request the pleasure of
....

at the marriage of their daughter
Samantha Jane *to* Mr James Harris
At Westminster Register Office
On Saturday 6 June 2000 At 1.00pm
AND AFTERWARDS AT
The Savoy Hotel, London WC2N
RSVP

Civil wedding with the bride's parents as hosts

Mr and Mrs John Hardy
Request the pleasure of
....

at the marriage of their daughter
Samantha Jane *to* Mr James Harris
At St Mary's Church, Kensington, London
On Saturday 6 June 2000 At 2.00pm
AND AFTERWARDS AT
The Roof Gardens, Kensington, W1
RSVP

Traditional wedding with the bride's parents as hosts

Miss Samantha Hardy and Mr James Harris
Request the pleasure of
....

at their marriage
AT WESTMINSTER REGISTER OFFICE
ON SATURDAY 6 JUNE 2000 AT 1.00PM
AND AFTERWARDS AT
The Savoy Hotel, London WC2N
RSVP

The couple as hosts

Mrs John Hardy
Requests the pleasure of

. . . .
at the marriage of her daughter
Samantha Jane *to* Mr James Harris
At St Mary's Church, Kensington, London
On Saturday 6 June 2000 At 2.00pm
AND AFTERWARDS AT
The Roof Gardens, Kensington, W1
RSVP

The pleasure of

. . . .
is requested at the marriage of
Miss Samantha Jane *to* Mr James Harris
At St Mary's Church, Kensington, London
On Saturday 6 June 2000 At 2.00pm

AND AFTERWARDS AT
The Roof Gardens, Kensington, W1
RSVP

Mr and Mrs John Hardy
Request the pleasure of

. . . .

At a reception at
The Roof Gardens, Kensington, London W1
On Saturday 6 June 2000 At 8.00pm
following the marriage of their daughter
Samantha Jane *to* Mr James Harris
RSVP

Mr and Mrs Michael Day
Request the pleasure of

. . . .

at the marriage of her daughter
Samantha Jane Hardy *to* Mr James Harris
AT ST MARY'S CHURCH, KENSINGTON, LONDON
ON SATURDAY 6 JUNE 2000 AT 2.00PM
and afterwards at
The Roof Gardens, Kensington, W.
RSVP

Mr John Hardy & Mrs Jemima Hardy
Request the pleasure of

. . . .

at the marriage of their daughter
Samantha Jane *to* Mr James Harris
At St Mary's Church, Kensington, London
On Saturday 6 June 2000 At 2.00pm
AND AFTERWARDS AT
The Roof Gardens, Kensington, W1
RSVP

Gift list heaven!

Traditionally, guests brought a present for the bride and groom to thank them for the opportunity to join in the celebrations of their wedding day. Usually the gift was chosen to contribute towards establishing a new home and life together. However, as most couples now live together prior to tying the knot, the element of starting a fresh life in a new home is not quite so applicable! And the emphasis on what gifts to give has changed accordingly.

As you will know if you have ever been to a wedding, it can be difficult to know what to buy, or whether you are duplicating other people's presents. It is also almost impossible to tell guests not to buy you anything! So to ensure you receive something that you can cherish and love and that will add to your established home, a gift registry is a perfect solution. If this seems a little calculated, just remember that your guests would much prefer to give you something that you will truly treasure as opposed to something that you only take out on their occasional visit!

Once you have decided on a gift registry company you will need to break it to your fiancé that you will both have to spend time going through a store, a catalogue or a website, taking down product details and codes to make your selection official. Most companies try to make this as stress-free and speedy as they can – however, understand that you will be dedicating at least a day to choosing a range of gifts in different price points and categories to suit a range of pockets.

There is no restriction on where you purchase from, so why not consider going to two stores to ensure you have a broad range of items for guests to choose from.

TIPS FOR LOOKING AFTER YOUR GUESTS

❧ Do send a map with the invitation. This may seem very obvious but it is important that people know where they are going! You can either send a photocopy of a road map with the appropriate places highlighted, or send a hand-drawn one. A professional artist can provide an amusing variation with cartoon characters of the bride and groom and caricatures of all that your area is famous for, coupled with an accurate map for your guest to use.

❧ When you are setting a time for your service do try to consider your guests' stomachs. Empty ones are not conducive to a party atmosphere! A one o'clock service may suit you perfectly, but consider people driving any distance to get to you. Even those who live near to the church will have to get ready at least an hour beforehand and will have no opportunity to eat lunch. Consider encouraging people to gather at a local pub for lunch an hour before the service. Put a note in with the main invitation and clearly mark the pub on the map. Perhaps get the groom and the ushers to go along as well. Guests will start the day relaxed and looking forward to the celebrations ahead.

❧ Consider setting up a booking service for the guests. This is an ideal job to give to a relative desperate to help! Put a small card in with the main invitation saying, '*Please call Joan Walters for hotel accommodation on . . .* ' Include a list of accommodation with price ranges to suit all budgets.

❧ If you do know where people are staying it is a really nice idea to put a small gift and card in their room ready for their arrival. This is a thoughtful gesture that shows how much you appreciate them having travelled to share in your celebration. Scented candles, fine chocolates, bath salts or other products, wine, flowers, fruit or cookies, all make ideal gifts and could be presented to tie in with your wedding theme.

❧ Do any of your guests have special needs? If anyone is disabled check the access to the church and the reception venue. Give the names of any elderly people to one of the ushers (preferably one that will know them by sight) to ensure that they are looked after.

❧ Don't wait to be told whether people are vegetarian or have any allergies, most of the time they forget to tell you when replying to your invitation! You will already know these things about most of your guests. Make arrangements with your caterers to have a couple of extra vegetarian meals standing by in case someone dislikes the main course you have chosen.

Heaven scent

Flowers can stimulate all the senses. They can inspire emotions of passion, love, flamboyance, style and drama. So remember, your flowers do a lot more than simply become your bouquet, they represent your individuality and style, and speak volumes about your personality.

Selecting the right florist

If you are marrying locally you may already know of a great florist. If not, a personal recommendation from friends or family is ideal as you know that they have been tried and tested. If you are marrying at a venue or in a place that you do not know well, try the following means of sourcing great florists.

❯ You can speak to your venue and see if they have a preferred florist.

❯ You can look in bridal magazines in their 'Where To Shop' section. This section advertises local stores and companies who can assist in the important finishing touches to your wedding.

❯ You can consult the telephone directory and choose a selection of florists and get some information sent to you to help simplify who will be best for you.

❯ You can try surfing the internet – there are many companies going on-line that are able to show their style of design without having to request too much information in advance.

❯ There is also a list of excellent florists and their contact details located at the rear of this book to get you started!

Once you have decided on whom you think you would like to work with you will need to call to make an appointment. This is a great opportunity to meet up and build a rapport with the florist and ensure they can do exactly what you want.

Key questions to ask and think about

❯ Request to see a portfolio of past work.

❯ Have some idea of the shape of bouquet that you would like. Check our list below of the range of shapes that you can have and which shape goes best with which gown

❯ It is best to have chosen your dress before meeting with your florist. Take a picture with you as this will help to ensure that you have chosen the best floral design to compliment it.

❯ Take pictures with you of designs you have seen and liked with colours and flowers that have caught your eye. The key here is communication. Her interpretation of your ideas may be very different to what you imagine in your mind.

❯ Remember that the sense of smell is the strongest sense of association. Choose a flower that you love the smell of, and it will forever become associated in your memory with your wedding day.

❯ Do think about what you or your bridesmaids will be wearing in your hair. Your florist can fashion a floral headdress to complement your bouquets, or wire individual flowers and leaves that can be interwoven into the hairstyle.

❯ Remember that flowers out of season will be more expensive. Check the list below to see which flowers are in which season. If you desperately want a particular flower, do check the price with your florist as it will be more expensive out of season.

❯ Please take samples of materials with you, if you can, of your gown, the bridesmaids' and even the groom's waistcoat! This will ensure that there will be no colour clashes on the day!

❯ You will need to speak to your florist about: your bouquet and the bridesmaids', any accessories for your hair or the bridesmaids', the groom's buttonhole, other buttonholes (remember to count up everyone who may want one plus one extra!), the venue's decorations (please see separate section).

The main thing to come away with from your first meeting is that you get on with them personally and you like their style. If you don't, simply move on and find one that you do like! Remember, you are the customer, do not be forced into anything you are not comfortable with as this will only add apprehension and bad feelings to pre-wedding nerves. You want to feel absolutely delighted with what you have chosen and looking forward to them adding to the enjoyment of the day.

Choosing the right bouquet

There are no taboos with flowers – think of fragrance, colour and what you will be wearing. Do you prefer traditional or contemporary styles? Think of your bouquet as an accessory that will complete your look on your wedding day. It must accentuate your gown and theme of the wedding without drowning out key details on your gown or your body.

Here are some helpful tips to make choosing the right bouquet for you easy and fun. There are several styles of bouquet that you can choose from and each style can compliment different gown shapes.

The bouquet

Shower or cascade: A bouquet that falls forward in a cascade. The idea with this bouquet is to elongate your silhouette and continue the line of your gown. Very traditional, but can be very dramatic if done properly. How about adding clematis strands, honeysuckle or jasmine? Or for a truly contemporary look, the exotic orchid?

The arm bouquet: A bouquet that is loosely held on one arm and is the modern way of carrying flowers. Tall, elegant flowers with a clean cut look need to be used, such as calla or arum lilies or tulips. Very modish.

The wired bouquet: A bouquet where the stems are individually wired into shape and the flowers have a less structured, more flowing look. Useful if you want to use lots of different flowers and greenery. This style can be used as a platform for alternative textures, such as shells, feathers or twists of material (perhaps using your bridesmaids material).

The teardrop: A contemporary shape that still encompasses an aspect of the traditional shower. Works well with deep colours as the shape is thus picked out easily against a light coloured gown.

Hand tied bouquet: Probably the most widely used method nowadays, as it is highly adaptable and suits a range of dress styles. Don't be afraid to work with other materials. How about adding some tassels to your bouquet? Or circling it with tulle or organza? The tulle can also be used over the top of the bouquet and pinned at certain points. You could also incorporate feathers or shells as with the wired bouquet. It can also look very chic if different colours and types of flowers are used in very tight concentric circles.

Pomander: A tightly constructed bouquet in a 3D shape (such as a globe or a heart), usually carried on the end of a rope or ribbon. Good if you want something really different and can be very effective again if using deep colours. Good for a range of dress styles.

The posy or nosegay: Simple and yet stylish. A bunch of lily of the valley or grape hyacinths would be very effective. A dramatic colour especially works well. Have you considered just one single flower such as the arum or calla lily?

Different and stylish: For a dramatic, but simple bouquet, have a skilled florist fashion one very large flower using many blossoms (such as rose petals) to construct a stunning oversized rose bloom, twelve or fourteen inches in diameter.

The gown

Straight dress If your gown has a straight silhouette the following bouquets should be considered; SHOWER OR CASCADE, ARM BOUQUET.

Full dress If your gown is full and romantic it is important to accentuate the flow and curves of the body and elongate the shape. Try WIRED BOUQUET or TEARDROP.

Princess line/a-line Your gown may have an empire waist or princess line which flows beautifully away from the body. Try HAND TIED.

Informal or contemporary outfit You may have chosen to wear a suit or a less structured dress. It is really important to give a special finish to your outfit with some of the styles of bouquets listed above. Alternatively why not consider contemporary looks such as POMANDER, THE POSY or NOSEGAY, DIFFERENT and STYLISH.

Attendants' flowers

Bridesmaids are there to compliment and support the bride on her special day. There are some great opportunities to get the best look for your bridesmaids and here are some helpful hints as to how to plan to accent their look with flowers.

It is best to try and look at the bridal bouquet and take a theme that will follow through. Think again of the colour, texture, shape or materials that you want to use, but on a smaller scale.

TIPS AND IDEAS

❧ If you have very young bridesmaids it is best to have either a small basket or a pomander. Sometimes it may be easier to give them a headband or head wreath of flowers as this will help to stop fidgeting and flying posies later in the day!

❧ Your youngest bridesmaid could have a basket full of rose petals. These can be gently scattered as they walk down the aisle (gently perfume them with a fragrance of your choice which will then permeate the air as they are scattered).

❧ You could choose for adult bridesmaids an exact replica of the bridal bouquet but on a smaller scale or in a posy form.

❧ A tight posy of roses is a beautiful option. Why not give a different colour for each bridesmaid?

❧ Each bridesmaid could carry a bouquet of a different type of flower, but matched to the same colour as the bridal bouquet.

❧ For bridesmaids wearing the same style dress but in different colours, either have the same flowers as the bridal bouquet but tied with ribbon in the same colour as the individual dresses, or have bouquets made up in the individual colours, but give them to different bridesmaids. (NB. especially important to take samples of material to the florist.)

❧ Select a single flower from the bride's bouquet and use it in masses for the bridesmaids

❧ Have the bridal flowers in the same colour of the bridesmaids' dresses and their flowers in the colour of the bride's dress (i.e. cream or ivory).

❧ If you have a lot of female friends you would like to include in the wedding and yet do not wish to choose between them for bridesmaids (or perhaps would just like children as bridesmaids or simply to cut costs by having none) you could reach the top of the aisle at the beginning of the wedding service and each friend could come up to you in turn and present you with a flower (for best effect, flowers that easily make a beautiful posy, such as lilies, gerberas or roses). The last friend or perhaps your mother, would simply gather them and tie them with a ribbon to become your bouquet.

Don't forget!

❤ **If it is a hot day, put all the flowers into the fridge as soon as they arrive**

❤ **If any females (such as mothers of the bride and groom) are to be wearing buttonholes, ask them what colour their outfits are going to be so you can arrange for the appropriate colour (better still ask them to call the florist to sort it out themselves!)**

❤ **Always carry your bouquet low, below your navel. This will make you look taller and slimmer**

❤ **Remember to put the delivery of your flowers onto your CONFIRMATIONS list. Put on your RESPONSIBILITIES list who is collecting the buttonholes for the groom's party**

❤ **You may want to keep your bouquet and have it pressed or professionally preserved for a keepsake (please see suppliers in the appendix). If so, and you would still like to keep with the old tradition of tossing your bouquet, then order a smaller, lighter and less expensive version of your bouquet for this purpose.**

Unique is chic!

- If you do not want to carry a traditional bouquet there are many other options. If you are having a winter or autumnal wedding, you could add a muff to your outfit and have a corsage pinned onto it. You can carry a small elegant bag with flowers spilling out of it, or if you wanted to be really contemporary then a low slung belt or a wrap made from flowers or rose petals. Your florist can also make a beautiful headdress or tiara for you.

- Place two special flowers in your bouquet – on your way up the aisle present one to your mother and on your way back down present one to your new mother-in-law.

- All flowers have their meanings. Why not put a little paragraph about this in your order of service, perhaps on the back page: 'Sophie has chosen for her bouquet: ivy for fidelity, lilies for purity and roses for love', or more in depth 'Sophie has chosen lily of the valley for her bouquet as it symbolises the return of happiness. Its scent is said to lure the nightingale from its nest and lead him to his mate'. It is a good touch and keeps guests occupied before the ceremony begins.

- Placing a few details about the reasons for your choice of flowers in your order of service is a lovely idea. It lends a feeling of a personal touch to your service and makes the day a little more special for everyone. For example 'Sophie has chosen hyacinths for her wedding bouquet as they were the first flowers that Simon ever gave to her', etc.

- Have very small posies (two or three flowers) made up for the female guests as they enter the church. This is especially effective for sweet smelling flowers such as sweet peas. Ask your florist for a price on this. Have either someone at the reception venue putting them into water to be claimed at the end of the day, or leave a large shallow vase at the entrance of the reception for them to put there themselves (with a notice saying please claim at the end of the day).

- Instead of tossing your bouquet, ask all the wives of married couples to come onto the dance floor. Ask those who have been married less than five years to leave, then less then eight, twelve etc., until you are left with the longest married wife. Present the bouquet to her and ask her to lead everyone in a dance.

- How about dispensing with real flowers, and using two or three large, dramatic ones made out of beads, false jewels or organza, tied neatly with a ribbon (perhaps tie this up with the buttonholes) Please see list of stockists in the appendix.

Buttonholes

The groom is an extremely important part of the wedding day and so should have the chance to feel as special as the bride.

The groom's buttonhole can be completely different or simply larger. A tasteful, masculine look may be created from just a few blooms – tight rosebuds, stephanotis blooms, a single gardenia, several lily of the valley or a huge gerbera! If you would like his buttonhole to be completely different to the rest of the flowers, do try to link one aspect, such as colour or type of flower.

Did you know

That the tradition of tossing the bouquet came from an earlier custom where the newly-wed bride threw her left shoe over her shoulder to indicate her new status and departure from her old life and the one that caught the shoe would be the next to marry! It is thought that the bouquet replaced the shoe as it was much more convenient to the bride rather than hobbling about for the rest of the day!

Amaryllis meaning PRIDE. The name comes from a Greek word meaning dazzling. The meaning is thought to come from how the amaryllis grows so strongly and holds its head so proudly.

Camellia meaning PERFECTED LOVELINESS. Victorian ladies were supposed to show their feelings towards a suitor by wearing a white or red camellia.

Clematis meaning MENTAL BEAUTY. Perhaps the significance of this is the fact that the clematis has no healing properties and is grown solely for its appearance.

went down stream he shouted, 'Forget me not!'. And she named the flowers in his memory.

Honeysuckle meaning SWEETNESS. You only have to suck the honey out of the centre of the flower to understand how it got its meaning.

Iris meaning MESSAGE. Iris was the messenger of the ancient Greek Gods. The Kings of France used the flower as their emblem and called it the Fleur de Lis.

to lure the nightingale from his nest and lead him to his mate.

Orchid meaning A BELLE. We think of these as exotic flowers but we have many varieties growing wild in the hedgerows. Said to have been growing at the feet of Jesus Christ as he was crucified and his blood dripped onto them causing their spots.

Pansy meaning THOUGHTS. Simply from the French word *pensée*, and people used to send them to their nearest and dearest for them to remember them by.

Rose meaning LOVE. One of the oldest flowers known to man. Was said to be created by Chloris, the Greek goddess of flowers, out of a lifeless body of a nymph. She asked the help of Aphrodite, the goddess

flower meanings

Cornflower meaning DELICACY. A young boy loved Flora, the goddess of flowers. When he was found dead Flora turned him into a cornflower to signify his love and sensitivity.

Daffodil meaning REGARD and CHIVALRY. There is hardly a poet who has not written of it! Reference the famous Wordsworth poem 'I wandered lonely as a cloud'.

Daisy meaning INNOCENCE. The daisy is a children's flower, evoking memories of games such as 'he loves me, he loves me not'. At night the daisy folds up its petals as if going to sleep.

Forget-me-not meaning TRUE LOVE. A knight was walking with a lady by a river. He picked these blue flowers but as he gave them to her he slipped and fell into the river. As he

Ivy meaning FIDELITY. Ivy is not able to support itself but depends upon something to climb. But once it has gained hold nothing can separate it and thus its meaning.

Jasmine meaning GRACE and ELEGANCE. The Hindus gave it the beautiful name, Moonlight of the Grove.

Lily meaning PURITY. The lily is dedicated to the Virgin Mary in honour of her purity and why many brides like to have it in their bridal bouquet.

Lily of the Valley meaning RETURN OF HAPPINESS. This is not surprising as it is the sweetest flower imaginable! Its scent is said

of love, who gave the nymph beauty, Dionysus, the god of wine, added nectar to give her a sweet scent, and the three graces gave her charm, brightness and joy. And thus the rose was born.

Tulip meaning LOVE. Cultivated and prized like jewels by the Turks and the Persians (who gave them their name 'tulipant' meaning turban). Holland took the flower to heart but the sale of the bulbs caused such a frenzy that their economy was put in jeopardy and England passed a law limiting their price!

Violet meaning MODESTY. The plant is often described as modest for hiding its beauty away in the long grass and for flowering so fleetingly.

spring

Arum or Calla lily
Bluebell
Broom
Camellia
Daffodil
Forget-me-not
Foxglove
Gardenia
Iris
Jasmine
Lilac
Lily of the Valley
Pansy
Rose
Tulip

summer

Bougainvillea
Bouvardis
Delphinium
Fuchsia
Gardenia
Honeysuckle
Hydrangea
Lily
Ox Eye Daisy
Peony
Rose
Sunflower
Wax flower

Seasonal flowers

autumn

Amaryllis
Bouvardis
Crabapple
Eucalyptus
Heather
Hydrangea
Ivy
Orchid
Sunflower

winter

African violet
Amaryllis
Anemone
Arum or Calla lily
Crocus
Holly
Hyacinth
Ivy
Jasmine
Orchid
Snowdrop
Tulip
Violet

YOUR WEDDING DAY WILL BE ONE OF THE MOST MAGICAL DAYS OF YOUR LIFE. YOU WILL TREASURE YOUR MEMORIES OF IT FOREVER, SO THINK SERIOUSLY ABOUT THE BEST WAY TO CAPTURE YOUR DAY ON FILM.

You've been framed

Don't leave it to the last minute to find a photographer. Allow yourself enough time to shop around and find exactly what you are looking for.

The wedding photographer

The most important thing about any photographer is that they put you at your ease and inspire a feeling of confidence. With this in mind, you may have to spend some time finding someone you both feel comfortable with. Most people hate having their photographs taken at the best of times, and so to know that you have found someone who will coax a natural smile from you and who you can spend time with without feeling uncomfortable or shy will make all the difference on the day. By the end of the wedding you should hope to feel as though this person is more of a friend than a professional doing a job for you.

Experience is paramount. A wedding photographer needs to be flexible and confident enough to deal with any situation that might arise – from bad weather and additional family shots not previously discussed, to knowing the best place for photographs at the chosen church or venue, and how you and your guests will respond to instructions in a natural, happy way – and at the same time make the whole process fun!

Things to look out for...

View previous work and ask to see a dozen exceptionally good shots from one wedding rather than one or two good shots from a cross-section of weddings. Proof of consistently excellent pictures is the ultimate aim.

A recommendation from a friend or colleague can help to narrow your search and give you confidence in the photographer's skills.

The photographer's local knowledge of churches, venues, florists and car hire companies should be extremely good. If they are unsure of your particular venue or church they should be keen to go and view the location in advance of the day.

Your photographer should be willing to run through some poses with you prior to your wedding to get the best out of you on the day.

Check to see if the photographer belongs to an affiliated body such as the Master of Photographers Association with either Kodak or FujiFilm as this will mean they have a professional accreditation to support them.

Videography

Don't forget the moving picture! Many people now have their own video camera, but as this is a special day, why not consider asking your friends and family to video as many aspects of the day as possible, and also book a professional videographer to capture the key moments. You will then have a complete reminder of the whole day, from walking down the aisle to the speeches and first dance.

A professional videographer will usually offer an editing service, and if requested could probably take any other films and edit them into his own to create a complete overview of the day, from your own stand point as well as that of your guests.

Make sure you speak to your clergy or registrar to request the presence of a videographer at your service – some churches will ask for restraint until after the vows have been said, so double check your position before booking an expensive professional who won't be able to capture exactly what you require.

Ensure you choose a videographer who has been recommended to you or has a clear affiliation with a professional body. You don't want an amateur at your wedding. So make sure you ask questions and see video footage of his/her previous work before placing a booking.

Choosing the style to suit you

With all the new technology available today, and so many individual and creative wedding options, there are lots of different styles of photography to choose from. Your day can be captured in anything from modern digital high tech to sepia old-school styling – the choice is yours! Your photographer should assist you with your decision and be prepared to take risks to get exactly what you are looking for. A mixture of traditional formal and candid reportage photography is the in thing at the moment and will enable you to get the best variety of pictures.

Traditional old-school

Giving the photographer a list of all the combinations of groups you would like to have photographed will make his/her job easier. It will also mean that the important members of the family are included and you won't have any gaps, such as grandparents, or distant friends that you have not seen for a long time. These shots can also be extremely romantic, and as long as your photographer is good and the prints are strong they will stand the test of time!

Reportage or storybook style

This is a very popular style of photography: the photographer mingles with guests and family to capture moments spontaneously. Be it a group hug outside the church or dancefloor hysterics at the end of the day, the impromptu shots are fun and will show the genuine excitement of the day. Reportage photography can be continued throughout the day and evening to give the full story of the whole event!

Digital styling

This style of photography is growing in popularity. It enables the photographer to capture images on disc and then produce standard high quality printouts or give the discs to the bride and groom for them to e-mail to friends and family.
It is also possible, via a computer, to make slight changes to any imperfections that may have occurred on a photograph, or to take the main characters within a photograph and place them on different backdrops or alter their images in a fun way. These can then be sent as a joke or a card to loved ones!

Sepia and black-and-white photography

Sepia photography is very warm and reminiscent of old school photographs. It gives a lovely tone to photographs, especially those taken up close and personal. The soft tones and warm brown hues take the sharpness away from dazzling sunny days and give a glowing ambience that is hard to create in colour or black-and-white photographs.
Black-and-white photography mixes well with traditional colour to give a different, modern edge to photographs. It is also very complimentary to the images that are taken as it contrasts light with dark in an atmospheric way.

TIPS

❧ Tell your make-up artist and hairdresser which style of photography you have chosen. They can accent different parts of your make-up and hair accordingly.

❧ Think about the little touches that may be picked up in the photographs. Your nails should be manicured just in case you choose a close-up shot of the giving of rings, the wedding cake being cut or the signing of the register.

❧ Ask your chief bridesmaid to carry a powder and lipstick so you can freshen up your make-up during the day.

A suggestion list of shots you may want to capture

Divide the day into preparations, ceremony, reception and evening. Go through the lists with the photographer, the ushers and bridesmaids before the day.

Preparations: Photographs at home or at the place where you are getting ready

Bride

Bride with mother

Bride with father

Bride with mother and father

Mother and father

Bride with family present

Bride with maid of honour or chief bridesmaid

Bride with bridesmaids

Bride finishing make-up

Bride and father getting into car

At the ceremony

Bridegroom arriving at church

Bridegroom with best man

Bridegroom with best man and ushers

Guests arriving at ceremony

Bride and father getting out of car

Bride and father and bridesmaids going into church/ceremony

Groom and best man at altar

Church service

Bride and father walking down aisle

Bride and groom exchanging vows

Organist/soloist/musicians

Signing the register

Bride and groom coming back up aisle

Group shot of all coming up aisle

Bride and groom outside church/ceremony

Bride and groom and immediate family outside church/ceremony

Formal shots at venue or church

Bride and groom

Bride and groom with bride's parents

Bride and groom with groom's parents

Groom with his parents

Groom with bride's parents

Bride with her parents

Bride with groom's parents

Bride and groom with bridesmaids and ushers

Bride and groom with groom's family

Bride and groom with bride's family

Bride and groom with friends

Bride and groom with entire family

Bride and groom with entire family and friends

At the reception

Bride and groom arriving

Bride and groom with drinks

Some location shots

Bride and groom going into reception

Receiving line

Table shots

Cake table

Cake cutting

Bride and groom toasting

Speeches

Bride and groom's first dance

There are many more options but the above list is fairly comprehensive and will take around two hours to complete.

THE SUCCESS OF YOUR
RECEPTION IS COMPLETELY
DEPENDENT ON THE MOOD OF
YOUR GUESTS. GET THEM
EXCITED AND IN THE PARTY
MOOD RIGHT FROM THE START
AND THE DAY IS GUARANTEED
TO GO WITH A BANG!

The reception

Wedding transport

As far as wedding transport is concerned, so long as whatever you choose gets you from A to B, anything goes! The most important thing is that you get to the church, and from the church to the reception!

If you choose to travel by car, there are a couple of things you may want to consider. Firstly, try to find a company that has its own cars rather than one that shares them with another company or hires them from someone else. That way you can guarantee your choice will be available on the day. Ideally, choose a company that has been recommended by a friend, or at least try to get a reference; this will dramatically reduce the possibility that the chauffeur will turn up late or drive into things! Take a look at some of the cars to see what general condition they are in.

When it comes to signing contracts, specify the type and colour of the car, that it will be washed and clean, the expected length of service, the destinations and obviously the date and the time.

Alternatively, you could ask a friend who has a nice car to play chauffeur. Most people are delighted to help, so don't be afraid to ask. Remember to thank them with a tank of fuel and a small gift, and don't forget to pay for the pre-wedding wash – that way you can be sure it will be done!

If you decide to do things a bit differently, why not try one of the following ideas:

a horse-drawn carriage – nothing could be more romantic!

if you are a keen horsewoman, then trotting to your church would make for some wonderful photos

if you are near a river or the sea, why not take a speedboat or even a gondola

a pedicab like the tuk-tuks in Bangkok would be fabulous if there wasn't far to go

for the ultimate in style, why not go for a helicopter or a hot air balloon!

a motorbike – not for the faint-hearted or those with large dresses!

Depending on exactly where the ceremony and reception venues are in relation to one another, you may wish to provide transport for the guests as well. This is a thoughtful gesture if you have any spare budget as the guests then arrive together – and any rows about map reading are prevented! If all the guests are staying in the same place, arrange for the transport to come and collect them at the end of the reception. Everyone will love you for this as it will mean they can drink and not drive!

You could hire a large coach on which to transport everyone, or try one of the following more unusual ideas:

❧ rent a large red double-decker bus for all your guests. Make sure there are some refreshments on board, even if it is just a short journey

❧ have a stream of horse-drawn carriages take your guests back and forth if the reception is not far away. You only need hire approximately five for eighty guests, and they will remember the experience forever!

❧ if the reception can be reached by water, a canal barge with refreshments on board is a great idea!

The seating plan

circle

refectory

This can seem a daunting task, particularly as you have to leave it relatively close to the day itself before you can complete it; ask someone to chase up any outstanding RSVPs prior to the wedding so you have a decent amount of time to plan the seating. Even if you are having a buffet, it is wise to have a seating plan. If guests do not know where they are supposed to sit at the reception, it makes them uncomfortable and leaves those who know relatively few people very much out in the cold and feeling unwelcome – the last thing you should want to inflict on your guests.

There are many ways to make the whole process as painless as possible; indeed, you can even stamp your individuality on to this aspect of the day!

Firstly, think about whether you would like a top table or not. Even if you decide the top table should just consist of yourself and the groom, it should be central to the whole proceedings. Alternatively, and more traditionally, your top table could also consist of the bride's parents, the groom's parents, the best man and chief bridesmaid, the ushers and bridesmaids, or any combination of these. It is completely up to you. Remember, the only rule is that you and the groom have to sit next to each other!

Secondly, consider your table arrangement. Ask your reception venue or your furniture supplier about the different sorts of tables they provide. The choices are:

circular · oblong · arc.

Always ask for the measurements of each one (useful if you are having any table decorations) and how many the table sits. They can be set out in a number of different ways, the most popular being:

in a circle

in an E-shape

in a refectory style

in a zig-zag

in a horseshoe.

Or you can create your own individual table layout. Do ask your reception venue if the plan you propose is viable and give them an exact diagram to ensure there are no mistakes on the day.

- Allow yourselves at least a week to create a seating plan. Give the phone numbers of those who haven't replied over to a relative so they can finalise the numbers.
- As soon as you know the final numbers, inform your caterers and the reception venue. Confirm the final table arrangement with the venue.
- Sit down with the groom and draw out a large table plan that is easy to work with. Write everyone's names on pieces of paper so you can manoeuvre them around your plan.
- Don't create a sole singles table as this may make people feel a little conspicuous. Place groups of singles among couples.
- Sit people with similar interests or who may have something in common together.
- Let your guests know where they're sitting either via waiters showing the plan around during the drinks or with a large scale plan taped up on a board for all to see. You could also create individual cards with the guests' table name and position on them, to be handed out or collected during the drinks. This could save the huge amount of work involved in making a large scale plan, and also work to your advantage if any last-minute changes need to be made.
- Certain companies can create beautiful seating plans for you (they are also a wonderful memento of your day). They will sketch out a design of your table plan and then add in individuals' names the week before.
- If your table arrangement consists of particularly large tables, consider asking all the men to move two places to their right between each course to finally end up next to their partners. It is a great way for people to get to know each other!
- If you are having smaller tables, then instead of just numbering them, name them! Use the names of places you have visited together or which are of particular significance to you both (birth places, where you met, your first date, where he proposed, and so on), or how about things that your hometown is famous for. Use your imagination and create a great talking point!
- Seat all the teenagers together.
- Consider having a separate table for younger children, situated away from the main tables with supervision. Children can get very bored and hungry if they have to observe the adults' rules.
- Take into consideration your guests' special needs. For instance, if they are elderly it would be nice to seat them in well-lit areas and away from the noise of the band.

horseshoe

zig-zag

plan ahead

E-shape

Food and drink!

These are probably the most important elements of your wedding reception – guests will remember a wonderful meal forever . . . unfortunately, the same applies to a terrible one. But look on the bright side – you and your future husband can spend some glorious evenings sampling prospective menus! And don't feel faint at the thought of all that expense, because good food need not be expensive. There are now so many options to choose from that all budgets are catered for!

Choose your caterer wisely

In-house caterers

More often than not the reception venue will have its own caterers. You need to ensure that you can afford them, that they are flexible enough to give you what you want, and that they supply good food and good service. There are several advantages to an in-house caterer:

you don't have to go to all the trouble of finding one of your own
they won't sap your valuable time as they will already be familiar with the layout of the venue and will supply all the linen, tables, crockery and cutlery
you will probably have a smoother ride on the day as they will have gone through the process many times before!

The disadvantage is that they normally cost a great deal more than outside caterers. Do ask if you can bring in your own people, but the answer will probably be no. And if they do agree, be aware that they will charge you a venue fee and you may be forced to buy all your booze through them or suffer a corkage fee.
If you decide to go with the in-house caterers, make sure you sample their menu at the venue itself so you can see the waiting staff in action. If the meal is not up to scratch, consider hosting the reception elsewhere.

Independent caterers

These can range from one extreme to another. Some specialise in keeping it simple; they supply the food and nothing else. All other elements have to come from you – the drinks, dinnerware, tables and chairs, even the waiters and waitresses. This can be an advantage as you can then shop around not only for the best price but for exactly what you want. The disadvantage is that it will take you an inordinate amount of time.
Another caterer may provide food and waiting staff, while yet another may offer food, waiting staff and

furniture, until you work your way up to the all-singing, all-dancing, do everything service. If you do opt for the latter, go through every conceivable item so you know exactly what you are getting.

If you want to save money, discuss various options with your chosen caterer. For instance, you may decide to do without canapés, to put wine bottles straight onto the tables for guests to help themselves, to serve all the vegetables in large platters on the tables, or to serve a cold starter instead of a hot one – each of these options will save on waiting staff.

QUESTIONS

❥ What is the final price of the food? Most caterers will quote you an estimate and then ninety days before the wedding, when they know the exact food prices at the time, will give you a final cost per head. Ask to what extent the price may vary between the estimate and the final cost.

❥ What does that cost per head actually include: the waiting staff, the linen, the crockery, the glassware, the cutlery and the furniture? Ask to inspect these elements prior to the event.

❥ What type of meal service are they offering? Buffet or sit-down? Go through each individual element, right down to how the vegetables are to be served. Can you choose from various options?

❥ Do they specialise in any particular cuisine and could they design a menu especially for you? Can they take care of different food needs, vegetarians, vegans, nut allergies or diabetics?

❥ If you would like to have canapés, ask for a separate quote so you can see the individual costs.

❥ What will the ratio of staff to guests be? Will that be enough to cover everything? How will the waiting staff be dressed? Think about tipping the waiting staff in advance of the wedding, or perhaps give them a small gift from yourself and the groom. Happy staff give excellent service and ensure the reception goes well.

❥ Can they supply some refreshments for the disc jockey, videographer, photographer and any other entertainers?

❥ What do they do with the leftover food? As you are paying for it you may want it boxed up and sent to charity.

❥ Is there a cake-cutting fee? Some caterers make a charge for cutting up your wedding cake and circulating it.

❥ Will the staff be responsible for clearing up at the end of the evening?

When you finally find a caterer or a venue that satisfies all of your criteria, get everything in writing and don't leave anything to chance.

What style of meal do you want?

The next thing to decide on is your preferred style of meal. Will it be a buffet or a sit-down meal? Canapés with drinks or an open bar? This will largely depend on your budget. Whatever you do, don't stretch your finances to serve a second-rate sit-down meal; go for a sumptuous buffet instead.

A sit-down meal

This will usually consist of at least three courses, served by waiting staff. The staff serve all the wine during the meal, and then the coffee. They also clear the tables.

Russian-style!

The tables are set with the starter course when the guests sit down. Waiting staff clear the tables and then bring in a large platter of food which they place in the centre of six people. The guests help themselves from the platter. Waiting staff serve dessert, wine and coffee.

A semi-buffet

The tables are set with the starter course (usually cold) when the guests sit down. The guests then go up to the buffet table for the main course. Waiting staff serve the wine, dessert (also usually cold) and coffee.

A buffet

The guests help themselves throughout. No starter is served and the guests also go up to the buffet table to help themselves to dessert and coffee. Bottles of wine are placed on each table for guests to serve themselves.

You could vary the traditional idea of a buffet by having stations – several buffet tables serving different types of food. Try a pasta station or a carving station, or use foods from around the world as a theme – the options are endless and will dramatically cut down queues and give your guests the luxury of choice!

Welcome drinks

When your guests first arrive at the reception it is customary to serve them a complimentary drink. This is the first thing your guests will experience at your reception, so try to make it impressive and memorable.

- Do the traditional champagne with a twist; pour glasses from impressive Methuselahs (equivalent to eight bottles).
- Or go for champagne cocktails, the ultimate in class! Sugar cubes soaked in Angostura bitters, a small shot of brandy and topped up with champagne – delicious!
- Serve refreshing mimosas (fruit juices and champagne). Be imaginative with the juices – try peach, mango or passion fruit.
- Serve vodka and Red Bull – folks will know you mean business!
- Go mad for cocktails! Have an impressive cocktail bar serving individual orders, or choose your favourite cocktail and have it served en-masse!
- For cold days, think of a warming winter drink, for example mulled wine or hot buttered rum. Why not try egg nog!
- Pimms No 1 Cup is a delicious, refreshing summer drink. Serve it with mint and fresh strawberries.
- Have bowls of different, refreshing punches that staff ladle out.
- A Bloody Mary is the perfect drink for an afternoon reception.
- For those on soft drinks, add an element of excitement by serving them with ice cubes in which you have frozen pieces of fruit.

Canapés or hors d'oeuvres

Ask your caterer if they can do something a little different – again, exciting canapés will add to the party mood. Try a selection of the following.

- Oyster shooters: fresh oysters in a Bloody Mary mix, gulped back in shot glasses.
- Spoon canapés: smoked salmon or caviar on crème fraiche or soured cream on a spoon. The spoons are then artfully arranged; the guest simply picks up the spoon and eats!
- Soup sups. A stylish little number: cold soup in a shot glass. Try gazpacho (spicy Spanish tomato soup), vichyssoise (leek and potato) or borscht (beetroot).
- Take your favourite foods and downsize them! Imagine deep fried whitebait and slender chips served in newspaper cones. Miniature bite-sized burgers and hot dogs; fajitas and crispy duck pancakes.
- Follow a heart theme! Use heart-shaped serving bowls, cut out cucumber hearts with prawns, and arrange the canapés in heart shapes.

The main event

A luncheon party

Invite guests to witness a noon ceremony and then serve lunch by half-past-one. Serve Bloody Marys to start the proceedings, and have a harpist playing gently in the background to add an air of unmistakable elegance.

MENU

Brie baked in Filo Pastry and stuffed with Wild Mushroom Forcemeat

Roast Stuffed Monkfish with Serrano Ham and Capers

Trio of Sorbets: Mango, Passion Fruit and Lychee served with Lemon Wedding Cake

A wedding breakfast

This is a wonderful idea for a bride and groom who want something low key but very classy. It is also a great option if you haven't long to plan your wedding, as the venue of your choice will almost certainly be free for a wedding breakfast at about eleven o'clock in the morning. You could serve the guests croissants and coffee on arrival, prior to the ceremony, and afterwards waiters can pass around trays of mimosas (fruit juice and champagne).

MENU

Fresh Figs served with Acacia Honey and Ricotta Cheese

Creamy Scrambled Eggs served with Smoked Salmon on Rye Bread

Vanilla Wedding Cake served with Whipped Cream and Peaches

Afternoon tea

Afternoon tea has a wonderful atmosphere of age-old elegance. You can serve beautiful food as a buffet with just a couple of waiting staff and no one will expect anything more! Have a string quartet playing in the background, and serve tea from silver teapots into delicately patterned cups and saucers.

MENU

Finger Sandwiches of:

Smoked Salmon, Lemon and Black Pepper

Cucumber

Celery and Brie with Cranberry Sauce

Finest York Ham

Freshly Baked Scones served with Strawberry Jam and Clotted Cream

Fresh Viennese Fancies

Chocolate Wedding Cake served with Whipped Cream and Fresh Raspberries

A cocktail reception

A chic way to entertain your guests! Greet them with cosmopolitan cocktails such as Manhattans or Martinis, and hire a jazz band or pianist to create an upbeat feel!

MENU

Prawn and Cucumber Tartlets with a Sweet Chilli Sauce

Gazpacho Soup Sups

Oyster Shooters in a Bloody Mary

Quail's Egg with a Spicy Mayonnaise Dip

Caviar Eclairs

Mini Burgers in Buns

Lettuce-wrapped Falafels with Hummus

Peking Duck Pancakes

Summer Berry Tartlets

Lemon Syllabub Puffs

Wedding Fairy Cakes

afterwards...

> **Serve chilled pudding wine with the dessert.**
> **Serve a slice of your wedding cake to each guest.**
> **Don't just offer ordinary coffee – include some flavoured ones for fun! Try Highland Grogg, Chocolate Praline, or Hazelnut. And how about hot chocolate and a range of fruit teas as well!**
> **If you really want something beautiful to finish with, why not serve the real thing – liqueur coffees. There is nothing better than Irish whiskey with sugar and fresh cream.**
> **Don't serve mints with the coffee – do something different! Try fortune cookies, fruits dipped in sugar, or raisins soaked in brandy and then set alight.**
> **Hand around port and cigars with the coffee. This will add an air of elegance to the evening.**

Wedding cakes

Your wedding cake is a symbol of your love and happiness – and a sumptuous focal point of your celebrations! The wedding cake of today is seen as an opportunity to create a fabulous statement. Whether it has a humorous tone or a spectacular presence, most brides and grooms have great fun selecting a cake that suits not only their personalities, but also the style of wedding – and most importantly their taste buds! There are countless options to choose from, but try to design the style, size, colour and filling to complement your chosen wedding theme and catering style.

Tradition

THE MODERN WEDDING CAKE HAS EVOLVED OVER MANY CENTURIES. IT DATES BACK TO ROMAN TIMES, WHEN A LOAF OF BREAD WAS BROKEN OVER THE BRIDE'S HEAD TO SYMBOLISE FERTILITY. THE GUESTS THEN ATE THE CRUMBS, WHICH WERE BELIEVED TO BE GOOD LUCK.

Consider the following questions:

what style of wedding are you planning – simple, dramatic, colourful, elaborate? If you have decided on a simple, contemporary wedding you may want a simple, contemporary cake with clean, pristine lines that will complement the overall ambience of the day.

how large is your reception venue and does it have high ceilings? The scale can be extremely important. For example, a large room with vaulted ceilings could be emulated with a tall, elegant cake.

is the weather likely to be very hot? A high temperature is not the best thing for a delicate cake of spun sugar or a chocolate extravaganza!

Something to tickle the taste buds!

Remember that your cake is in fact edible! Why not serve it either as the dessert following your main course, or as an additional sweet option for a buffet held later in the evening. Think of your cake as a culinary treat for your guests!

Nowadays, the variety of cakes that caterers or specialist cakemakers can create for you is practically without limit. So instead of going for the traditional fruit cake, why not select something a little unusual – let your imagination run wild!

❧ Have a different filling for each layer of your cake. You and your fiancé may prefer different types of cake, and this can be overcome by dedicating a layer to each of your preferred sweet sensations!

❧ If you do go for the traditional fruit cake and decide to serve it as part of the dessert menu, why not add a special accompaniment such as hot brandy sauce or a whipped cream sensation

Talk to the experts

Once you have found a baker or caterer that you trust, make sure you ask lots of questions.

❧ What size of cake do you need for the number of guests you are having? Are you limited to a particular size and shape?

❧ What choice of flavours and frostings do they have? Could you have different flavours for different layers?

❧ Can they create a fake layer to add height, and would this reduce the cost compared to a genuine layer?

❧ If you are having a novelty cake, look at some pictures of the caterer's past work. Ensure that you are both talking about the same thing regarding shape and size, and show them sketches and measurements.

❧ Can they mould decorations and personalise your cake? Why not include symbols of love such as cherubs, hearts, doves, maidens, and rings linked together.

Doing it yourself

If you have a very clever aunt, mum or friend who wants to make your cake for you, it is wise to have a trial run well in advance of the real thing. This will not only set your mind at rest and show you that you can achieve what you really want, but if things don't turn out as well as planned you still have the option of talking to your caterer or local baker.

❧ Dressings such as ribbons, lacework, swirls of frosting, marzipan fruits, sugared fruits and flowers, and sugar paste can be found at local specialist food decoration shops or bakers'. Ask the assistants at these stores how they would apply certain decorations so that you can experiment if you are not too sure.

❧ The table on which the wedding cake is displayed should be one of the focal points of the room. Make sure it is beautifully decorated and positioned for full impact. Think carefully with a liquor base to give it body and complement the flavours of the cake. Make sure you include the fact that you are having your wedding cake as dessert on your menu (this will save guests' confusion later on).

❧ A dense vanilla wedding cake with fresh apricot filling and vanilla butter cream frosting is the perfect accompaniment to a spring day.

❧ A light lemon wedding cake with a trio of fruit sorbets is divine for a summer wedding. An ice cream or sorbet mix served in a tulle basket means that your guests have the option of adding an accompaniment if required.

❧ Angel food wedding cake with a cinnamon brandy butter would be fitting for an autumnal theme.

❧ A white chocolate cake with milk chocolate filling, surrounded by flakes or curls of white chocolate and fresh raspberries and served with a dark chocolate sauce, is a very popular option that not only looks tempting but suits a whole range of wedding themes.

❧ A dense chocolate wedding cake with a mocha hazelnut filling and chocolate coffee beans has a strong aroma as well as a flavour that will tickle more than just your taste buds!

❧ Ask to taste some of their cakes. Ensure that on the day you will get exactly what you have tasted. Make sure they use the best ingredients, for example butter instead of vegetable shortening.

❧ Never move a cake yourselves! Ask the caterer to place it straight onto the cake table at the reception. As always, double check the date, the time of delivery, and give them a map so they can find the venue.

❧ Can a small portion of the cake be prepared with brandy or another form of alcohol? This will allow you to follow the tradition of freezing and sharing a piece of cake with your husband on your first anniversary or using the top tier of your cake for the christening cake of your first child.

about the display of the cake on the day. The stand and cake knife are equally important elements. Most bakers will hire out cake stands, and caterers or venues will normally have a cutting knife. Make sure you ask in advance of the day!

❧ For a minimalist look, ensure the same linen is used as for the rest of the tables, and centre the cake with the cutting knife to the left side. If you want to create a more dramatic effect, you can drape tulle or net swags over the table linen in

different (and complementary) colours and pin them up with fresh flower corsages.

❧ Alternatively, strew the table with rose petals or glitter confetti to add a softer look around the base of the cake stand. As with all focal points, ensure that the lighting is good and that there are no awful pictures or other background distractions that could ruin any pictures taken during the cutting of the cake!

Creative alternatives

❧ If you would like to serve your cake as a dessert and yet want something a little different, why not think about a French croquembouche, which is a dramatic pyramid of profiteroles wrapped in spun sugar. Or how about a similar shape using baby meringues – a delicious variation on a pavlova.

❧ Ask your baker to make a selection of miniature cakes, decorated in silver or an equally vibrant shade of icing, and stack them in tiers on a beautiful glass plate.

❧ How about a cheesecake? This is perfect as a dessert and can be decorated to look just like a traditional cake.

❧ How about reviving the old tradition of a groom's cake – usually a fruit cake. These can last indefinitely (unfrozen) if wrapped in greaseproof paper and then in foil and periodically spiked with brandy.

❧ It is nice to give your guests a piece of wedding cake to take home with them, and also to send a piece to those who were unable to attend your wedding. You will need little boxes in which to distribute them; these could also bear your names and the date of the wedding.

Cutting the cake

❧ The cake used to be cut just before the dessert was served so that if the cake was to be the dessert it could be taken away and divided up by the caterers. However, the cake can be cut whenever you choose, usually following any formal speeches. If you plan to have an afternoon tea or cocktail reception, it should be cut quite early to be used as a dessert.

❧ Your master of ceremonies or toastmaster should announce the fact that you are cutting the cake. Use an heirloom cake knife tied with a ribbon, or perhaps a sword that could be ceremoniously presented to you. The groom should place his hand on top of yours and together you should slice the cake.

The evening's entertainment

As you will have seen by now, there are countless ways to make your day unique, and the selection of your evening entertainment is another element that can add a special touch to the day. Continuing the ambience of the service through the reception and on to the evening party will help the day to flow and add to the overall enjoyment of yourselves and your guests.

When you start planning your evening reception, make sure you discuss your particular tastes in music. Your wedding is a perfect place to play music that suits both personalities, and if your tastes differ dramatically – one likes jazz, the other likes disco – there is no reason why you can't have both; it's just when and how they are presented that will need consideration.

Musical entertainment

Once you know what you both want to listen to it's time to decide how you want it played.

Jazz band If Harry Connick Junior tickles your fancy, there are many good jazz bands that can replicate the swooning tones of his music.

Lookalike bands There are many great bands that copy popular bands such as Abba, the Bee Gees, Steps, and the Spice Girls. Why not have a wild night of partying to your all-time favourite group.

Country and western bands If a line dance or barn dance is your thing, or something that you've always wanted to try, why not get your guests to join in with some of the dances or clap along to your antics!

Instructors Hire an instructor to teach Le Roc, Latin American salsa, and get everyone up to dance!

Live bands These don't have to cost the earth. You usually pay for the musicians' time, so if your budget is restricted you can negotiate what you're prepared to pay.

Karaoke Find out if your guests are truly gifted singers by dedicating part of the evening to Karaoke!

A disco The most popular choice to round off the evening festivities or as the main act to get everybody up and partying. There is a wide choice of DJs, so have a good look around and make sure the one you choose plays the music you want to hear. A song list is recommended so that he/she will know your taste and style of music.

The first dance

The song played at the beginning of the evening reception is dedicated to the bride and groom. You and your partner may have a song that you call your own, but just in case you need a helping hand, the following list of smoochy numbers are perfect for that special moment!

Three Times a Lady *The Commodores*

Wind Beneath My Wings *Bette Midler*

Someone To Watch Over Me *Gershwin*

Let's Face The Music And Dance *Irving Berlin*

S'Wonderful *Gershwin*

It Had To Be You *Harry Connick Jnr*

You'd Be So Nice To Come Home To *Cole Porter*

Let's Do It *Cole Porter*

When I Fall In Love *Nat King Cole*

Is This Love? *Bob Marley*

At Last! *Etta Jones*

Everything I Do *Bryan Adams*

I Will Always Love You *Whitney Houston*

Unchained Melody *Righteous Brothers*

Love Is All Around *Wet, Wet, Wet*

You Send Me *Sam Cooke*

Grow Old With Me *Mary Carpenter*

Wonderful Tonight *Eric Clapton*

When a Man Loves a Woman *Percy Sledge*

Sea of Love *Honey Drippers*

Utterly Beloved *Neville Brothers*

Wedding Song *Kenny G*

From This Moment *Shania Twain*

What A Wonderful World *Louis Armstrong*

Alternative entertainment

As well as the musical entertainment, why not surprise your guests with one of the following.

❧ Have a magician wandering through the reception venue doing tricks.

❧ Set up a casino table on which to place bets with pretend money and have a prize for the guest with the largest winnings!

❧ A vodka luge is not only a striking addition to the drinks table but will add an element of daring to the party mood!

❧ Hire a caricaturist to draw your guests and give away the portraits as keepsakes at the end of the day.

❧ A fortune teller can be a great attraction. They can impart wonderful news – like who'll be getting married next . . . ? When will the patter of tiny footsteps be heard . . . ?

❧ A tattooist who can put great designs on crazy parts of the body (obviously they won't be permanent!).

❧ A bucking bronco or even a jousting match! This would be a great entertainment if set up in the grounds of a castle venue!

Don't forget the kids!

If children are invited to your wedding, you will want to enjoy their presence, not worry about what they are getting up to! You will also want the mums and dads to relax and have a fabulous time, so why not incorporate some kiddie-related entertainment.

❥ If you can squeeze an additional table into your reception room, make it available to the children and stock it with colouring pads, streamers, jigsaws, books, party horns, party hats, masks – anything that will keep them occupied and happy. Tell the parents that this will be available during the meal and get them to bring the children's favourite toys to add to the fun.

❥ Create some fun bags for the kids containing mini gifts that they can use on the day and then take away with them.

❥ Book a clown or a children's entertainer to keep them occupied and happy during the meal and speeches.

❥ Hire a crèche for the day to allow the parents the opportunity to join in the fun.

IF YOU WANT THE WEDDING
OF YOUR DREAMS, THIS IS
PROBABLY THE MOST
IMPORTANT (AND MOST
TEDIOUS!) CHAPTER OF THE
BOOK. THERE IS NO POINT
SPENDING VAST AMOUNTS
OF TIME CREATING THE
PERFECT WEDDING, ONLY TO
SEE IT RUINED BECAUSE
YOU HAVEN'T CHECKED THAT
THE SIMPLE THINGS HAVE
BEEN TAKEN CARE OF.
HERE'S A QUICK GUIDE TO WHAT
YOU SHOULD DOUBLE CHECK.

Last-minute
checklist

Ask everyone who will need electricity on the day for their requirements. They should give them to you in either watts or amps; ask for one version or the other. Then add them all together and ask whoever is providing the electricity if they think you will have an adequate supply. If you are holding your reception in a marquee, a generator either as your main supply or as an emergency would be a good idea.

Do have a wet weather plan for the day. Keep a supply of umbrellas handy and ask the hotel what happens if you can't have your summer reception on the lawn.

Ensure that the reception venue has adequate restrooms for both sexes; there is nothing more annoying than waiting in a queue of 40 equally desperate females.

If you are having a marquee, do consider the average temperature for the time of year. No one will appreciate any of your unique, lovingly planned details if they are freezing cold, and heaters may be your best investment yet.

Don't run out of booze! Use the following measurements as a guide: there are six flutes to one 750ml bottle of champagne or sparkling wine; five medium glasses to one 750ml bottle of wine. As a general rule of thumb, allow for two glasses per person before the meal and three during the meal. Have equal quantities of red or white wine available, and don't forget the champagne or the sparkling wine for the toast!
At the bar after the meal, have all the general spirits available – gin, whisky and vodka, as well as wines, beers and mixers such as orange juice, soda, tonic, dry ginger ale, tomato juice and cola. If you want a fuller bar then add tequila, brandy, rum and vermouth. Don't forget lemons for slicing, any other garnishes, and a bottle of Worcestershire sauce!

Ask the best man and the groom to carry their mobile phones with them (preferably switched on!) the day before the wedding, and even on the day itself so you can get hold of them with any last-minute questions and changes of plan.

Ensure your musicians, caterers, etc., know the exact location of the venue and are aware of the date and time to arrive.

For a really thorough final check, walk through the day both as yourself and as a guest. Look for anything missing or lacking.

4

show time!

Wedding day countdown

Perfect presents

The speeches

Dramatic exits

FOR A STRESS-FREE

WEDDING DAY THAT WILL

FLOW SEAMLESSLY,

USE THIS BASIC SCHEDULE

TO KEEP THINGS RUNNING

PRETTY MUCH ON TIME!

THE TIMETABLE OF EVENTS

CAN BE CRAFTED TO

SUIT YOUR OWN WEDDING

CELEBRATION.

Wedding day countdown

It is useful to make a plan of your chosen sequence of events and to give copies to the best man, the chief bridesmaid, the caterers, the photographer and the entertainers so that everyone will know what is expected of them.

Countdown to success

The most popular time for a wedding ceremony is 1pm, so we have used this time to illustrate how the morning and afternoon events might flow. Adapt the timings to suit your own plans.

Try to get a good night's sleep before your wedding day. This will be easier said than done, however the more relaxed and rested you are the more energy you will have on the day and the more you will enjoy yourself.

8.00am You may be surrounded by family members and your chief bridesmaid on the morning of your wedding. Whoever is with you must make sure that you have a good breakfast as you will need all the energy you can get. A glass of bubbly or bucks fizz always goes down well with a strawberry or two to create the right ambience for the celebrations ahead.

8.30am Take time to pamper yourself with a long soak in a bath.

9.00am Go to the hairdressers or start styling your hair. This may be time-consuming, depending on the style you have chosen and the length of your hair. Your veil and headdress will probably be secured during this time; make sure you ask for plenty of hairspray as you don't want to worry about your hair once it has been done.

10.00am Now is the time for either yourself or your make-up artist to apply your make-up. You should have had at least one practice run before the day so you know you feel comfortable with what you are going to look like. Allow at least an hour to apply make-up to ensure any minor corrections won't interfere with your schedule. Your mother and your bridesmaids may want a little touching up, but this will only happen if there is enough time after you have finished.

11:00 AM

11:30 AM

12:30 PM

12:45 PM

Service

1:00 PM

11.00am You will need at least 30 minutes to get into your lingerie, hosiery, dress, shoes and accessories. Your excitement will really be starting to kick in as you get to see the finished you! Try to savour it – this is your special day!

11.30am Your photographer will arrive at least an hour and a half before your departure for the service. He/she should have been to the house prior to the day to check location shots and can be setting up for a first shot whilst you are applying your finishing touches.
Your family and bridesmaids should now be present, dressed and ready.
Photographs will take at least one hour and will include shots of you with your parents, with your bridesmaids, getting into your car, and any special individual shots you have asked the photographer to include.

12.30pm The photographer will leave before you to get to the church or venue to take some shots of the groom and best man before the service.

12.45pm The arrival of the bride at the church or venue. It is customary for the bride to be a few minutes late, however if you can get there slightly early you can take your time capturing some great photographs as you get out of the car and walk up to the church or venue.

1.00pm It is customary for the bride and her father to walk down the aisle first. However, it is becoming popular to send the bridesmaids ahead of the bride to give an added air of anticipation to the bride's arrival. A Catholic service will take at least one hour; Church of England 30 minutes; venue or register office 15–20 minutes.

2:00 PM

2.00pm Photographs following the service. These can take between 30 minutes and an hour depending on the focus given to structured formal shots.

3.00pm Confetti throwing and departure of bride and groom for the main reception.

On to . . . the party

3:30 PM

3.30pm Cocktails and canapés will be served to guests whilst the bride and groom have their photographs taken in the grounds or within the venue.

4.30pm A receiving line can be held by the bride and groom, either as the guests arrive at the venue, or in a more formal line leading into the main dining area.

5:00 PM

5.00pm Announcement that dinner is served.

5.15pm The bride and groom are welcomed and a blessing given. The starters are served to the top table first.

7:15 PM

7.15pm The toasts follow the leisurely dinner, and are usually introduced by the best man or toastmaster after the dessert.

8.00pm Cutting the cake and further photographs.

8:20 PM

8.20pm The bride, groom and guests remove themselves to the room in which the party will start in earnest.

9:00 PM

9.00 PM THE FIRST DANCE...*then, very late – the bride and groom may want to throw the bouquet and sling the garter to the girl and guy destined to marry next! At this point they usually make their departure. However, most brides and grooms like to stay to the very end to savour every moment of their special day.*

TRADITIONALLY, FIVE SUGARED ALMONDS WERE USED TO REPRESENT HEALTH, WEALTH, FERTILITY, HAPPINESS AND LONG LIFE; THE BITTERNESS OF THE ALMOND IN THE SUGAR COATING ALSO REPRESENTED AN IMPORTANT PART OF THE WEDDING VOW – 'FOR BETTER, FOR WORSE' – AND THUS THE GUEST SYMBOLICALLY HONOURED THE MARRIAGE.

Perfect presents

Wedding favours are simply a thank you to your guests for having made the effort to share your special day with you. Nowadays, almost anything can be used as a favour, and they are one of the most personal details of the wedding.

Wedding favours

Encase your favours in bags, boxes or pouches, but be creative! Display your offerings as impressively as possible, whilst at the same time using materials that will complement the style of your wedding. Given a little time and effort you can always hand craft your presentation. Make bags and pouches from felt or ribbon, or use opulent velvets and tassels. Little boxes lined with coloured paper are charming containers for cookies or chocolates and can be made months in advance.

Make sure that your gift contains a message somewhere, for example a handwritten luggage label or a little card. Or try putting it in an unexpected place – the inside of a fortune cookie, or printed on the inside of the wrapping paper.

If the favours are all arranged together, make sure your guests know to take one home. Place a handwritten card among them, with the words: 'PLEASE PICK A FAVOUR', 'PLEASE ENJOY', or 'FOR YOU'. Alternatively, ask the bridesmaids to hand out the favours from baskets.

Edible favours are always popular. If you do decide to give a piece of your wedding cake as a favour then present it beautifully. Buy miniature boxes to serve it in (find a company that will print your names and the date of the wedding on the box, or on ribbon to tie around the box), arrange the boxes into tiers and intersperse with fresh flowers to mimic the wedding cake.

If you decide to give the traditional almonds, don't just tie them in tulle! Tuck them into tiny boxes decorated with silk flowers and arrange them en-masse.

Present silver or gold dragees in boxes with flowers on top, or in aluminium tins with see-through lids.

Little luxury cookies are perfect if presented well! Place two different flavoured cookies into cellophane bags. Or why not go for novelty cookies in the shape of hearts, stars, or daisies, and iced in beautiful, vibrant colours.

Give each guest a bulb planted in a small terracotta pot or smart aluminium bucket, or even in small pebbles in a clear glass.

Marzipan fruits nestled in a small tin make a beautiful and colourful favour.

Tiny pots of honey symbolise a sweet and fruitful marriage. Either pot them up yourself or buy miniatures. Look for really unusual ones that no one will have tried before, like thyme or lavender honey.

Fill little cake cups with sweets, and tie with a ribbon.

Scented candles in unusual containers are a lovely gift. You could even make your own using shells or empty coconut halves.

Buy or make some gorgeous soaps and present them in little pouches tied with a glorious ribbon.

A lottery ticket in an envelope with some confetti and a personal note from the bride and groom is a really different and potentially lucrative favour!

Give your guests the seeds of the flowers that make up your bouquet. Take them out of the seed packets and put them into little pockets of wax paper, place simple handwritten planting instructions in with them and tie the top with a piece of ribbon. Perhaps include the meanings of each of the flowers (see page 132).

Plant little grasses or cacti in miniature buckets or pots.

Create a fun bag for each guest! Include a miniature bottle of liqueur, a scented candle, and a small bottle of bubble bath. Throw in a couple of foil-wrapped aspirins for the morning after!

Represent your region with pride! Your area must be famous for something or someone; whether it is pork pies or Winnie the Pooh, present them as your favours with a note explaining their significance.

Thank you gifts

Many people have willingly contributed huge amounts of time and effort towards your big day
and the ideal way to thank them is with a gift. In the rush and chaos of the lead-up to the day itself
it is easy to forget to thank someone or to tell them how much their efforts have meant to you –
a beautifully wrapped and thoughtful present with a personal note attached will let them know how
you both feel.

Prepare your gifts and cards months in advance and place them in your 'Reception' box. Anyone
who has made an extra special effort on your behalf (such as your mother or best friend, perhaps)
should be thanked properly during the speeches and presented with their gift.

Who you should be thanking

Bridesmaids • **Best man** • **Ushers** • **Mother of the bride** • **Mother of the
groom** • **Service performers** *(readers, singers, etc.)* • **Helpers** *(all those who
may have helped with the decorations, cakes or organisation)*

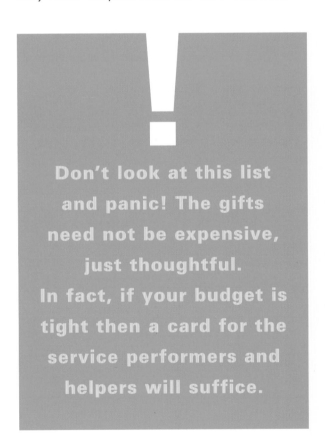

Don't look at this list
and panic! The gifts
need not be expensive,
just thoughtful.
In fact, if your budget is
tight then a card for the
service performers and
helpers will suffice.

For bridesmaids

❧ Underwear – treat her to the luxury of a beautiful gift set of bra and briefs.

❧ A beauty or natural therapy treatment or a day at a health spa.

❧ A piece of jewellery inkeeping with her taste – a small pendant or set of earrings is a lovely thought.

❧ Fill a basket with the most decadent toiletries you can find, preferably her favourite!

❧ Personally decorated china. Inscribe a plate with the date and place of the wedding and her name, or something personal to yourselves.

❧ Fill a tin with her most favourite things! This can be a cheaper option but is deeply personal. Include her favourite biscuits, alcohol, chocolates, bubble bath, soap and video.

❧ A subscription to a magazine of her choice.

❧ A pot of rosemary for remembrance.

❧ Subscription to a chocolate/wine/cheese or pudding club, that delivers an item each month for twelve months!

For best man and ushers

❧ Underwear for them too! Buy silk boxers or special wedding varieties with 'usher' or 'best man' printed all over them.

❧ A day at the races – either horse racing or Silverstone.

❧ Cufflinks. There are so many to choose from, including wedding varieties.

❧ An engraved hip flask.

❧ A bottle of wine or port that can be 'laid down'. Ask the recipient to lay it down for 5/10/15 years, then open it on your wedding anniversary and toast you.

❧ A golf lesson with the local pro.

❧ Men get stressed too! Book them a massage at their local health spa.

❧ A chill out box! A bottle of wine, a cigar, their favourite CD and some massage oil.

For mothers

It is traditional to give the mothers bouquets of flowers, which do make a delightful gift, but if they will also be taking the decorative flowers from the day home with them they could be a little overwhelmed! So why not try something different...

❧ A gift box of their favourite perfume, complete with body lotion and soap.

❧ A piece of jewellery.

❧ A day at their local health spa.

❧ Tickets to a play or show.

❧ A mother's ruin box – a large bottle of gin, a lemon, a wooden massager and foot balm for tired feet, to show how much you appreciate all their running around!

❧ A tree sapling to remind them of you as they watch the marriage tree grow strong.

❧ A rose variety called 'Wedding Days'.

❧ A pashmina or wrap; something luxurious they wouldn't buy for themselves.

For service performers and helpers

Keep these gifts simple to make it easy on yourself; it is really touching for the people concerned just to know that they have been remembered. Wrap up several boxes of chocolates (always include a couple extra, just for those last-minute thank yous), place them in your 'Reception' box together with the thank you cards and a list of the people you intend to give them to. Either ask someone to place them at the appropriate person's place setting or give them out yourself. If some people are not present at your reception, ensure that they are thanked beforehand or ask a relative to pass on a card and/or present shortly afterwards.

Presents for each other

Your mind will undoubtedly be on other things on your wedding morning, but it is really nice to let your loved one know, amidst the stress and trauma, what this day is actually all about. The gesture does not have to be great – a post-it note somewhere he will find it, or a present he will treasure for the rest of your lives together. Try one of the following possibilities.

❧ Record your favourite song, or one that you think sums up how you feel about each other. Leave the tape either in a Walkman in his bag or in his car with a note.

❧ Give him a 'wedding day' card.

❧ Leave him a joke to make him smile or remind him of a funny incident.

❧ Buy him some special wedding day boxer shorts with lurid love hearts all over them!

❧ Cufflinks.

❧ A beautifully engraved fountain pen or watch.

❧ Something he has always been dying to do – a hot air balloon trip or a bungee jump!

THE SPEECHES ARE A LONGSTANDING TRADITION AT WEDDINGS. USUALLY PERFORMED BY THE BRIDE'S FATHER, THE GROOM AND THE BEST MAN, THEY PROVIDE AN OPPORTUNITY TO THANK ALL THE CLOSE FRIENDS AND FAMILY THAT HAVE COME TOGETHER TO SHARE IN YOUR HAPPY CELEBRATION.

The speeches

Nowadays, the speeches are less formal, and many couples add their own fun and inspirational angles to personalise this aspect of their day. Many brides, mothers and friends also want to say a few words, so do draw up a plan so that you know the timing of the speeches will be just right.

If you have never written a speech before, this chapter aims to help you put together a few words that you will be comfortable repeating in front of an audience, and allow you to walk away happy, having maintained some of your credibility!

Understanding the responsibility

The honour of being the best man or the father of the bride brings with it the responsibility of having to tell a large number of people (most of whom you will already know!) how privileged you are to be a part of such a special occasion, and to express openly and in a light-hearted manner the love and happiness that you feel for the happy couple.

This is not an easy task. So to make things easier for yourself, take time to prepare, plan, and above all practise.

The father of the bride

In the 21st century, the position of the father of the bride can now be taken by a number of different people. For example, mothers often like to say a few words on behalf of herself and her husband, or it could be a brother, or a best friend of the family. The choice is yours, however a few words from the father who has given his daughter away on this special day is a tradition that gives substance to the speech format.

The father usually goes first in the order of speeches. It is his opportunity to:

* **welcome the groom to the family**
* **offer his congratulations and restate his happiness at the union**
* **say a few words about his daughter and the new life she is entering.**

It is usually an emotional day for both families, so keep the speech short and endearing, unless you are a confident speaker and wish to impart a few fun anecdotes about your daughter and her partner.

The best man's speech

Traditionally, the main elements to be covered by the best man's speech are as follows:

* **to thank the groom for his toast to the bridesmaids**
* **to read any telegrams from absent friends or family**
* **to introduce the cutting of the cake.**

There are no set rules, however the best man is expected to deliver at least one anecdote about the groom's past, preferably with a touch of humour. To make your life easier, call the parents, brothers, sisters and friends of the groom to glean some juicy, fun stories that will be acceptable for the entire audience, not just the young or single guests present. Remember, this speech is to celebrate the union of two special people, and the most effective are simple and have lots of toasting at the end!

Things to avoid

DO NOT mention ex-girlfriends or recount stories that will make grandmothers blush with embarrassment.

DO NOT swear or make lewd jokes at the expense of the bride or groom.

DO NOT include 'in jokes' that most people will not understand.

DO NOT tell endless jokes and forget the true purpose of your speech.

DO NOT drink too much prior to your speech – save that for later...!

Delivery is key!

Practising your speech out loud in the car or in front of a mirror will give you confidence and will enable you to get used to hearing your own voice. Remember to lift your normal voice level so that you will be heard; nerves can sometimes make you drop your voice and be too quiet.
Once you have confidence in the contents of your speech, choose someone close to you to try it out on so that they can give you constructive feedback.

Preparation

There are many ways in which to write a speech about a person that you know. The following examples are about the same person, but with different approaches. There may be a style that will suit you, or you may wish to use one as a guideline and adapt it to your personal style.

Background to the speech: the best man has known the groom for nearly 10 years, since they met at college at the age of 20. The groom is extremely ambitious, although he did not start out that way!

STYLE ①
rhyme

Some may find it easier to put a speech into rhyme or verse. It is a light-hearted, modern approach that is fun to create and will certainly be remembered!

This speech should be formatted in a style that suits you. It can be shorter or use less rhyme, however it helps to keep it simple so that the audience can pick up quickly what you are relaying to them.

Practise saying the verses out loud to find where the pauses work best. They should usually fall where you think the audience may appreciate certain comments or where the verse needs to be clearly highlighted, such as at the end of a profound statement.

The speech also needs to be delivered slowly – there will be a desire to race through the verses as they will flow nicely, however a steady, easy pace will get the response you are after.

Introduction

Ladies and gentlemen...

WHO YOU ARE For all those of you who don't know me, I'm supposed to be the witty best man! For all of you who do know me, please be gentle with me!

This is the hardest part of my duties today and so I have decided to turn to verse to present some of the stories that I have managed to collect about Roger over the years. Please bear with me as this is the first time that I have turned my hand to poetry and it took quite a lot of working out, as you will see! So here goes!

Let me take you through years gone by
What was Roger doing, we can only ask why
To tell you about Roger's childhood days
Inform you about his now manly ways

With the opposite sex Roger's really quite nifty
His first true love though was well into fifty
Roger used to disappear for an hour a day
What could he be doing, was he getting his way!
A waitress on holiday when he was just eight
She sure was indulging him with her chocolatey cake!

Roger getting drunk has been a sight we've all seen
All sorts of behaviour, some quite obscene
His first experiences were quite benign
pink champagne at the tender age of nine

Roger was generally a good boy at home
It only went pear-shaped when left alone
With parents away and sisters to mentor
Drink and parties would be top of the agenda
Lights left on and gas taps left blazing
Roger had to do a lot of explaining!

THERE'S MORE...

Trendy or camp I want you to hear
Cos Rog had an earring in his left ear
For more than 2 years he wore it with pride
Then saw the resemblance to a girl guide!

In Roger's college life he had a mission
To drink lots of beer and watch television
It's fair to say he would party all day
Studying truly got in the way
Missing exams and bunking the odd lecture
Passing with Honours was a University gesture!

I lived with Roger for almost a.year
Two men in one bedroom, it was kind of queer
Roger and his spooning was such an ordeal
If the truth is but known I could only appeal.

In his working life Roger towed the corporate line
Customers and clients he'd wine and dine
He bought the boss's car to try to improve
Very neat and extremely smooth!

Roger's aspirations are really quite high
The sky's the limit, you'll soon know why
From sessional temp to company Group Operations
  Director
He's known as GOD in the Leisure sector!

Life hasn't always been this way
whilst receiving his weekly GLL pay
From naked swimming to drinks behind the bar
All he needed was the fast car

It's quite clear to see that Roger's now maturing
His meeting with Abby will be truly enduring
It wasn't this way when first they did meet
Roger was shy and extremely sweet.

To Abby and friends he would play it real cool
When it comes to love though Roger's nobody's fool
He wouldn't admit it at the very start
But Roger was falling for Abby with his heart

Now they are married, the deed has been done
We wish them lots of happiness and bags of fun

Here ends my little verse and I must take this opportunity to thank you on behalf of the bridesmaids and myself for your kind words and to ask you all to once again be upstanding and raise a toast to Roger and Abby – 'Lifelong happiness'.

The bride and groom will now cut the cake.

THE END

Speeches

STYLE ❷
short and sweet

This style of speech is short and sweet and is best suited to someone who is not confident with public speaking. The style is a little more formal but is timely and says everything that really needs to be said.

It is ideal when you cannot pull together enough information for the main body of your speech.

If your groom is such a nice guy that you can only find a few past stories and anecdotes, then don't try to force a funny, jokey speech.

This type of speech is appropriate for many formal occasions and can be adapted to suit your own tone. Remember to deliver the speech in a controlled and clear manner with the pride that you feel for being best man on this special day in evidence.

Practise speaking out loud; don't think that because your speech is short and concise that it doesn't need to be rehearsed. People who are overconfident usually make mistakes or stumble when they realise the enormity of the occasion. So be prepared!

Introduction

Ladies and gentlemen...

WHO YOU ARE I am not a worldly wise speaker, and having heard the wonderful words from the groom and the bride's father I will be keeping mine short but extremely sweet!

I have had the pleasure of knowing Roger for a number of years and during this time we have been through many experiences, both fun and mad! What I have gathered throughout my time of knowing him is that he is a great friend with a great sense of adventure and energy, which captivates everyone who knows him.

Today is no exception. He has managed to marry a fabulous girl whom I know has been the apple of his eye for quite some time – even if he tried to cover it by acting cool and nonchalant at times! Well done Abby for making him wait!

But today is a huge celebration of the beginning of their lives together and I am extremely proud to have been asked to be his best man and to have the chance to ask you all to be upstanding and join with me in toasting 'The Bride and Groom'.

I would also like to say a big, big thank you on behalf of the bridesmaids for your kind words and toast earlier.

And without further ado, the bride and groom will now cut the cake.

THE END

The groom

Traditionally, the groom's speech includes:

thanking the bride's father and mother for their support and for giving him permission/approval to marry their daughter

giving out flowers or gifts to the mothers on both sides, thanking them for their love and support

toasting and thanking the attendants for their help and support on behalf of the bride.

More recently, thanks have also been included for the best man's support during the build-up to the day and for organising the stag night.

The content of this speech therefore is mainly thanks – and is a perfect opportunity for the groom to say a few words to his new wife.

The bride

It is a regular 21st-century occurrence for the bride to say a few words at her wedding, usually to reinforce what her new husband has said.

There is no real format to follow or outline of what should be included;

as long as the words are from the heart, anything goes!

THE CUSTOM OF TYING SHOES

ONTO THE BACK OF THE

HONEYMOON GETAWAY CAR

DATES BACK TO WHEN THE

FATHER OF THE BRIDE GAVE

HIS DAUGHTER'S SHOES TO

HER NEW HUSBAND,

SIGNIFYING THAT SHE WAS

NOW THE GROOM'S PROPERTY.

THIS GIFT FROM THE FATHER

TO THE GROOM LEGALLY

SEALED THEIR AGREEMENT.

Dramatic exits

You have probably been so busy planning the various aspects of your wedding that you haven't even considered your exit! Remember, this will be the guests' last memory of the two of you on your wedding, and if you organise your exit properly it can be the perfect end to a perfect day. Why not do it in style!

the perfect end

- Have a beautiful going away outfit to hand and arrange to throw your bouquet.
- Have your going away car decorated with the traditional 'JUST MARRIED' banner and trailing tin cans. Ask someone you know well to do this so you don't end up with any horrible surprises!
- Rent a flash car – a Ferrari, Porsche, or Bentley.
- Have the disco play 'Auld Lang Syne' as a tribute to your friends.
- A South African tradition is for all the guests to form a human arch that the bride and groom duck through.
- Why not rent a helicopter for the ultimate send off!
- If there is a river running through the venue's grounds, ask a friend to row you both around the corner and out of sight as a farewell. Decorate the boat with tin cans and streamers – it will be a great photo for the album!
- As your car departs down the drive, arrange for fireworks to go off on either side of the drive.
- Rent a Harley Davidson, and you and your new husband can zoom off into the sunset.
- If you are both proficient horse riders, why not canter away down the drive, tossing your bouquet over one shoulder as you go.
- If you are leaving at sunset, why not hire a hot air balloon to whisk you both away!

Honeymoons and first night magic

Your honeymoon should be discussed when you start planning your wedding. You should consider the amount you would be happy to spend and have a few ideas of where you would like to go. Once the wedding celebrations are over it will be your first opportunity as a married couple to escape the limelight and spend some special time together, so don't pressurise yourselves into thinking you must have a holiday of a lifetime; just think about how this time could be enjoyed together.

Nowadays, many couples choose to spend their first night as a married couple at or near their wedding reception venue. It gives them the chance to see friends and family the morning after the wedding, before they are whisked away to their honeymoon destination.

First night preparations

If you need to travel from your reception venue to the hotel where you will spend your first night, make sure you ask the best man to check what time your transport will be picking you up.

Prepare your luggage well in advance so that you can give it to the best man to take to your hotel so that everything is in place when you arrive.

Try not to give too much away about where you will be staying. You don't want any unwanted surprises in your room!

Honeymoon bliss!

Make sure you give yourselves enough time to get to the first destination on your honeymoon trail, whether it's an airport or ferry terminal. Don't give yourselves the headache of having to race around; you should be relaxing and enjoying each moment. You will be happily exhausted after your wedding day and things will have passed by in a blur, so take your time and don't get stressed – consider the possibility of not going on honeymoon for one or two days following the wedding to allow yourselves time to recover.

TIPS

❧ Look into honeymoon destinations as early as you can. Take your time to choose exactly where you want to go and what you want to do when you're there.

❧ Narrow your choices down to a handful of destinations, then get the travel agent to do the hard work of finding the perfect retreat for you.

❧ When booking your honeymoon make sure you consider all additional costs. If you choose an all-inclusive resort holiday make sure it is with a reputable company like Sandals or Couples. Sometimes, drinks, tips and airport tax are not included in the overall price of the holiday, so make sure you have a kitty to cover these expenses.

❧ If you choose a destination that requires vaccinations, ensure you get them done as far in advance of your wedding as possible. You don't want to risk a reaction that may cause a rash or even symptoms of the flu on your big day.

❧ Make sure your passport details match your booking reservations. If you do want to change your name on your passport you will need the registrar to sign the relevant passport application form. Make sure you take your wedding certificate along on your travels to verify your change of status.

❧ Take out some travel insurance to cover your holiday. Remember that things don't always go as planned.

❧ Go with the flow and enjoy every minute together.

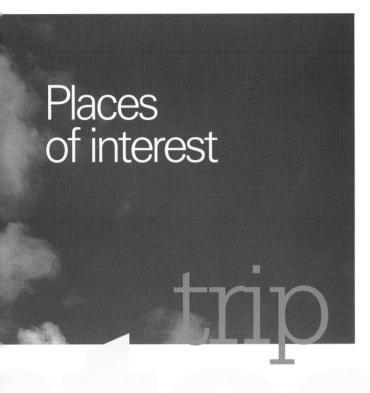

Places of interest

Adventure

For the adventurous couple who want to explore and who have a passion for something a little different, why not try one of the following.

Kenya offers a fabulous destination in terms of both wildlife and climate. Why not combine a resort holiday to restore your energies, with a safari to visit the spectacular untamed and unparalleled beauty of Kenya's wilderness.

New York The Big Apple is always buzzing – visit tourist spots like the Empire State Building or the Statue of Liberty. Take a helicopter ride over this magnificent city or visit trendy Greenwich village or Soho for a truly cosmopolitan experience.

Exotic

For those of you who have always craved the exotic, why not try the Orient and experience the beauty of Thailand or Singapore.

Thailand is a great destination for romance, in 5-star luxury hotels and resorts with spectacular beachside locations. What more could you ask for!

Singapore offers a wealth of culture, excitement and shopping heaven. It's also a good destination if you want to travel onto other Far Eastern delights such as Bali, Lombok or Bintan – smaller islands that offer a tropical paradise in which to pamper and bathe the senses.

Romantic

For the romantics among us, try one of the following.

Bahamas These islands are popular for honeymooners. There are 700 to choose from, so you can make your dream trip totally unique and special. Try glass bottom boat trips, wind surfing, sailing and snorkelling in the tropical azure sea and romantic walks across sun-drenched beaches.

Barbados, Grand Cayman, St Lucia, the Seychelles and Jamaica are also popular romantic destinations. All offer facilities which include horse riding, wind surfing, cruises, 24-hour dining, golf, scuba, excursions and waterskiing.

Effortless

For something a little closer to home, why not try Europe.

Portugal offers a superb mix of excitement and relaxation! Lisbon is a vibrant city to explore and sight-see, with the advantage of beautiful beaches nearby to allow you to escape and find peace and tranquillity.

Paris is a city of love, with some fabulous sights to visit, shops to indulge in and cuisine to salivate over!

Italy has some incredibly beautiful cities, as well as some wonderful beach resorts to escape to. Why not do a two-centre-style holiday and get the best of both worlds!

Suppliers & sources

Part 1
First things first

The engagement

Announcing the engagement

The Times   020 7782 7347
The Guardian   020 7713 4069
The Daily Telegraph   020 7538 6870
The Daily Mail   020 7938 6427

For details of your local newspaper, see Yellow Pages

The engagement ring

Allen Brown Gallery
Heart of the Country
Swinfen
Nr Lichfield
Staffs WS14 9QR
01543 481948
www.allenbrown.co.uk
Specialist in unique handmade pieces of jewellery.

Asprey & Garrard
167 New Bond Street
London W1
020 7493 6767
www.asprey-garrard.com
Beautiful, timeless, elegant pieces of jewellery.

Beverly Hills Jewellers
108 Hatton Garden
London EC1
020 7405 4847
One of the largest ranges of engagement and wedding rings in the country.

Bramwells Jewellers
23–24 Post House Wynd
Darlington DL3 7LP
01325 464175
and
24 Elvet Bridge
Durham DH1 3AA
0191 386 8006
Have been helping couples to choose their wedding rings for more than 100 years.

Electrum Gallery
21 South Molton Street
London W1
020 7629 6325
Unique and exciting contemporary jewellery.

Tiffany
25 Old Bond Street
London W1
020 7409 2790
www.tiffany.com
For the ultimate engagement ring.

Christian Bauer
08000 640840
Branches nationwide.

H. Samuel
0800 389 4683
www.hsamuel.co.uk
Branches nationwide.

The National Association of Goldsmiths
78a Luke Street
London EC2
020 7613 4445
The professional trade association for jewellers. Can supply a list of members in your area, as well as advice on buying your rings.

Timing is everything

Wedding co-ordinators

Siobhan Craven-Robins
Wedding Co-ordinator
020 7481 4338
All the help and advice you need in planning your perfect day.

Debbie Dwek
Wedding Co-ordination
0208 446 9501
debbi.dwek@lineone.net
www.deborahdwekweddings.co.uk

Patricia Rogerson
020 8449 3372
www.patricia-rogerson.com
One of the UK's leading wedding co-ordinators.

Wedding Co-ordination by
Marvellous Moments
01789 267728
www.weddingcoordinatorsuk.com
Draws on a wide range of contacts and experience to create the wedding of your dreams.

The Wedding Design Company
01252 350678
www.yourweddingdesign.com
A unique service from a young, energetic company.

How to tie the knot

Church of England
Enquiry Centre
Church House
Great Smith Street
London SW1P 3NZ
020 7898 1000
www.church-of-england.co.uk

Church of Scotland
121 George Street
Edinburgh EH2 4YN
0131 225 5722

Catholic Enquiry Office
The Chase Centre
114 West Heath Road
London NW3 7TX
020 8458 3316

General Register Office of
England & Wales
PO Box 2
Southport
Merseyside PR8 2JD
0151 471 4200

General Register Office for Scotland
New Register House
Edinburgh EH1 3YT
0131 314 4447

General Register Office for
Northern Ireland
49–55 Chichester Street
Belfast BT1 4HH
028 90252000

General Registrar for Dublin
00 353 1671 1000

Jewish Marriage Council
23 Ravenhurst Avenue
London NW4 4EE
020 8203 6311

For civil ceremony venues, see Themed
Weddings.

Marrying abroad

Contact Marks and Spencer for travel
insurance 0800 068 3918

Airtours
08702 412568

British Airways Holidays
0845 6060 747
www.batravelshops.com

Caribbean Connection
01244 355300
www.classic-connection.co.uk

Caribbean Expressions
020 7431 2131
www.expressionsholidays.co.uk

Cosmos
0161 480 3929
www.cosmos-holidays.co.uk

Couples Resorts
0208 900 1913
www.couples.com

Elegant Resorts
0870 908 2329
www.elegantresorts.co.uk

First Choice
0161 742 2262

Hayes & Jarvis
0870 8989890
www.hayes-jarvis.com

Italia Romantica
020 8830 2090
www.italiaromantica.co.uk

JMC
0870 789 3911
www.jmc.com

Kuoni
01306 747007
www.kuoni.co.uk

Sandals
0800 742 742
www.sandals.com

Thomson
0870 550 2555
www.thomson-holidays.co.uk

Tradewinds
0870 751 0009
www.tradewinds.co.uk

Tropical Places
0800 083 6662
www.tropicalplaces.co.uk

Unijet
0870 2424 247
www.unijet.com

Virgin Holidays
01293 456789
www.virgin.com

www.weddingdreams.com
The authority on weddings in Las Vegas.

www.weddings-abroad.com
*Over 400 locations for your overseas
wedding.*

Snowland, Lapland
00 358 16 316302
www.fintravel.com
Get married in the Snowcastle!

If music be the food of love...

Horizon Music
01569 764457
Music for every occasion.

Music At Your Service
01905 358474
*Choirs, soloists and organists.
Nationwide.*

Music For A While
01923 291633
*Trumpeters, string quartets, harpists,
vocalists, pianists and choirs. Nationwide.*

The Professional Musicians Network
020 7639 3331
*Contact for a list of musicians in your
area.*

Sternberg-Clarke
020 8877 1102
www.sternberg-clarke.co.uk
*Supplied the orchestra for Posh and
Becks' wedding!*

The Wedding Music Company
020 8293 3392
www.weddingmusic.co.uk
*Offers a wide variety of music for civil
and church ceremonies and receptions.
Nationwide.*

The price of love

Wedding Insurance

Marks and Spencer wedding insurance
0800 316 5985

Part 2
Doing it your way

Themed weddings

Civil ceremony and reception venues

Valentine

Eastnor Castle
Ledbury
Herefordshire HR81RL
01531 633160
www.eastnorcastle.com
The perfect fairytale castle.

Hedingham Castle
Castle Hedingham
Halstead, Essex
01787 460261
*One of the best preserved Norman keeps
in England.*

Chillingham Castle
Chillingham
Nr Alnwick
Northumberland NE66 5NJ
01668 215359
*A medieval fortress set in Italian gardens
featuring a lake and stunning views.*

Powderham Castle
Exeter EX6 8JQ
01626 890243
*Picturesque medieval castle set in a deer
park.*

Thornbury Castle
Thornbury
Nr Bristol
South Gloucestershire BS35 1HH
01454 288182
*A magnificent Tudor castle-palace set in
historic gardens and parkland.*

Easter

Cambridge Cottage
Kew Gardens
37 Kew Green
Royal Botanic Garden
Kew
Richmond TW9 3AB
020 8332 5641
A Grade II listed 18th-century building set in 300 acres of Kew Gardens.

Longleat
The Estate Office
Warminster
Wiltshire BA12 7NW
01985 845424
The Orangery at Longleat is set in informal gardens featuring the Maze of Love and a secret garden.

The Orangery
Margham Park
South Wales
01639 881635
Set in acres of beautiful ornamental gardens.

Tatton Park
Knutsford
Cheshire WA16 6QN
01625 534406
Owned by the National Trust and overlooking an Italian garden, deer park and lakes.

Temple of Concord and Victory
Stowe Landscape Gardens
Buckinghamshire MK18 5EH
01280 822850
Classic temple with views over Grecian valley.

Under the sea

Carlyon Bay Hotel
St Austell
Cornwall
01726 812304
Set on craggy cliffs on the Cornish riviera, with spectacular sea views.

London Aquarium
County Hall
South Bank
London SE1
020 7967 8000
www.londonaquarium.co.uk
Host your reception surrounded by sea life!

Royal Naval College
Greenwich
London
0800 389 3341
A magnificent Baroque building, designed by Christopher Wren.

SS Great Britain
Great Western Dock
Gas Ferry Road
Bristol BS1 6TY
0117 922 5737
A romantic Victorian luxury passenger ship.

Temple Island
Henley-on-Thames
Oxfordshire
01491 572153
Georgian folly on a picturesque island on one of the most beautiful stretches of the Thames; you and your guests approach the island by boat!

Autumnal flair

The London Dungeon
28–34 Tooley Street
London, SE1
020 7403 0606
www.thedungeons.com
For a truly dramatic wedding reception!

Bassetsbury Manor
Bassetsbury Lane
High Wycombe HP11 1BB
01494 421889
A 17th-century manor house overlooking the Rye River, next to a millstream.

Coombe Abbey
Brinklow Road
Coventry CV3 2AB
01203 450450
A 12th-century abbey which has been tastefully restored into a luxury hotel.

The Celtic Manor
Coldra Woods
Newport
Gwent
01633 413000
www.celticmanor.com
One of the UK's most impressive hotel and golf resorts, with stunning views of the Usk Valley.

Grafton Manor
Bromsgrove
Worcestershire B61 7HA
01527 579007
www.graftonmanorhotel.co.uk
A 16th-century manor house, with its own chapel, perfect for a blessing after the ceremony.

Christmas

Armathwaite Hall
Bassenthwaite Lake
Keswick
Cumbria CA12 4RE
01768 776551
A 17th-century stately home, now a family-owned hotel featuring wood-panelled rooms and log fires.

Bailiffscourt Hotel
Climping
Littlehampton
West Sussex BN17 5RW
01903 723511
www.hshotels.co.uk
A listed building featuring oak beams, log fires and four-poster bed.

Hambleton Hall
Hambleton
Oakham
Rutland
Leicestershire LE15 8TH
01572 756991
www.hambletonhall.com
A luxury hotel with Michelin-starred restaurant and views over Rutland Water.

Knowsley Hall
Knowsley Park
Prescott
Merseyside L34 4AG
0151 489 4827
A stately home and safari park, which can be let complete with butlers and maids.

Rudding Park House
Rudding Park
Follifoot
Harrogate
North Yorkshire HG3 1JH
01423 871350
www.rudding-park.co.uk
A Grade I listed Regency house set in extensive grounds featuring woodland and lakes.

Contemporary

116 Pall Mall
London SW1Y 5ED
020 7451 3107
A Grade I listed building designed by architect John Nash.

One Aldwych
London
020 7300 1000
The ultimate in minimalist cool.

Burgh Island Hotel
Burgh Island
Bigbury-on-Sea
South Devon
01548 810514
Ultra-stylish Art Deco hotel on its own island.

House for an Art Lover
Glasgow
0141 353 4770
Designed by Charles Rennie Mackintosh; perfect for lovers of 20th-century art.

Roof Gardens
Kensington High Street
London W8 5ED
020 7937 7994
English Heritage roof garden club set in over an acre of landscaped gardens and fountains.

Other venues of interest

BA London Eye
020 7654 0813
Tie the knot on the Millennium Wheel for city romance at its best.

Chelsea Football Club
Fulham Road
London SW6 1HS
020 7385 5545
The perfect venue for Chelsea fans. Contact the ground of your own favourite team as most are now licensed for civil weddings.

Crazy Horse Saloon
Frontierland Theme Park
Marine Road West
Morecambe Bay LA4 4DG
01524 410024
Cowboys and Indians are on hand at this western-style saloon bar situated in an American theme park.

Granada Studio Tours
Water Street
Manchester M60 9EA
0161 832 9090
Host your reception on Baker Street or in the Rovers Return.

Holdsworth House
Holdsworth
West Yorkshire
01422 240024
The pretty gazebo is Britain's smallest licensed venue; perfect for an intimate ceremony.

Le Manoir Aux Quat' Saisons
Church Road
Great Milton
Oxon OX44 7PB
01844 278881
Raymond Blanc's 15th-century manor house and famous Michelin-starred restaurant.

London Zoo
Regent's Park
London NW1 4RY
Arrive at this venue by canal boat, and host your reception in one of the animal houses.

National Railway Museum
Leeman Road
York YO 26 4XJ
01904 621261
Dine on the central platform with your guests!

Odeon Leicester Square
London, WC2
020 7930 6111
Tie the knot in front of the big screen at Britain's most famous cinema.

Pump Room and Roman Baths
Stall Street
Bath BA1 1LZ
01225 477782
The perfect place for an elegant civil wedding.

Ritz Hotel
150 Piccadilly
London W1V 0BR
020 7493 8181
The ultimate in stylish glamour!

Royal Pavilion
Brighton
West Sussex
01273 292815
George IV's fantasy seaside palace provides a romantic setting for a wedding.

Silverstone Circuit
Silverstone
Towcester
Northants NN12 8TN
01327 320415
The perfect venue for the motor racing fanatic! Hold your wedding overlooking the famous start line.

Stephen Joseph Theatre
Westborough
Scarborough
North Yorkshire Y011 1JW
01723 370540
As many as 400 guests can be seated in the audience as you take centre stage in this 1930s cinema.

For further venues, contact:

Country House Wedding Venues
01244 572012
www.wedding-venues.co.uk

Perfect Wedding Venues
01476 571081
www.perfectvenues.co.uk

The Location Solution Company
07000 494373

Local Services
Office of National Statistics
Smedley Hydro
Trafalgar Road
Southport
Merseyside PR8 2HH

Themed wedding 'dress'

Carousel Costumes
120 Shrubland Street
Leamington Spa CV31 2AR
01926 881356
Outfits for medieval weddings.

Angels and Bermans
119 Shaftesbury Avenue
London WC2H 8AE
020 7836 5678
www.fancydress.com
Outfits from film and TV shows; a huge range of costumes.

Costume Company
Tyn-y-bwlch
Glan-yr-afon
Corwen
Denbighshire
North Wales LL21 0HE
www.themedweddings.co.uk
Historical designs for all periods.

Royal Exchange Costume Hire
47–53 Swan Street
Manchester M4 5JY
0161 932 6800/0161 833 9333
Costumes and made-to-order dresses.

Personalising your day

Bougainvillea
01404 811467
www.bougainvillea.uk.com
A stunning array of natural and biodegradable bougainvillea confetti.

Forever Memories
01384 878111
www.forevermemories.co.uk
Personalised cameras and other wedding accessories.

Ice Creations
01580 892977
www.icesculpturesuk.com
Stunning personalised ice sculptures.

National Weaving Company
01834 861757
Personalised woven tape/ribbon.

Paperchase
020 7467 6200
Handmade papers for cones, metallic confetti, useful boxes and bags. Branches nationwide.

Picture Perfect Cameras
01684 311800
www.pictureperfectcameras.co.uk
Wedding table cameras.

Prices Candles
110 York Road
London SW11 3RU
020 7228 3345
Supplier of candles for Themed weddings section.

The Real Flower Petal Confetti Company
01386 555045
www.confettidirect.co.uk
Beautiful naturally dried flowers in all their original colours.

RTL
01592 263352
Personalised miniatures and personalised labels for your wine.

V.V. Rouleaux
54 Sloane Square
London SW1
020 7730 3125
Fantastic selection of ribbons, silk and fabric flowers.

The Very Nice Company
01884 232152
www.verynicecompany.co.uk
Confetti in all colours and styles, chocolate dragees, organza bags.

The Wedding Camera Store
020 7622 4323
Personalised cameras.

Wedding Bubbles
01288 353838
Wedding-themed bubble blowers.

Wedding Candles
01689 828994
www.weddingcandles.co.uk
Beautiful, individually hand-crafted candles.

Wedding Collection by Liquid Assets
01279 428899
www.liquidassets.co.uk
Personalised labels for bottles.

www.confetti.co.uk
For disposable cameras, a wide range of confetti, and countless other unique wedding-related items.

Also see Alternative entertainment and Wedding favours.

Part 3
Behind the scenes

The bride

Before visiting any of the stockists listed below, please call first in case an appointment is needed.

The dress

Berkertex Bride
www.bbride.com
Stockists nationwide.

Bliss Bridal Centre
178–180 St Georges Road
Bolton BL1 2PH
01204 385249
and
149 Great Ducie Street
Manchester M3 1FB
0161 839 2266
Stockists for all the top designers and manufacturers.

Bridal House of Chester
66–68 Northgate Street
Chester
01244 340707
Leading brideswear specialist.

The Bridal Room
31 Sun Street
Hitchin
Hertfordshire
01462 432889
Designerwear without the designer price tag.

By Storm
11 Chiltern Street
London W1
020 7224 7888
and
156 Milngavie Road
Bearsden
Glasgow G61 3EA
0141 942 8900
www.bystorm.co.uk
Inspired and individual designs.

Caroline Castigliano Boutiques
62 Berners Street
London
020 7636 8212
Dresses by leading designers and an in-house label.

Chanticleer
The Wedding Shop
21 Regent Street
Cheltenham
Gloucestershire
01242 226502

Anna Christina
Unit C
Oakfield Works
Oakfield Road
Walthamstow London E17 5RP
020 8527 7001
Exclusive designer bridalwear.

Confetti and Lace
Farsley
Nr Pudsey
Leeds
0113 236 0652

The Cotswold Frock Shop
3 Talbot Court
Stow-on-the-Wold
Gloucestershire
01451 832309
Made-to-measure and ready-to-wear designer dresses and two in-house labels.

Neil Cunningham
28 Sackville Street
London W1X 3DA
020 7437 5793
Exquisite dresses from this leading designer.

Catherine Davighi
121 Adnitt Road
Northampton
01604 604122
Contemporary and traditional silk gowns.

Eleganza Sposa
117 Quarry Street
Hamilton
Lanarkshire
01698 303050
Exclusive wedding dresses.

Elizabeth of York
12 Blake Street
York Y01 2QG
01904 658600
In-house designs and ready-to-wear designer dresses.

Farideh
32 John Street
Sacriston
Durham DH7 6HH
0191 371 1137
Ready-to-wear and made-to-measure dresses.

Favourbrook
19–21 Piccadilly Arcade
Jermyn Street
London SW1Y 6NH
020 7491 2337
www.favourbrook.com
Combining exclusive and luxurious fabrics with elegant and sophisticated styles.

Diana Gray
11a Upper Northgate Street
Chester CH1 4EE
01244 378220
*Ready-to-wear and made-to-measure
dresses.*

Gypsophilia
205–207 Bacup Road
Rawtenstall
Rossendale
Lancashire
01706 213242
Individual bridalwear.

Alan Hannah
7A Chaseside Works
Chelmsford Road
London N14 4JN
020 8882 0007
www.alanhannah.co.uk
Leading wedding dress designer.

Trudy Hanson
All Saints Road
Notting Hill
London W11 1HE
020 7792 1300
www.trudyhanson.co.uk
*Couture bridalwear, shoes, veils, tiaras,
lingerie, bridesmaids' dresses.*

Sharon Hoey
19 Upper Mount Street
Dublin
Ireland
353 676 2772
*Contemporary classics for the modern
bride.*

Hoops a Daisy
219 Barnsley Road
Sandal
Wakefield
West Yorkshire WF1 5NU
01924 240312
www.hoopsadaisy.a39.com
*Superb collection of over 200 bridal
gowns.*

Isobel Love
70–72 Antrim Street
Lisburn
Northern Ireland
02892 669911

Jeni Kershaw
83 High Street
Brampton
Cambridgeshire
01480 412310
*Couture hand-embroidered gowns and
designer dresses.*

Rena Koh Collection
61a Queens Street
Edinburgh EH2 4NA
0131 225 8955
Ready-to-wear dresses.

Kiss Bridal Design
3 Talbot Court
Stow on the Wold
Gloucestershire GL54 1BQ
01451 832309
*One of the smallest bridal shops in the
UK, but the selection and advice given is
first rate.*

Lace Bridal Fashions
154 Ashley Road
Hale
Cheshire
0161 941 7374
The latest fashions for the modern bride.

Lesley's Bridalwear
The Old Chapel
225 Warwick Road
Solihull
West Midlands
0121 706 6060
*A huge variety of styles, including many
designer gowns.*

The London Designer Bridal Room
3rd Floor
Dickins & Jones
Regent Street
London W1
020 7434 3966
A fabulous selection of gowns.

London Bride and Groom
201 Walworth Road
London SE17 1RL
020 7703 6796
www.londonbrideandgroom.co.uk
*A wide range of competitively priced
gowns.*

Matchmaker Bride
137 & 139 Kings Road
Brentwood
Essex CM14 4DR
01277 263500
www.matchmakerbride.co.uk
Stunning collection of bridal gowns.

Mirror Mirror
37 Park Road
London N8 8TE
020 8348 2113
www.mirrormirror,uk.com
A mecca for stylish brides and celebrities.

Morgan Davies
62 Cross Street
Islington
London N1
020 7354 3414
*An amazing selection of dresses from
some of the top British and European
designers.*

Suzanne Neville
44 High Street
Harrow on the Hill
Middlesex HA1 3LL
020 8423 3161
www.suzanneneville.com
*A leading couture wedding dress
designer.*

One and Only
81 Newton Road
Mumbles
Swansea
Wales
01792 361477
*Own-label gowns for the fashion-
conscious bride.*

The Pantiles Bride
Tunbridge Wells
Kent
01892 514515
www.pantilesbride.com
*Winner of the Best Emporium Award in
the Bridal Buyer Retail Awards for the
Millennium.*

Anne Priscilla
8 Dixon Street
St Enoch's
Glasgow
0141 222 2504
Made-to-order dresses.

Evangeline Rose
15A Church Street
Godalming
Surrey GU7 1EL
01483 415199
www.evangeline-rose.co.uk
Designs to suit every modern bride.

Donna Salado Bridalwear
28 Abington Grove
Northampton NN1 4QX
01604 792869
www.donnasaladobridalwear.com
Designer bridalwear.

Serafina
Redloh House
2 Michael Road
London SW6 2AD
020 7731 5215
Elegant, sophisticated dresses.

Silkworm
4 Golden Square
Aberdeen
01224 646 481
Stockist of silk designer ranges.

Surrey Brides
10 Castle Street
Weybridge
Surrey
01932 846812
Made-to-measure designer dresses.

Angela Vickers Handmade Bridal Design
Studio 1
Fashion Designer Studios
69–73 Lower Parliament Street,
Nottingham
0115 941 5616
*Over 100 couture gowns, both modern
and historical in style.*

Catherine Walker
46 Fulham Road
London SW3
010 7581 8811
Made-to-measure and couture dresses.

Watters and Watters, via Virgin Bride
(020 7766 9001) and Mirror Mirror (020
8348 2113) in the UK
www.watters.com
Dresses for extraordinary occasions.

The Wedding Centre
Maple House
21–23 Little Marlow Road
Marlow
Bucks
01628 478888/477367
www.weddingcentre.com
Made-to-measure designer dresses.

The Wedding Company of Warwick
76 Smith Street
Warwick
01926 494929
*An excellent selection of top designer
and manufacturer gowns.*

The Wedding Studio
59 Queens Road
Weybridge
Surrey KT13 9UQ
01932 841066
Stock gowns by many leading designers.

The Wedding Vault
21 High Street, Pewsey
Wiltshire SN9 5AF
01672 563337
www.theweddingvault.co.uk
*Stunning designer gowns and
accessories.*

Young Bride and Groom
98 The Parade
Watford
Herts
01923 249664
www.youngbrideandgroom.co.uk
*Ready-to-wear and made-to-measure
dresses.*

Basia Zarzycka
52 Sloane Street
London SW1
020 7730 1660
www.basias.com
High-quality, imaginative gowns.

Wedding dress services

The Bridal Gown Exchange
The Mill House
Badger
Burnhill Green
Wolverhampton
01746 783066
Once-worn designer dresses to buy.

The Wedding Dress Exchange
44 Lavengro Road
London SE27
020 8473 4416
*Immaculate once-worn and sample
gowns.*

The Royal School of Needlework
020 8943 1432
For embroidery details on your dress.

Designer Alterations
2 Queenstown Mews
Battersea
London SW8 3QG
020 7498 4360
*Alterations and repair work on your dress.
Also offer hand-finished valeting and
secret storage service.*

Accessorising the bride

Headdresses and veils

Blossom
Unit 3
Itchel Home Farm
Itchel Lane
Crondall
Farnham
Surrey
01252 851733
www.blossom.co.uk
Tiaras and veils.

Butler & Wilson
20 South Molton Street
London W1
020 7409 2955
Tiaras and hair accessories.

Cant Bridal Headdresses
14 Dewhurst Road
Harwood
Bolton BL2 3NE
01204 533303
*Tiaras/hair accessories designed
exclusively for Cant.*

Polly Edwards
01903 882127
www.pollyedwards.com
Headdresses and tiaras.

Philippa J. Eyland
020 7729 7350
Headdresses and tiaras.

Halo & Co.
36 High Street
Repton
Derby
01283 704305
Tiaras.

Irresistible
01403 871449
*Tiaras, headdresses, combs, flowers,
veils and hats.*

Joyce Jackson Bridal Veils
01745 343689
www.joycejacksonveils.com
Wide range of veils.

Linzi Jay
Units 104–108
Glenfield Park Site One
Phillips Road
Blackburn
Lancashire BB1 5PF
01254 665104
www.linzijay.co.uk
*One of the leading suppliers of bridal
accessories in the UK and Europe.*

Johnny Loves Rosie
020 7375 3574
Hair accessories, fake flowers and tiaras.

Isabel Kurtenbach Design
18 Earls Court Square
London SW5 9DN
020 7854 9647
www.isabelkurtenbach.com
Handmade tiaras and bridal accessories.

Rhapsody Headdresses
2 Corporation Road
Loughor
Swansea SA4 6SD
01792 893214
www.weddingheaddresses.co.uk
Exclusive range of handmade tiaras.

Serendipity
01342 713828
Designer tiaras.

Stupid Cupid
74 Fairview Road
Taplow
Berkshire SL6 0NQ
01628 542730
www.stupidcupid.co.uk
Tiaras and veils.

Jenny Wicks Designs
0161 434 6855
www.jennywicks.com
Exquisite individual headwear.

www.veilsdirect.co.uk
*A selection of exquisite handmade veils
and bridal accessories.*

Lingerie

Agent Provocateur
6 Broadwick Street
London W1V
020 7439 0229
and
Pont Street
London SW1X
020 7235 0229
www.agentprovocateur.com

Bravissimo
0700 244 2727
www.bravissimo.co.uk
Larger size bras.

Charnos
01159 322191
Nationwide.

Gossard
01525 859769
Nationwide.

La Perla
163 Sloane Street
London SW1
020 7245 0527

La Senza
020 8561 9784
Nationwide.

The Lingerie Company
www.the-lingerie-company.co.uk

Janet Reger
10 Beauchamp Place
London SW3
020 7584 9368

Rigby and Peller
2 Hans Road
London SW3
020 7589 9293
and
22A Conduit Street
London W1
020 7491 2200

Triumph
01793 720232
Nationwide.

www.simplylingerie.com

Garters

Arsenic and Old Lace
01244 811721

E & P Designs
01733 840455

HKE
01323 728988

Shoes

Anello & Davide
47 Beauchamp Place
London SW3
020 7225 2468
Bridal shoes and bags.

Joseph Azagury
73 Knightsbridge
London SW1X 7RA
020 7259 5074
High-fashion shoes.

Jimmy Choo
20 Motcomb Street
London SW1
020 7235 0242
The ultimate designer shoes.

Diane Hassall
020 8223 0505
Handmade bridal shoes.

HKE
01323 728988
*Silk and satin shoes for adults and
children.*

Emma Hope
53 Sloane Square
London SW1W 8AX
020 7259 9566
Elegant bridal shoes.

Rainbow Club/Else/Gabriella & Lucido
Hennock Court
Hennock Road
Marsh Barton
Exeter EX2 8RU
01392 207030
www.rainbowclub.co.uk
*One of the largest bridal footwear
manufacturers, using the world's best
dyeable fabrics.*

Wedding Shoes Direct
01782 635515
www.weddingshoesdirect.co.uk
Over 8,000 pairs of shoes in stock.

Bride's bouquet

See Heaven scent.

Hair and beauty

Carolyn K Make-up
020 8614 1951
www.carolynk.co.uk
Offers full bridal make-up service.

Clarins
020 7629 2979
*Over-the-counter makeovers and make-
up lessons in Clarins studios nationwide.*

C n C Beauty
020 8778 2911
*Professional photographic make-up
artists.*

Hair Extensions by Jealous
079 463 99011
www.JealousHAIR.com
For fairytale, celebrity-looking hair.

Marianne Kerr
020 8340 5789
A leading film hair and make-up artist.

Molton Brown
020 7499 6474
www.moltonbrown.co.uk
*Offer in-store make-up consultations and
lessons. Branches nationwide.*

Moving Make-up and Hair Artistry
9 Willcocks Close
Chessington
Surrey KT9 1HG
020 8391 4201
www.movingmakeup.co.uk
*A complete mobile make-up and
hairstyling service.*

The bride's attendants

Elizabeth Amys
01453 751204
For little bridesmaids.

Sophie English Couture
020 7828 9007
*An exclusive range of glamorous
bridesmaid dresses.*

Eternity
01423 565444
Flowergirl dresses for girls aged 2–14.

Head Over Heels
366 Malden Road
Worcester Park
Surrey KT4 7NW
020 8330 2950
*An interesting collection of bridesmaid
gowns.*

Hyacinth
020 8852 2212
Perfect for trendy bridesmaids.

JLM Couture
0800 328 1531
Beautiful bridesmaid dresses.

LouLou Bridalwear
Studio F20
Europa Trading Estate
Fraser Road
Erith
Kent DA8 1QL
01322 440225
www.loulou.co.uk
*One of Britain's leading bridesmaids
companies.*

Serafina
Redloh House
2 Michael Road
London SW6 2AD
020 7731 5215
*Simple, elegant outfits for bridesmaids,
flowergirls and pageboys.*

Vertbaudet
0500 012345
Special occasion wear for ages 0–16.

Virgin Bride
The Grand Buildings
Northumberland Avenue
London WC2
020 7321 0866
www.virgin.com/bride
*The largest bridal emporium in the UK
stocking a stunning array of bridesmaid
dresses.*

Watters and Watters, via Virgin Bride
(020 7766 9001) and Mirror Mirror (020
8348 2113) in the UK
www.watters.com
*Stunning contemporary bridesmaid
dresses.*

Also see Brides – The dress, as many of
the outlets listed will also stock
bridesmaid dresses.

The hen party

Activity Superstore
01799 526526
www.activitysuperstore.com
Offers activities such as parachuting.

The Adventure Company
01768 775351
www.stagandhen.co.uk
*Offers a wide range of events across the
UK and Europe.*

The Body Shop Direct
08459 050 0607
*At-home hen nights perusing a selection
of Body Shop products.*

The Chocolate Society
01423 322238
www.chocolate.co.uk
Host a chocolate testing party!

Evening Entertainment Company
0800 328 5628
www.eveningentertainment.com
*Nights out for groups of any size.
Nationwide pick-up and drop-off service.*

Great Escapades
01432 830083
www.greatescapades.co.uk
*Try paint balling, riding, sailing or
quad biking.*

Party Gifts Limited
01989 750903
partygifts@hotmail.com
*Offers an array of gift packs dedicated to
hen nights.*

The Party Bus
020 7233 0022
www.partybus.co.uk
*Travel to various nightclubs on a double
decker bus with on-board DJ.*

Red Letter Days
020 8442 2000
www.redletterdays.co.uk
Offers a wide variety of themed days out.

Red Seven Leisure
0127 367 1177
www.henparty.co.uk
The perfect hen party.

Ann Summers Party Hotline
020 8645 8200
www.annsummers.com
For G-strings and giggles at home.

www.hens.org
0870 787 5959
Tailor-made hen weekends.

www.lastminute.com
*For last minute bargain getaways and
events.*

Health spas

The Sanctuary Spa
12 Floral Street
Covent Garden
London WC2E 9DH
08700 630300

Champneys
Wigginton
Nr Tring
Herts HP23 6HY
01442 291111
and
21 Piccadilly
London W1
020 7255 8000

Hoar Cross Hall
Hoar Cross
Nr Yoxall
Staffordshire DE13 8QS
01283 575671

Nirvana Spa
Wokingham
0118 977 4976

The groom

Menswear

Gary Anderson
36 Chiltern Street
London W1U 7QJ
020 7224 2241
and
34–35 Savile Row
London W1X 1AG
020 7287 6661
www.garyanderson.co.uk
Leading designer and menswear retailer.

Anthony
53 High Street
Billericay
Essex CM12 9AX
01277 651140
www.anthonyformalwear.co.uk
Exclusive formalwear.

Fantasy waistcoats
Rynkild House
Burnett Road
Streetly
Sutton Coldfield
West Midlands B74 3EL
0121 353 2848
www.fantasywaistcoats.com
*An extensive range of waistcoats in all
sizes.*

Favourbrook
19–21 Piccadilly Arcade
Jermyn Street
London SW1Y 6NH
020 7493 5500
www.favourbrook.com
High-quality, timeless English tailoring.

Geoffrey (Tailor)
57–59 High Street
The Royal Mile
Edinburgh EH1 1SR
0131 557 0256
www.geoffreykilts.co.uk
For all your Highland dress requirements.

Tom Gilbey
2 New Burlington Place
London W1
020 7734 4877
Bespoke and ready-to-wear suits.

London Bride and Groom
201 Walworth Road
London SE17 1RL
020 7703 6796
www.londonbrideandgroom.co.uk
*A wide range of competitively priced
menswear.*

Moss Bros Hire
020 7447 7200
Branches nationwide.

Neal and Palmer of Jermyn Street
Jermyn Street
11 Piccadilly Arcade
London SW1Y 6NH
020 7495 4094
www.nealandpalmer.com
Groomswear specialists.

The Pantiles Groom
The Pantiles
Tunbridge Wells
Kent TN2 5TE
01892 548511
www.pantilesgroom.co.uk
An exciting range of formal attire.

Virgin Bride Menswear
The Grand Buildings
Northumberland Avenue
London WC2
020 7766 9110
www.virgin.com/bride
An excellent choice of both traditional and contemporary suits and accessories.

Marc Wallace
261 New Kings Road
London SW6 4RB
020 7731 4575
www.marcwallace.com
Suits, waistcoats, shirts and accessories.

Young Bride and Groom
98 The Parade
Watford
Herts
01923 249955
www.youngbrideandgroom.co.uk
One of the finest collections of menswear.

The stag night

Red Letter Days
020 8442 2000
www.redletterdays.co.uk
Offers a wide variety of themed days out.

www.lastminute.com
For last minute bargain getaways and events.

www.stags.org
0870 787 5959
Tailor-made activity weekends.

www.lastnight-stag.co.uk
www.lastnightoffreedom.co.uk

Bands of gold

www.ultimateweddingband.co.uk
See also Engagement rings.

The guests

Stationery

Marks and Spencer
From invitations to orders of service, wedding stationery is a reflection of individual style and personality, capturing the spirit of your special day. Our exclusive selection offers a host of different looks – traditional, humorous and contemporary – with distinguishing touches such as luxurious finishes, foil embossing, laser-cut details, and decorative ribbons and tassels. Every set includes: a wedding invitation, an evening invitation, an order of service, a thank you card which is also designed to be used as a reply card and place card. We offer a choice of invitation wordings including options for church weddings, evening receptions and civil ceremonies. If you have any queries or would like to request samples, chat to our professional advisors at the Personalised Stationery Centre on 0870 241 5893 between 8.30am and 5.30pm, Monday to Friday, and 9am to 5pm, Saturday (excluding bank holidays).

Gift list heaven!

Marks and Spencer
01952 858502
www.marksandspencer.com/giftregistry
Branches nationwide.

Heaven scent

Ace Floral Designs
Headington
Oxford OX3 8RY
01865 762816
www.acefloraldesigns.co.uk
Silk flower specialists – perfect for allergy sufferers and weddings abroad.

Angel Flowers
60 Upper Street
Islington
London N1 0NY
020 7704 6312
www.angel-flowers.co.uk
Voted by Tatler magazine as among the top five florists in London.

Bluebird Flower Market
350 King's Road
Chelsea
London SW3 5UU
020 7559 1141
www.conran.com
Superb fragrant flower market – create wonderful floral designs.

The Country Garden
01824 705179
Bridal and reception flowers throughout the country.

The Flower Store
282 Seven Sisters Road
London N4
020 7561 9287
An impressive array of flowers.

Sophie Hanna Flowers
Arch 48
New Covent Garden
London SW8 5PP
020 7720 0841
www.sophiehannaflowers.com
Strives to make your wedding different and special.

Heavenly Scent Floral Designs
The Garden Workshop
Duckmead Lane
Liss
Hampshire GU33 7JS
01730 892161
www.heavenly-scent.co.uk
Excellent reputation and extensive media coverage.

James James-Crook
102 Fitzalan Road
Arundel
West Sussex BN18 9JY
01903 883239
www.pineappleheads.com
Floral architecture.

McQueens
126 St John's Street
London EC1
020 7251 5505
Suppliers of the flowers shown on pages 100–101.

Jane Packer Flowers
56 James Street
London W1
020 7935 2673
www.jane-packer.co.uk

Michael Pooley Flowers
21 Arlington Way
London EC1
020 7833 5599

Paula Pryke Flowers
20 Penton Street
London N1
020 7837 7336
www.paula-pryke-flowers.com
One of the most innovative florists in the world.

Something Special
Kelsick Road
Ambleside
Cumbria
LA22 0BZ
01539 433848
Dutch flower specialists.

Mary Jane Vaughan at Fast Flowers
609 Fulham Road
London SW6
020 7385 8400
www.maryjanevaughan.co.uk
Winner of the British Bridal Awards, 2001.

Willow Trading
De Courcy's Arcade
Cresswell Lane
Hillhead
Glasgow G12 8AA
0141 357 3915
www.willowtrading.co.uk
Co-ordinating flowers for modern brides and bridesmaids.

Woodhams
1 Aldwych
London WC2
020 7300 0777

Floral preservation

Delphinium Pressed Bridal Bouquets
0161 678 2891
www.pressedflowers.co.uk
Flower pressing.

Flowers Forever
0800 298 5880
Your wedding bouquet preserved and framed in 3D.

Pressed for Time
01489 574668
Bouquet preservation.

You've been framed

Albaphoto
01764 68181
www.albaphoto.com
Wedding photography Scotland-wide.

Fiona Baker Photography
Wood Cottage Studio
Horley
Nr Banbury
Oxfordshire OX15 6BJ
01295 738101
www.fionabaker.co.uk
Modern wedding photography with a feminine touch.

Jo Bradbury
0161 881 6925
www.jobradbury.co.uk
Modern wedding photography.

Camhire.com
0800 652 7384
www.camhire.com
Hire the latest in digital camcorder technology just for your big day.

Tim Fisher Photography
29 Tonbridge Crescent
Harrow
Middlesex HA3 9LE
020 8238 9131
www.t-f-p.com
A distinctive reportage style of wedding photography.

Funky Weddings
020 8452 3076
www.funkyweddings.co.uk

Leigh Goodsell Photography
Kings Lynn
Norfolk PE31 8AY
01485 210841
www.goodsell.ws
Informal, fun, reportage photography.

J & L Wedding and Video Services
020 8841 0239
www.jlvideo.co.uk
Wedding video specialists offering complete, discreet coverage.

Kodak Weddings
0800 0855145
www.KodakWeddings.com
Quality and professional service direct from Kodak.

Memorable Moments Video
Keswick
Sunningvale Avenue
Biggin Hill
Kent TN16 3BZ
0800 174482
www.mmvideos.co.uk
Highly experienced, professional videography.

Oliver Murray Photography
020 8367 3360
www.olivermurray.com
Traditional or informal coverage of your wedding day.

Millhook Video
35 Church Street
Weybridge
Surrey KT13 3DG
01932 843384
www.millhookvideo.co.uk
Creative, artistic videography.

Picture This Photography
01491 671864
www.picturethisphotography.co.uk
Award-winning photographer.

Photography by Liam Bailey
020 7928 7635
www.liambaileywedding.net
Innovative reportage wedding photography.

Salthouse Digital
07989 600038
Professional film-makers of the highest calibre and technical quality.

Steven Pugh
5 Park Lane
Kemsing
Sevenoaks
Kent TN15 6NU
01732 763269
www.stephenpugh.co.uk
International award-winning photographer.

UC Images
London SE23
0870 742 4118
www.ucimages.co.uk
High-quality, artistic work.

The Wedding Photo Agency
01483 860172
Experienced fashion styled wedding photography.

Wedding Videos Direct
0800 917 8251
www.weddingvideosdirect.co.uk
World-class wedding videos.

Other useful contacts:

British Institute of
Professional Photography
01920 464011

Guild of Wedding Photographers
07000 484536

Master Photographers Association
01325 356555

Society of Wedding and
Portrait Photographers
01745 815030

Association of Professional Videomakers
01529 421717
www.apv.org

Institute of Videography
0845 7413626
www.iov.co.uk

The reception

Reception
Event management
DJ-ing services

Chance Organisation
020 7376 5995
Full event management.

The Classic Party Company
01904 468666

The Core Group
020 8871 2232
Full event production.

The Fifth Element Event Design Ltd
020 7610 8630
Full event management.

Jongar Event
020 8443 3333

Moodies
01428 644310
www.moodies.co.uk
One of the most successful and reliable hospitality companies in the UK.

William Bartholomew Party Organising
020 7731 8328
Full event management.

Marquee hire

Raj Tent Club
020 7376 9066
www.rajtentclub.com
Exotic moghul-inspired tents, from a huge Maharajah tent to small Pergola.

Cheshire Marquees
Gatley
Cheadle
Cheshire SK8 4NB
0161 428 1862

HSS Event Hire
0845 7282828
www.hss.com

The Main Event Marquee Company
East Sussex TN19 7QS
01580 860318

Millennium Marquees
01606 737670

Furniture/crockery hire

ABC Hire
010 8641 6700
www.abchire.co.uk
Everything you need for your reception to suit your colour scheme.

Ever Trading
020 8878 4050 for stockists
Engraved glassware and ornate cutlery.

HSS Event Hire
0845 7282828
www.hss.com

The Pier
020 7814 5020
Glassware and china.

Wedding transport

American Classic Hire Co.
01895 421962
Travel in Roy Orbison's 1955 Cadillac!

Austins Vintage Taxi Hire
London
020 8767 0817
www.vintagetaxi.com
Original 1930s taxis and Rolls-Royces.

Mike Berry Vintage Car Hire
Hertfordshire
020 8449 2954
www.wedcars.co.uk
Specialise in 1930s London taxi cabs and Rolls-Royces.

Bespokes
01923 250250
www.bespokes.co.uk
Classics and sports cars. Nationwide.

The Classic Taxi Limo Service
Essex
020 8252 4288

Fleetwood Classic Limousines
London
020 7624 0869

Lord Cars
London
020 7435 1114
and
Hertfordshire
01707 262520
www.lordcars.co.uk
Vintage, classic or modern wedding cars.

Northern Sports Car Hire
01977 668068
www.sportscarhire.net

O'Brien Car Hire
Kent
01322 400123
www.obriencarhire.co.uk

Vintage Wedding Cars
Buckinghamshire
01753 883234

www.vintageweddingscars.co.uk
One of the largest fleet of vintage cars in the country.

Horse-drawn carriages

Capital Carriages
01277 372082
www.capitalcarriages.co.uk

Cinderella's Magic Coach
01491 413322

Courtyard Carriages
01784 482937

Haydn Webb Carriages
0118 988 3334

Orchard Poyle Horse Drawn Carriage Hire
01784 435983

Food and drink!

Annie Fryer Catering
020 7351 4333
www.anniefryer.com
Specialises in providing private clients with individually tailored party planning.

Blue Food Catering
020 7739 0727
Friendly and flexible service and affordable menus. Client list includes Jennifer Lopez and 20th Century Fox.

By Word of Mouth
020 8871 9566
Party organisers and caterers.

Champagne Information Bureau
020 7495 4909

Cooks and Partners
020 7731 5282
Over 30 years experience of creating memorable and stunning weddings nationwide.

Interwine
01628 473 920
Wine supplied to event organisers or private clients.

Lodge Catering
020 8960 5794
www.lodge-catering.co.uk
The official caterers to the Royal Geographic Society, they will tailor-make their service to suit your needs.

Phoenix Catering
01327 351679
www.phoenix-catering.co.uk
First-class service at a venue of your choice throughout the UK.

Sapna Caterers
020 8843 1111
Specialise in authentic Halal cuisine for weddings nationwide.

Simply Delicious
01653 692725
Catering for all occasions.

Tophies Mobile Bar service
01403 217547
Provide drinks and service for your wedding day.

Wedding cakes

Jane Asher's Party Cakes
24 Cale Street
London SW3 3QU
020 7584 6177
www.jane-asher.co.uk
Party cakes and sugarcraft.

Linda Calvert Cakes
01273 474739
Beautiful wedding cakes.

Cake Designs
020 7354 3699
Delivers in London and the south-east.

The Cake Shop
101 Avenue 3
The Covered Market
Oxford OX1 3DY
01865 248691
www.the-cake-shop.co.uk
All wedding cakes individually made to style.

Choccywoccydoodah
47 Harrowby Street
London W1
020 7724 5465
and
27 Middle Street
Brighton BN1 1AL
01273 329462
www.choccywoccydoodah.co.uk
Decadent Belgian chocolate wedding cakes.

David Cakes of Distinction
0151 931 3331
www.davidcakes.co.uk
Cakes by an internationally renowned cake artist.

Helen Houlden
28 Station Terrace
Radcliffe on Trent
Nottingham NG12 2AH
0115 933 3751
www.helenhouldencakes.co.uk
Specialising in cakes with the 'oooh' factor!

Purita Hyam
Acorns
3 Fieldgate Close
Monks Gate
Horsham
West Sussex RH13 6RS
01403 891518
www.chocolateweddingcakes.co.uk
Wedding cakes handmade from the finest ingredients.

Karen's Cakes
2 Arlingham Mews
Waltham Abbey
Essex EN9 1ED
01992 717217
www.karenscakes.co.uk
Breathtaking, mouthwatering wedding cakes.

Konditor and Cook
020 7261 0456
Suppliers of square fondant cakes on page 152.

Louise's Simply Cakes
94 Watling Street
Radlett
Herts WD7 7AB
01923 859849
www.louisessimplycakes.co.uk
Design and create your own wedding cake.

Maison Blanc
020 8838 0848
www.maisonblanc.co.uk
Deliciously decadent wedding cakes.

Rachel Mount
020 8672 9333
Individually designed cakes for customers.

Pat-A-Cake Pat-A-Cake
83 Dartmouth Park Road
London NW5 1SL
020 7485 0006
Supplier of cakes and biscuits on pages 59 and 148–149.

The evening's entertainment

Musical entertainment

Absolute Musicians
020 8558 0977
www.absolutemusicians.com
Represents bands across the UK – from classical to the funkiest dance bands.

Barn Dance Weddings Limited
020 8657 2813
www.barn-dance.co.uk
A barn dance is the perfect entertainment for every occasion. The band will guide you through the moves!

Bob's Big Bad Boogie Band
020 8994 4990
A seven-piece band who play Jools Holland-style good time blues, jive and boogie woogie.

Box Around the Clock
020 8948 1884
Hire an all-singing, all-dancing old-style juke box to play your favourite classics and latest hits all night long.

Espree Music Management
020 8293 1132
www.espreemusicmanagement.co.uk
Represents various professional bands, including spectacular 70s tribute band Boogie WonderBand.

International Highlanders
07000 4274737
www.pipermusic.co.uk
Create a dramatic impression with a Highland piper.

Joffins Travelling Discotheques
0800 072 3073
www.joffins.co.uk
Excellent music accompanied by fantastic sound and light shows.

Jumpin'
01908 526786
www.jumpin.co.uk
An energetic four-piece band who play non-stop party music from the 60s through to the 90s.

National Entertainment for Weddings
0800 328 6364

Original Counterfeit Beatles
020 8777 1309
Relive the excitement of Beatlemania with the closest sounding act to the real thing.

Original ID
020 8368 9778
www.original-id.com
A collection of highly experienced musicians – one of the best live bands to play at any function.

Prima Artists
08707 493093
www.prima-artists.com
Provide any style of music or entertainment to suit your day.

Reel Blend Ceilidh Band
01235 817101
www.reelblend.com
A three-piece ceilidh band who promise you a night to remember!

Shades Discotheque
01732 363675
www.shadesdiscotheque.co.uk
Sound and lighting of the highest quality, with sky trackers, star cloths, video projection and pyrotechnics.

Ultimate Wedding Band
01708 788066
A diverse band that can adapt to any function.

Upbeat Management
020 8773 1223
www.upbeat.co.uk
The best in music and entertainment for your wedding.

Alternative entertainment

Cabaret Casino Associates
01932 867486
www.cabaretcasino.co.uk
Treat your guests to the sophisticated and enthralling atmosphere of a casino.

The Complete Talent Agency
01702 427100
www.entertainers.co.uk
A wide range of entertainment for any type of function.

Fanfare 3000
020 8429 3000
www.fanfare.co.uk
Provide entertainers for private events.

Magical Weddings UK
01903 211519
www.natzler.com
Top magicians for your special occasion.

Monte Carlo Casino Entertainment
01489 601000
www.montecarlocasino.co.uk
Bring all the fun of a genuine casino to your wedding.

Party Props
01252 792787
Kids' party accessories.

What a Palaver!
01623 811467
www.whatapalaver.com
All-round comedy duo – fire eating, bed of nails, etc.

Fireworks

Aurora Fireworks
0800 975 6573
www.AuroraFireworks.co.uk
Firework displays to capture your imagination.

Firework Factors
01531 640441
www.efireworks.co.uk
Put together display packs; also offer one-fuse fireworks (one fuse starts the whole display).

Lightech Sound & Light
01260 223666
www.lightech.co.uk
Fireworks, and lighting and power rental for marquees.

Pains Fireworks
01794 884040
www.painsfireworks.co.uk
Professional firework displays.

Bouncy castle hire

Absolutely Bouncy Castles
01403 790053

CJ Inflatables
01858 469394

HSS Event Hire
0845 7282828
www.hss.com

Creche services

Crêchendo
020 8675 6611
www.crechendo.com
Creche service supplying balloons, children's entertainers, etc.

The Wedding Creche Service
01483 202490
www.weddingcreche.com
Safe, fun childcare, offering wedding-themed activities.

Perfect presents

Wedding favours

BB Favours
01832 275191
www.favours.fsnet.co.uk
Italian-inspired bomboniere.

Bomboniere by Natalie
020 8202 6579
Supplier of favours for Themed wedding section (pages 56–77).

Eleganza Sponsa
01698 303050
Beautiful and simple favours – scented candles, almonds, chocolates, heart-shaped trinket boxes. Mail order.

Favours by Francesca
020 7437 2916
Exclusive Italian almond favours.

Forever Favours
020 8550 8053
Italian favours, decorative boxes and keepsakes.

Graceful Favours
01423 526531
www.graceful-favours.fsnet.co.uk
Favours handmade to your specifications.

Totally Crackers
0113 278 5525
Personalised wedding crackers. Mail order.

Truely Scrumptious
020 8932 7932
www.truelyscrumptious.com
Designer range of inspirational and fun products, including fortune cookies.

The White House
01905 381149
www.the-whitehouse.uk.com
One of the UK's leading wedding favour suppliers.

The speeches

Keith Anderson
0800 389 8568
www.crispandcheerful.co.uk
Specially written humorous speeches.

Tongue Tied
0117 946 6048
Contemporary, casual and colloquial poems and speeches.

Dramatic exits

Contact Marks and Spencer for travel insurance 0800 068 3918

UK honeymoons

British Tourist Authority
020 8846 9000

Country Cottages in Scotland
0870 444 1122

English Country Cottages
0870 585 1155

The Landmark Trust
01628 825925
A charity which restores and lets out listed historic buildings.

National Trust Holiday Cottages
01225 791133
www.nationaltrustcottages.co.uk
Offers 260 cottages in England, Wales and Northern Ireland.

Rural Retreats
01386 701177
Manages a select group of countryside properties in Great Britain.

Scottish Tourist Board
020 7930 8661

The Vivat Trust
020 7930 8030
A charity which restores and lets out listed historic buildings.

Wales Tourist Board
0292 0475226

For details of honeymoons abroad, see Marrying abroad.

Other useful contacts/ links to more suppliers

Bridal House
398 Farnham Road
Slough
Berkshire
01753 570080/531100
www.bridalhouse.co.uk
One of the largest one-stop wedding shops in the UK.

The Wedding Shop
171 Fulham Road
Chelsea
London SW3
020 7838 1188
Plan your gift and choose your dress – all under one roof!

The National Wedding
Information Service
01992 576461
Offers comprehensive listings of suppliers.

www.confetti.co.uk

Picture credits

Index